Embed ⎰Systems and
Compu ⎱Architecture

Embedded Systems and Computer Architecture

G. R. Wilson

Newnes

OXFORD   AUCKLAND   BOSTON   JOHANNESBURG   MELBOURNE   NEW DELHI

Newnes
An imprint of Butterworth-Heinemann
Linacre House, Jordan Hill, Oxford OX2 8DP
225 Wildwood Avenue, Woburn, MA 01801-2041
A division of Reed Educational and Professional Publishing Ltd

 A member of the Reed Elsevier plc group

First edition 2002

British Library Cataloguing in Publication Data
A catalogue record for this book is available from the British Library

ISBN 07506 5064 8

Typeset by Florence Production Ltd, Stoodleigh, Devon
Printed and bound in Great Britain

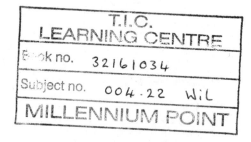

FOR EVERY TITLE THAT WE PUBLISH, BUTTERWORTH-HEINEMANN
WILL PAY FOR BTCV TO PLANT AND CARE FOR A TREE.

Contents

Preface

This book is about how a computer works and how it is programmed. No previous knowledge of digital logic or computers is assumed. *Embedded Systems and Computer Architecture* is intended for students taking a first-level introductory course in electronics, computer science or information technology. Whoever you are, if you want to understand what goes on inside the box containing your computer, or to build your own small computer, this book is written for you.

The **accompanying software** provides you with the facilities of a system's development laboratory entirely on your PC. Using this, you can develop and test computer systems that are typical of those that are embedded within very many 'smart' products. Input and output devices, such as keyboards, a liquid crystal display, a stepper motor, a calendar, and others may be incorporated into your embedded system.

The book is divided into three parts. **Part 1** introduces the basic digital devices, gates and flip-flops, from which all microprocessors are made. After considering how numbers may be represented using only the digits 0 and 1, we see how logical expressions are formed. The simplification of these expressions is next discussed with the aid of software. Various logical building blocks are discussed, as is the design of sequential circuits. The accompanying software animates some combinational and sequential digital circuits. Part 1 ends with the design of circuits to perform arithmetic.

Part 2 is the main part of the book. We begin by analysing how manual computation is performed and identify the major components of an automatic computer. The basic digital devices, explained in Part 1, are interconnected to form a simple microprocessor. We then consider the sort of instructions that the microprocessor must be able to execute. The resulting design is called the G80 because it is very similar to the classic Z80[1] microprocessor. Example programs illustrate the use of important program control structures and data structures. The accompanying software allows you to step through these programs, one instruction at a time, to see them as they are executed. After designing some circuits for small computers, we add input and output ports. Then, we investigate the various methods used to transfer data between a computer and an input/output device. These methods are illustrated using a variety of input/output devices, all of which may be added to your simulated computer and controlled by your program.

The operation of the assembler tool is described. Its use, together with the linker tool, in making large programs is illustrated. Finally, two ways of designing the control unit of a microprocessor are considered.

---

[1] Z80 is a registered trade mark of Zilog Inc.

Part 3 explores how a small microprocessor may be developed into one that is capable of meeting the demands of a general-purpose computer. Faster operation is achieved by making the memory and the data bus 32 bits wide. Registers inside the microprocessor are also expanded to 32 bits. Ways of further speeding the access to the contents of the memory are considered. The advantage gained from the use of a memory cache is discussed and various ways of organizing a cache are considered. Finally, we see how memory management techniques allow a computer to run programs that are too large to fit into the main memory.

Each chapter contains **exercises**, or projects to test your understanding or to present you with typical engineering challenges. Some of these have a single answer and some of these are available from the associated website. However, many exercises require you to write a program to meet a given specification. There is no single, 'correct' solution to these. Essentially, you have a working solution if your code meets the required specification. Nevertheless, some working solutions are more elegant than others; some of the author's solutions are modestly made available on the website.

The author thanks Alan R. Baldwin of Ohio for permission to base the assembler and linker tools on his original code. Any bugs introduced are the responsibility of the present author.

Finally, it is hoped that this book will help you to develop your engineering creativity, and enjoy the satisfaction that results from creating a solution to an engineering problem.

Website The website associated with this book and its software is at www.bh.com/companions/0750650648. Here you can access solutions to some of the problems posed in the book and download the latest versions of the accompanying software. The author welcomes comments via email at grwilson@iname.com, although he cannot reply to every message.

Notation used in the text

- An asterisk (*) on a section title indicates that the section contains more detailed information that you may choose to skip without affecting your understanding of subsequent sections.
- The names of program menu items and buttons are in this font.
- Program names are in this font.
- X = = Y is to be read as 'the value of X is the same as the value of Y'.
- X = Y is to be read as 'the value of X is changed to be the same as the value of Y'.
- <XYZ> = = <UVW> is a short way of writing X = = U, and Y = = V, and Z = = W.
- <XYZ> = <UVW> is a short way of writing X = U, and Y = V, and Z = W.

PART 1

The Building Blocks

1 Binary numbers

Our study of computing machines begins by looking at the basic components from which a machine might be constructed. We begin by asking how numbers may be represented in a machine.

1.1 Numbers within a computing machine

The simplest numbers that we want to represent in the machine are the **unsigned integers**. These are whole numbers without a sign, for example, 0, 1, 2, 3, … The mechanical calculators of yesteryear and the car mileage meter of today both store unsigned integers on what are effectively cogs having ten numbered teeth[1]. Thus a simple two-digit calculator capable of addition and subtraction will comprise two cogs, one indicating units, the other indicating tens, Figure 1.1.

A simple device moves the tens cog one position every time the units cog completes a rotation and passes from 9 back to 0. Thus, if the tens cog currently indicates 4 and the units cog indicates 9, when the units cog is moved forward one position, so adding 1, the cogs correctly display the result 50. The 'carry' from the units cog to the tens cog is thus automatic[2].

Decimal[3] numbers are represented by using the ten digits 0, 1, 2, … 9 in such a way that each digit is interpreted according to its position in the number. That is, a three-digit number represented on the cogs as $<d_2, d_1, d_0>$ is interpreted as

$$100.d_2 + 10.d_1 + 1.d_0$$

or $\quad 10^2.d_2 + 10^1.d_1 + 10^0.d_0$

e.g. 406 is said to represent the number *four hundreds, no tens, and six units*.

The digits are **weighted** according to their position in the number; in general, digit d_J has a weight of 10^J.

Now consider four imaginary cogs having just two teeth, labelled 0 and 1. Again, a simple device moves the cog to the left one position every time

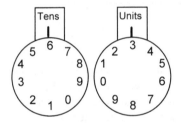

Figure 1.1 *Two cogs representing the two-digit number, 63*

---

[1] There is nothing special about the number ten other than it happens to be the number of fingers and thumbs with which most people are born. We could let the cogs have any number of teeth, so long as the number is greater than one: a one toothed cog would not be able to move to a different position and so would not be able to count!

[2] A machine of this type was first made by Blaise Pascal in 1642. It performed addition and subtraction. In 1674 Gottfried von Leibnitz made a machine that performed multiplication and division as well as addition and subtraction.

[3] Decimal comes from the Latin *decimus* meaning tenth.

Cogs $\langle b_3, b_2, b_1, b_0 \rangle$	Interpretation in decimal
0000	0
0001	1
0010	2
0011	3
0100	4
0101	5
0110	6
0111	7
1000	8
1001	9
1010	10
1011	11
1100	12
1101	13
1110	14
1111	15

Figure 1.2 *Successive positions of four cogs, each having two teeth*

a cog completes a rotation and passes from 1 back to 0. When advanced one step at a time the cogs will display the sequence shown in Figure 1.2.

The cogs now have weights of 8, 4, 2 and 1 and when they indicate $\langle b_3, b_2, b_1, b_0 \rangle$, the value of the number, in decimal, is obtained from:

$$8.b_3 + 4.b_2 + 2.b_1 + 1.b_0$$

or $\quad 2^3.b_3 + 2^2.b_2 + 2^1.b_1 + 2^0.b_0$

e.g. the number 1101 is interpreted as one 8, one 4, no 2s, and 1 unit or $1.8 + 1.4 + 0.2 + 1.1 = 13$, in decimal notation.

This method of representing numbers is called **pure binary** notation[4]. We use this notation to represent unsigned integers. The digits 0 and 1 are called **binary digits**, or **bits**. The four-cog mechanism represents numbers using 4 bits and so can represent only the 16 numbers, 0000 to 1111. If we use 5 bits to represent a number, the extra bit allows us to represent twice as many numbers, 0000 to 11111. In general, if we use N bits to represent a number, we have 2^N different numbers. An N-bit number $\langle b_{N-1} \, b_{N-2} \, \ldots \, b_2 b_1 b_0 \rangle$ has the decimal value $2^{N-1}.b_{N-1} + 2^{N-2}.b_{N-2} + \ldots + 2^2.b_2 + 2^1.b_1 + 2^0.b_0$.

---

[4] Binary from Latin *binarius*, meaning two together.

1.2 Adding binary integers

The familiar rules for adding two decimal digits are shown, in part, in Figure 1.3(a). Note that the addition of two one-digit numbers results in a two-digit number; we call the right-most digit the sum digit and the left-most digit the carry digit. Decimal addition proceeds as shown in the example Figure 1.3(b). Starting with the right-most pair of digits, the sum digit is written down and the carry digit is carried into the column to the left. The sum of this column of digits therefore requires that we add three digits. Note that, if the number mechanism holds only two-digit numbers, the sum in this example has overflowed; that is, the sum is too big to be held in the mechanism.

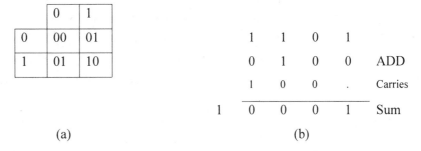

	0	1	2	...	9
0	00	01	02	...	09
1	01	02	03	...	10
2	02	03	04	...	11
...	...	...	...	...	...
...	...	...	...	...	...
9	09	10	11	...	18

(a)

	7	6	
	5	2	ADD
1	0	.	Carries
1	2	8	Sum

(b)

Figure 1.3 *(a) Part of the rules for adding two decimal digits; (b) decimal addition*

	0	1
0	00	01
1	01	10

(a)

	1	1	0	1	
	0	1	0	0	ADD
	1	0	0	.	Carries
1	0	0	0	1	Sum

(b)

Figure 1.4 *(a) Complete rules for adding two binary digits; (b) binary addition*

The rules for the addition of two binary digits are much simpler, Figure 1.4.

1.3 Representing signed integers

Signed integers are numbers such as $-3, -2, -1, 0, +1, +2$. Let there be a number <0111>. Counting down gives the sequence shown in Figure 1.5. Note that when the bits reach <0000>, the next lower number is <1111>, which we regard as the number 'one less than zero', or -1. (Imagine a car mileage meter that is turned back from 00000 to 99999.) These numbers may

$\langle b_3,b_2,b_1,b_0 \rangle$	Interpretation as signed decimal number
0111	+ 7
0110	+ 6
0101	+ 5
0100	+4
0011	+ 3
0010	+ 2
0001	+ 1
0000	0
1111	− 1
1110	− 2
1101	− 3
1100	− 4
1011	− 5
1010	− 6
1001	− 7
1000	− 8

Figure 1.5 *Four bits counting down*

be evaluated by giving the bits the weight −8, +4, +2, +1. This method of representing signed integers is called **two's complement** representation. In general, the left-most bit of a two's complement number has a negative weight. For example, the signed integer $\langle p_3p_2p_1p_0 \rangle$ has the decimal value:

$$- 8.p_3 + 4.p_2 + 2.p_1 + 1.p_0$$

or $- 2^3.p_3 + 2^2.p_2 + 2^1.p_1 + 2^0.p_0$

e.g. 1101 represents $-8.1 + 4.1 + 2.0 + 1.1 = (-3)$

and 0010 represents $-8.0 + 4.0 + 2.1 + 1.0 = (+2)$

1.4 Addition and subtraction of signed integers

The two's complement representation of signed integers has the valuable property that two such numbers can be added using the **same arithmetical rules** as for unsigned integers. This has the great advantage that any mechanism we devise for the addition of unsigned integers will also work correctly for signed integers. Consider the following addition:

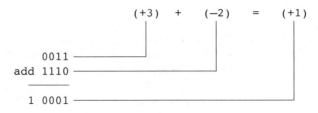

The fifth bit, at the extreme left, is called the **carry-out**. If this bit is ignored, what remains is the correct representation on the machine for the sum, $+1$. Similarly, the following addition gives a sum of <1111>, which is the correct representation for -1 on the machine.

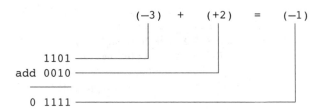

```
               (−3)   +   (+2)   =   (−1)


       1101
add    0010
      _____
     0 1111
```

The ability to add negative numbers implies that subtraction can be performed by the process 'change the sign and add' since:

$$(+A) - (+B) \equiv (+A) + (-B)$$

and $(+A) - (-B) \equiv (+A) + (+B)$

Thus, in order to perform subtraction on a machine that is capable of addition, the machine must also be capable of changing the sign of a number, that is, it must have the facility of multiplying the number by -1. This is quite simple when the numbers are represented in two's complement: we simply invert all the bits and add 1. For example:

```
+7 is represented by    0111  ⟩ invert the bits
                        1000
                           1  ── add 1
                        ____
                        1001  which represents −7
```

```
−7 is represented by    1001  ⟩ invert the bits
                        0110
                           1  ── add 1
                        ____
                        0111  which represents +7
```

1.5 Two's complement theory*

The English language is not very good at making clear the distinction between numbers and arithmetical operations. Thus, English uses 'plus' and 'minus' to indicate both the sign of a number and the arithmetical operations 'add' and 'subtract'. These double meanings, or ambiguities, are also evident in the use of '+' and '−' to indicate the sign of a number as well as 'add' and 'subtract'. In everyday use, the meaning of an ambiguous term such as 'plus' is understood by the reader who makes use of the context, that is, the other words or symbols in the sentence. Since our purpose is to design a machine for processing numbers, we must be absolutely clear about what it is we want the machine to do. Where there is any ambiguity, we shall use '+' and '−' to indicate the sign of a number, and use 'add' and 'subtract' to indicate an arithmetical operation.

Let a number be represented in pure binary by N bits; there are 2^N possible numbers in the range 0 to $2^N - 1$.

Let A and B be unsigned integers in the range 0 to $2^{N-1} - 1$.

Represent $(+A)$ by the pure binary number A, and represent $(-A)$ by the pure binary number $2^N - A$. For example, for N = 8, $(+3)$ is represented by 0000 0011 and (-3) is represented by $256 - 3 = 253 =$ binary 1111 1101.

Consider the four possible additions of A and B.

$(+A)$ add $(+B) = A$ add B, which is the correct representation of the required result.

$(+A)$ add $(-B) = A$ add $(2^N$ subtract B$) = 2^N$ subtract (B subtract A), which is the correct representation of $-$(B subtract A) or $+$(A subtract B), the required result.

$(-A)$ add $(+B) = (2^N$ subtract A$)$ add B $= 2^N$ subtract (A subtract B), which is the correct representation of $-$(A subtract B) or $+$(B subtract A), the required result.

$(-A)$ add $(-B) = (2^N$ subtract A$)$ add $(2^N$ subtract B$) = 2^N$ add 2^N subtract (A plus B). The first 2^N causes a carry-out of the left-hand end of the number. Ignoring this carry leaves 2^N subtract (A plus B), which is the correct representation of $-$(A add B), the required result.

Therefore, when signed integers are represented using two's complement, we apply the normal rules of binary addition and ignore any carry-out. This gives the correct result.

Earlier, we simply stated that to multiply a number by -1, we invert all the bits and add 1. To see why this works, consider an N-bit number, A. Invert all the bits to get the number B. Now $A + B = 111..1 = 2^N - 1$ always, so that $B = 2^N - 1 - A$. Adding 1 to this gives $2^N - A$, which is the required two's complement representation of $-A$.

1.6 Use of hexadecimal representation

While electronic computers represent both data and instructions as patterns of bits, it is inconvenient for humans to write down and read long patterns of 0s and 1s. Purely as a matter of convenience, the binary patterns are usually written in **hexadecimal**. This simply requires that the person reading the hexadecimal numbers remembers the first 16 pure binary numbers and their equivalent in hexadecimal, Figure 1.6.

Instead of writing 0011110010010101, group the bits into fours 0011 1100 1001 0101, and write the hexadecimal digit for each group:

Binary	Hexadecimal
0000	0
0001	1
0010	2
0011	3
0100	4
0101	5
0110	6
0111	7
1000	8
1001	9
1010	A
1011	B
1100	C
1101	D
1110	E
1111	F

Figure 1.6 *First 16 counting numbers in binary and hexadecimal*

3   C   9   5

This is much easier for a person to read once the above table has been memorized. This hexadecimal number is often written 0x3C95, 0X3C95, 3C95H, or 3C95h to distinguish it from a decimal number. Hexadecimal or 'hex' is widely used to represent patterns of 0s and 1s within computing machines; it is purely for human convenience – the computing machine, of course, works with 0s and 1s.

1.7 Problems

1 Write down the hexadecimal representation of the following bit patterns:
(i) 0001 1111   (ii) 1100 1101   (iii) 1001 0111 1111 1111.

2 Write down the bit patterns represented by the following hexadecimal numbers:
(i) 0x1F   (ii) 0xCD   (iii) 0x97FF.

3 An N-bit unsigned integer is written $b_{N-1}b_{N-2}..b_2b_1b_0$. Write an expression for its decimal value.

4 Convert the following unsigned integers to decimal:
(i) 1011   (ii) 0010   (iii) 0000 1111
(iv) 1111 1111.

5 How would the following numbers, written in decimal notation, be represented in 8 bits as unsigned integers?
(i) 1   (ii) 2   (iii) 127
(iv) 128   (v) 254   (vi) 255.

6   Obtain the sums of the following unsigned integers:
    (i)   1011 + 0010   (ii) 0000 1111 + 0000 0001
    (iii) 1111 1111 + 0000 0001.

    Check your answers by converting the numbers to decimal.

7   An N-bit signed integer, in two's complement representation, is written:
    $b_{N-1}b_{N-2}..b_2b_1b_0$. Write an expression for its decimal value.

8   Convert the following signed integers, written using two's complement
    representation, to decimal:
    (i)   1011   (ii) 0101   (iii) 0000 1111
    (iv) 1111 1111.

9   How would the following numbers, written using decimal notation, be
    represented in 8 bits using two's-complement representation?
    (i)   +1   (ii) +127   (iii) −1
    (iv) −128   (v)   +2   (vi) −2.

10 A number is represented by 16 bits. Answer each of the following ques-
    tions by writing the binary representation of the number and its decimal
    equivalent.
    (i)   What is the largest value of the number assuming the 16 bits repre-
          sent an unsigned integer?
    (ii) What is the smallest value of the number assuming the 16 bits
          represent an unsigned integer?
    (iii) What is the largest value of the number assuming the 16 bits repre-
          sent a two's complement number?
    (iv) What is the smallest value of the number assuming the 16 bits
          represent a two's complement number?

11 Multiply the following signed integers, written using two's complement
    representation, by −1:
    (i)   1011   (ii) 0101   (iii) 0000 1111
    (iv) 1111 1111.

    Check your answers by converting the numbers to decimal.

12 How would the decimal number −1 be represented in two's comple-
    ment notation using
    (i)   4 bits   (ii) 8 bits   (iii) 16 bits?

13 Obtain the sums of the following signed integers, written using two's
    complement representation:
    (i)   1011 + 0010   (ii) 0000 1111 + 0000 0001
    (iii) 1111 1111 + 0000 0001.

    Check your answers by converting the numbers to decimal.

14 Obtain the differences of the following signed integers, written using two's complement representation:
   (i)   1011 − 0010   (ii) 0010 − 1011
   (iii) 0000 1111 − 0000 0001 (iv) 0000 0001 − 0000 1111
   (v) 1111 1111 − 0000 0001   (vi) 0000 0001 − 1111 1111.

   Check your answers by converting the numbers to decimal.

15 Each bit of an N-bit unsigned integer is inverted and the result is added to the original number. What is the resulting pattern of bits and what is its decimal value?

16 Shift the 4-bit unsigned integer 0110 one place to the left. What is the arithmetical relationship between the original and the shifted number?

17 Shift the 4-bit unsigned integer 0110 one place to the right. What is the arithmetical relationship between the original and the shifted number?

18 Shift the 4-bit unsigned integer 0011 one place to the right. What is the arithmetical relationship between the original and the shifted number?

19 The 8-bit unsigned integer X = 0000 1001 is shifted two places to the left, then X is added to the result. What is the arithmetical relationship between X and the result of these operations?

2 Logic expressions

We begin our discussion of logic by asking how we can make an automatic device for controlling access to a bank vault. In finding an answer to this question, we shall arrive at a form of algebraic expression that always evaluates to either 0 or 1. To arrive at the simplest form of these expressions, you can learn a graphical method and a tabular method for simplifying logic expressions.

2.1 Logic – the bank vault

Three employees of a bank have access to the vault: the Manager, the Assistant Manager, and the Chief Cashier. In order to obtain access to the vault, any two of these persons must present themselves before an incorruptible person, the controller, who decides if access to the vault is permitted.

The controller makes a 'truth table', Figure 2.1, which he uses to determine whether access to the vault is permitted. When bank employees present themselves before him, he asks three questions, the answers to which are either 'Yes' or 'No':

Is the Manager present?
Is the Assistant Manager present?
Is the Chief Cashier present?

He then arrives at his decision by looking it up in the truth table. Note that there are eight possible sets of answers to these three yes/no questions[1].

The controller realizes he could arrive at his decision in a different way. He writes down all the conditions that make Allow_access equal to 'Yes', Figure 2.2.

In order to write the expression for 'Allow_access' more concisely, the controller writes the symbol M instead of 'Manager is present' and writes the symbol /M (read as 'not M') instead of 'Manager is NOT present'. He does likewise for the Assistant Manager and the Chief Cashier. The resulting expression is:

Allow_access =
/M AND A AND C
OR
M AND /A AND C
OR
M AND A AND /C
OR
M AND A AND C

[1] There are two possible answers to each of the three questions, so the number of possible answers to the three questions is $2 * 2 * 2 = 2^3 = 8$.

Is Manager present?	Is Assistant Manager present?	Is Chief Cashier present?	Allow_access
No	No	No	No
No	No	Yes	No
No	Yes	No	No
No	Yes	Yes	Yes
Yes	No	No	No
Yes	No	Yes	Yes
Yes	Yes	No	Yes
Yes	Yes	Yes	Yes

Figure 2.1 *The vault-access controller's truth table*

Allow_access =

(Manager is NOT present) AND (Assistant Manager is present) AND (Chief Cashier is present)

OR

(Manager is present) AND (Assistant Manager is NOT present) AND (Chief Cashier is present)

OR

(Manager is present) AND (Assistant Manager is present) AND (Chief Cashier is NOT present)

OR

(Manager is present) AND (Assistant Manager is present) AND (Chief Cashier is present)

Figure 2.2 *All the conditions that allow access to the bank vault*

More briefly:

Allow_access = /M.A.C + M./A.C + M.A./C + M.A.C

Here a dot is used as an abbreviation for 'AND', and a + is used as an abbreviation for 'OR'.

This expression has exactly the same meaning as the expression given in Figure 2.2. In order to arrive at his decision, the controller has to evaluate this logic expression every time bank employees present themselves before him. How does he evaluate this expression?

2.2 Evaluating the logic expression for the bank vault

If the Manager is present, the controller gives M the value 1; if the Manager is not present, the controller gives M the value 0. He also gives variable A a value of 0 or 1 according to the presence or absence of the Assistant Manager, and similarly for variable C.

For example, consider the situation where the Manager is present, the Assistant Manager is NOT present, and the Chief Cashier is present. The variables thus have the values $M = 1$, $A = 0$, and $C = 1$. To evaluate the expression for Allow_access, the controller applies the following rules[2].

Let x stand for a particular value, 0 or 1, then:

$$/0 = 1 \qquad\qquad /1 = 0$$
$$x.0 = 0 \qquad\qquad x.1 = x$$
$$x + 0 = x \qquad\qquad x + 1 = 1$$

The controller replaces the variables in the expression for Allow_access with their actual values, so that for this situation:

$$\begin{aligned}
\text{Allow\_access} &= /M.A.C + M./A.C + M.A./C + M.A.C, \\
&= 0.0.1 + 1.1.1 + 1.0.0 + 1.0.1 \\
&= 0 + 1 + 0 + 0 \\
&= 1
\end{aligned}$$

In more detail, the result of applying the rules given that $M = 1$, $A = 0$, $C = 1$:

$$/M = 0 \qquad /A = 1 \qquad /C = 0$$
$$/M.A.C = 0.0.1 = (0.0).1 = 0.1 = 0.$$
$$M./A.C = 1.1.1 = (1.1).1 = 1.1 = 1.$$
$$M.A./C = 1.0.0 = (1.0).0 = 0.0 = 0.$$
$$M.A.C = 1.0.1 = (1.0).1 = 0.1 = 0.$$

Finally, the logical OR of these four values is:

$$0 + 1 + 0 + 0 = (0 + 1) + (0 + 0) = 1 + 0 = 1$$

That is, the value of Allow_access is 1, which means that access to the bank vault is allowed.

All eight possible combinations of the values of M, A, and C are listed in the table of Figure 2.3 together with the corresponding evaluations of Allow_access. The evaluations give the required results.

Note that the term /M.A.C may be regarded as detecting <MAC> = = <011>. Similarly, M./A.C detects <MAC> = = <101>, M./A.C detects <MAC> = = <101>, M.A./C detects <MAC> = = <110>, and M.A.C detects <MAC> = = <111>. Since these logic expressions detect various combinations of the input variables they are known as **combinational** or **combinatorial** logic expressions.

Using this detection property gives a simpler way of evaluating Allow_access. In the table of Figure 2.4, we can quickly write down the value of each of these so-called **product terms**. In the column headed /M.A.C we write 1 where <MAC> = = <011> and write 0 everywhere else. We do

---

[2] These are the basic rules of Boolean algebra, first demonstrated by George Boole in his book *Mathematical Analysis of Logic*, 1847.

M	A	C	Allow_access = /M.A.C + M./A.C + M.A./C + M.A.C	Allow_access
0	0	0	1.0.0 + 0.1.0 + 0.0.1 + 0.0.0	0
0	0	1	1.0.1 + 0.1.1 + 0.0.0 + 0.0.1	0
0	1	0	1.1.0 + 0.0.0 + 0.1.1 + 0.1.0	0
0	1	1	1.1.1 + 0.0.1 + 0.1.0 + 0.1.1	1
1	0	0	0.0.0 + 1.1.0 + 1.0.1 + 1.0.0	0
1	0	1	0.0.1 + 1.1.1 + 1.0.0 + 1.0.1	1
1	1	0	0.1.0 + 1.0.0 + 1.1.1 + 1.1.0	1
1	1	1	0.1.1 + 1.0.1 + 1.1.0 + 1.1.1	1

Figure 2.3 *Evaluation of Allow_access = /M.A.C + M./A.C + M.A./C + M.A.C*

M	A	C	/M.A.C	M./A.C	M.A./C	M.A.C	Allow_access
0	0	0	0	0	0	0	0
0	0	1	0	0	0	0	0
0	1	0	0	0	0	0	0
0	1	1	1	0	0	0	1
1	0	0	0	0	0	0	0
1	0	1	0	1	0	0	1
1	1	0	0	0	1	0	1
1	1	1	0	0	1	1	1

Figure 2.4 *Alternative method for evaluating Allow_access = /M.A.C + M./A.C + M.A./C + M.A.C*

the same for the other product term columns. Finally, we write a 1 in the Allow_access column wherever one or more of the product term columns in the same row contains a 1.

This is a good time to try Problems 1 to 4.

2.3 Another solution

The controller might have seen that the vault access rule is effectively that any two of the Manager, Assistant Manager, and Chief Cashier must be present. This would lead him to the expression:

Allow_access = M.A + M.C + A.C

instead of:

M	A	C	M.A	M.C	A.C	Allow_access
0	0	0	0	0	0	0
0	0	1	0	0	0	0
0	1	0	0	0	0	0
0	1	1	0	0	1	1
1	0	0	0	0	0	0
1	0	1	0	1	0	1
1	1	0	1	0	0	1
1	1	1	1	1	1	1

Figure 2.5 *Truth table for Allow_access = M.A + M.C + A.C*

$$\text{Allow\_access} = /\text{M.A.C} + \text{M.}/\text{A.C} + \text{M.A.}/\text{C} + \text{M.A.C}$$

How do we know that these two expressions perform the same function?

We construct the truth table for the simpler expression, Figure 2.5 and compare it with the truth table of Figure 2.4. The Allow_access columns in both truth tables are identical, therefore the two expressions represent the same function.

A question now arises: given an expression for a particular function, how do we arrive at the simplest expression that performs the same function?

2.4 Simplifying logical expressions* Consider the members of an orchestra. We wish to classify the members according to what sort of instruments they play – string, wind, or percussion instruments. Some members play several types of instrument. We want to group the players on a rectangular field according to the types of instrument they play. How do we do this? Obviously we ask each member the three questions:

Do you play Strings?   If Yes, set S = 1, /S = 0
Do you play Percussion?   If Yes, set P = 1, /P = 0
Do you play Wind?   If Yes, set W = 1, /W = 0

Since there are eight, (2^3), possible sets of answers, we divide the field into eight squares, one square for each possible set of answers. We give each square a number according to the scheme shown in Figure 2.6; the numbering scheme is important. A square number is obtained by regarding the three 0s and 1s in <SPW> as á pure binary number: for convenience, we write the number in decimal notation. We shall refer to the field with squares arranged in this way as a **map**. Furthermore, we arrange the squares on the map such that all string players are in the bottom part of the map, all percussion players are in the right-hand part of the map, and all wind players are in the middle two columns of the map.

/S./P./W	/S./P.W.	/S.P.W	/S.P./W
Square 0	Square 1	Square 3	Square 2
S./P./W	S./P.W	S.P.W	S.P./W
Square 4	Square 5	Square 7	Square 6

(Percussion above columns 3-4; Strings labels right side; Wind below columns 2-3)

Figure 2.6 *Labelling the squares on the map*

The orchestra members in square 5, (= binary 101) are described by S./P.W, that is, they play strings, do not play percussion, and play wind. Similarly, the members in square 3, (= binary 011) are described by /S.P.W, they do not play strings, do play percussion, and do play wind.

And so on for all the eight squares.

It is usual to refer to terms such as S./P.W and /S.P.W as minterms. A **minterm** is the logical AND of all the variables in either their true or complemented form. Further, we can refer to a minterm by the number formed by writing 1 for a true variable and 0 for a complemented variable. Thus, minterm S./P.W becomes 101 or 5, and /S.P.W becomes 011 or 3.

2.4.1 Using the squares

Suppose we wish to find where the members who play strings AND play percussion are located. We can proceed as follows:

All those that play strings are in squares 4, 5, 6, 7.
All those that play percussion are in squares 2, 3, 6, 7.

Hence, all those that play strings AND play percussion, S.P, are in squares 6, 7.

So, those that play strings AND play percussion may be described by:

S.P = Squares 6,7
= S.P./W + S.P.W[3]

Note that S.P is a simpler way of expressing S.P./W + S.P.W.

Again, suppose we wish to find where the members who play strings OR percussion, (S + P), are located. We can proceed as follows:

All those that play strings are in squares 4, 5, 6, 7.
All those that play percussion are in squares 2, 3, 6, 7.

---

[3] Incidentally, this indicates that Boolean functions may be factorized: S.P./W + S.P.W = S.P.(/W + W) = S.P.1 = S.P.

Hence, all those that play strings OR play percussion, (S + P), are in squares 2, 3, 4, 5, 6, 7, giving:

$$S + P = \text{Squares 2, 3, 4, 5, 6, 7}$$
$$= \text{/S.P./W + /S.P.W + S./P./W + S./P.W + S.P./W + S.P.W}$$

Note that S + P is a simpler way of expressing

/S.P./W + /S.P.W + S./P./W + S./P.W + S.P./W + S.P.W

This is a good time to try Problems 5 to 11.

2.4.2 Simplified logic for bank vault access

Going back to the bank vault access problem, we can use a map to simplify the original design solution:

Allow_access = /M.A.C + M./A.C + M.A./C + M.A.C

It is convenient to write:

Allow_access(M, A, C) = minterm 011 + minterm 101 + minterm 110 + minterm 111

or Allow_access(M, A, C) = sum of minterms 3, 5, 6, 7

or Allow_access(M, A, C) = Σ3, 5, 6, 7

Note that it is necessary to write (M, A, C) to indicate the order in which the variables are written in order to obtain the numerical value of the minterm.

Draw a map, as shown in Figure 2.7 and write a 1 in each of the squares 3 (/M.A.C), 5 (M./A.C), 6 (M.A./C), and 7 (M.A.C). Squares 6 and 7 may be grouped together into a region described by M.A. Squares 5 and 7 group to become the region M.C, and squares 3 and 7 become A.C. So we can write the simplified expression by forming the OR of these groups:

Allow_access = M.A + M.C + A.C

We now have a graphical way of simplifying expressions.[4]

---

[4] This map method was originated by E. W. Veitch and modified by M. Karnaugh.

Veitch, E.W., 'A Chart Method for Simplifying Truth Functions', *Proc. ACM*, Pittsburgh, USA, pp. 127–133, May 1952.

Karnaugh, M., 'The Map Method for Synthesis of Combinational Logic Circuits', *Trans. AIEE*, Pt I, Vol. 72, No. 9, pp. 593–599, 1953.

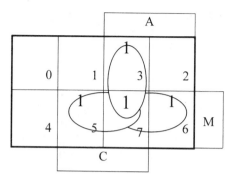

Figure 2.7 *Map of Allow_access = /M.A.C + M./A.C + M.A./C + M.A.C*

2.5 Rules for simplifying logical expressions using a map*

For the general function of three variables, F(C, B, A), output F depends on input variables C, B, and A. In order to simplify the function we use the following steps.

Step 1   Draw a map as in Figure 2.8. Label the bottom part C, the right-hand part B, and the middle part A.

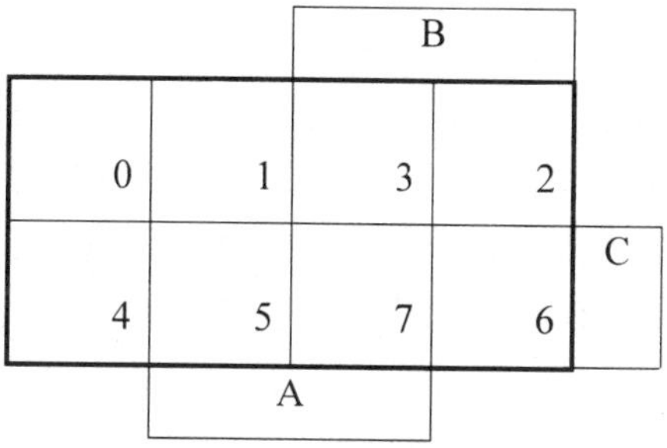

Figure 2.8 *Map for three variables, C, B, and A*

Step 2   Where F is to have the value 1, write 1 into the corresponding square(s).

Step 3   Identify in your mind, all possible groups of squares with a 1 written in them. A group *must* contain 1, 2, 4, or 8 squares in the shape of a rectangle. The groups *must* be as large as possible.
The right-hand and left-hand edges of the map are regarded as being the same edge – thus, for example, if squares 4 and 6 both contain a 1, they form a group of two.
A square containing a 1 may be in any number of groups.

Step 4   Examine each square containing a 1 – if there is only one group that contains that square, draw a loop around the group, or move onto another square containing a 1.

Step 5   Repeat step 4, until all squares containing a 1 have been examined.

Step 6 Re-examine any squares containing a 1 that are not in a group. These are those that may be grouped in more than one way. Choose a group for these squares.

Step 7 For each group, ask 'Is this group entirely within region C?' If it is, write C; if it is entirely outside region C, write /C. If the group lies *only partly* within C, do not write anything. Repeat this question for region B, then for region A. What you have written down is the logical description for that group.

Step 8 Repeat step 7 for all the groups.

Step 9 Write the result as the OR of the descriptions of all the groups.

Example 1

An output, F, depends on inputs C, B, and A. The function is F(C B A) = Σ0, 1, 4, 5, 6. The map of the function is:

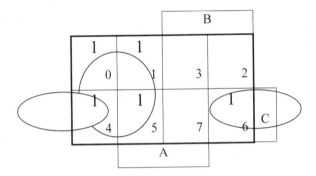

Simplification:

Group squares 0, 1, 4, 5, and ask the questions:

> Is the group wholly within C? Answer: part of it is but part of it is not; so write nothing.
> Is the group wholly within B? Answer: no; so write /B.
> Is the group wholly within A? Answer: part of it is but part of it is not; so write nothing.

Thus, the group is described by /B.

Group squares 4, 6, and ask the questions:

> Is the group wholly within C? Answer: yes; so write C.
> Is the group wholly within B? Answer: part of it is but part of it is not; so write nothing.
> Is the group wholly within A? Answer: no; so write /A.

Thus, the group is described by C./A.

Hence, F = /B + C./A.

Example 2

F(C, B, A) = C./B./A + C.B./A + A

The term C./B./A is minterm 100 and maps to square 4.
The term C.B./A is minterm 110 and maps to square 6.
The term A is not a minterm; it maps to squares 1, 3, 5, 7.
Therefore, the map is:

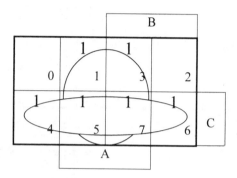

Simplification:

Group squares 1, 3, 5, 7, and ask the questions:

Is the group wholly within C? Answer: part of it is but part of it is not;
so write nothing.
Is the group wholly within B? Answer: part of it is but part of it is not;
so write nothing.
Is the group wholly within A? Answer: yes; so write A.

Thus, the group is described by A.

Group squares 4, 5, 6, 7, and ask the usual questions:
This group is described by C.
Hence, F = C + A.

Example 3

G(C, B, A) = C./B + C./A + /C./B

C./B maps to squares 4, 5. C./A maps to squares 4, 6. /C./B maps to squares
0, 1.
This is the same map as Example 1.

Hence, G = /B + C./A.

Example 4 – Map for four variables

The squares on a four-variable map are arranged and numbered as shown in
Figure 2.9 (Note that if the lower half of this map is folded over the top half,
the new squares have a minterm number that is eight more than the square
over which it now lies.) The new squares are labelled as region D.

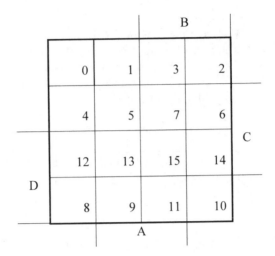

Figure 2.9 *Map for four variables, D, C, B, and A*

$$F(D, C, B, A) = /D./C./B./A + /D./C./B.A + D./C./B./A + D./C./B.A + /D./A.$$

The map of the function is made using:

/D./C./B./A is minterm 0000 and maps to square 0.
/D./C./B.A is minterm 0001 and maps to square 1.
D./C./B./A is minterm 1000 and maps to square 8.
D./C./B.A is minterm 1001 and maps to square 9.
/D./A is not a minterm; it maps to squares 0, 2, 4, 6.

So the map of F(D, C, B, A) is:

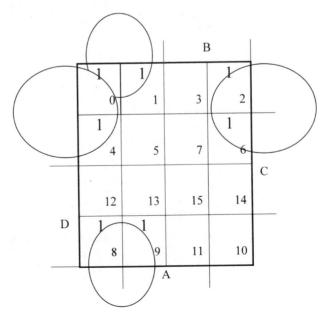

Simplification:

Group squares 0, 2, 4, 6 and describe the group by /D./A.

Group squares 0, 1, 8, 9 and describe the group by /C./B. (*Note that the top and bottom edges of the map are regarded as being the same, as are the left-hand and right-hand edges.*)

Hence, F = /D./A + /C./B.

This is a good time to try Problems 12 to 18.

2.6 Karnaugh–Veitch program, KVMap*

The KVMap.exe program automates the map method for four variables labelled D, C, B, and A. (For three-variable problems use only the top half of the map and ignore D in the solution.) Enter the data for the truth table either by typing the value in the truth table or by clicking on a square in the map. (The program allows a square to be set to X as well as 0 or 1: we shall see the use of the X in Chapter 3.) Possible groups of squares, called **prime implicants**, are looped and listed automatically. Often the required logic expression is the OR of all the prime implicants but this is not always so. This is because not all the prime implicants may be essential to implement the function; that is, some prime implicants are not needed in the simplest possible solution, as in the following case.

Consider the map of the function F(D, C, B, A) = Σ 0, 1, 5, 7, 10, 14, 15, shown in Figure 2.10. The prime implicant or loop (/D./C./B) covering minterms 0 and 1 is essential because it is the only loop containing minterm 0. Similarly, the prime implicant (D.B./A) covering minterms 10 and 14 is essential because it is the only prime implicant covering minterm 10. These two prime implicants /D./C./B and D.B./A are both flagged with an E to indicate that they are essential.

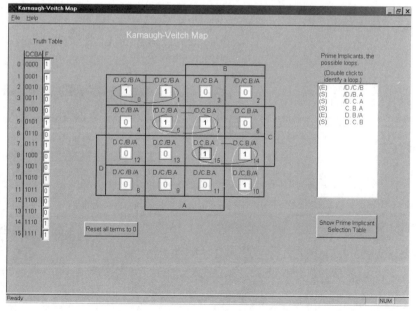

Figure 2.10 *Example of program KVMap.exe*

One way of looping the remaining minterms, 5, 7, and 15, is to loop minterms 1 and 5 (/D./B.A), and loop minterms 7 and 15 (C.B.A). Alternatively, minterms 5 and 7 may be looped (/D.C.A) and minterms 14 and 15 (D.C.B). All these prime implicants are flagged with an S, which indicates that it may or may not be needed; you, the designer, must make the choice. There are two possible solutions, both, of course, include the essential prime implicants.

$$F = /D./C./B + D.B./A + /D./B.A + C.B.A$$
$$F = /D./C./B + D.B./A + /D.C.A + D.C.B$$

Both solutions produce expressions that are equally simple.

2.6.1 Prime implicant selection table

Clicking on the **Prime Implicant Selection Table** button in program KVMap. exe gives a table that helps to select the prime implicants. For the current example, the table is shown in Figure 2.11. (You can print this table from the program.) The table shows all the possible prime implicants and the minterms that they cover. The second and third rows show all the minterms and their value, either 0 or 1. Reading across the row for prime implicant /D./C.B, the table shows that this loops minterms 0 and 1. Reading down the column for minterm 0, we see that this is the only prime implicant that loops minterm 0; this prime implicant must therefore be included in the solution, which is why it is flagged as essential, (E). We strike through this row and the columns for minterms 0 and 1. Similarly, we strike through the row for essential prime implicant D.B./A and the columns for minterms 10 and 14. The table now shows all the minterms that are looped more than once and are therefore to be selected by us. Thus we may choose to cover minterm 5 either by /D./B.A or by /D.C.A. Suppose we choose /D./B.A: we strike through the row for this prime implicant and the column for minterm 5. This

Prime Implicant	0	1	2	3	4	5	6	7	8	9	10	11	12	13	14	15
	1	1	0	0	0	1	0	1	0	0	1	0	0	0	1	1
/D./C./B (E)	#	#														
/D./B. A (S)		#				#										
/D. C. A (S)						#		#								
C. B. A (S)								#								#
D. B./A (E)											#				#	
D. C. B (S)															#	#

Figure 2.11 *Prime implicant selection table*

leaves minterms 7 and 15 still uncovered; the proper choice now is prime implicant C.B.A, which covers both these minterms.

2.7 Quine–McCluskey method*

The KV map method is useful for expressions having four, or fewer, variables. For more variables, the maps effectively become three dimensional and are difficult to interpret. Not surprisingly, reduction of combinational logic expressions is usually done with the aid of a computer. The computer programs are often based on the algorithm described here[5]. Since it makes use of tables, it is often called a **tabular** method. The algorithm detects all the possible implicants, that is, all the possible loops that can be made on the KV map of the function. However, unlike the KV map method, this algorithm can be applied to any number of variables. A word of warning: the algorithm takes much longer to describe than to do! Once the algorithm has been practised a few times, it is quite easy, though tedious, to simplify logical functions by hand.

2.7.1 Finding pairs of adjacent minterms

The arrangement of the KV maps is such that adjacent squares represent minterms that differ in one, and only one, variable. For example, adjacent minterms 6 (/D.B.C./A) and 14 (D.B.C./A) differ only in variable D. Two properties follow from this. First, adjacent minterms always have a numerical difference that is a power of 2. Second, there is always one more 1 in the binary number for one minterm than the other. We call the number of 1s in a binary number its **index**. Thus, in the example, 6 = 0110 has an index of 2, and 14 = 1110 has an index of 3. This suggests the basis of an algorithm for detecting adjacent minterms, which may then be combined into an implicant.

These two properties alone, however, are not sufficient to correctly identify adjacent minterms. Thus, minterms 7 (0111, index 3) and 9 (1001, index 2) have numerical values that differ by a power of 2, yet they are not adjacent. We overcome this by noting that the minterm with the higher numerical value must also have the higher index. These three properties of adjacent squares imply that:

if two minterms:
> have index values that differ by 1, and
> have numerical values that differ by a power of 2, and
> the minterm with the higher index also has the higher numerical value

then, the two squares are adjacent.

An unsophisticated implementation of this algorithm would be to compare every minterm with every other minterm and test to see if they are adjacent.

---

[5] The Quine–McCluskey method was devised by W. V. Quine in 1952 and 1955 and modified by E. J. McCluskey in 1956.

However, there is only a need to compare those minterms that have index values that differ by 1, so we will put the minterms into a list that is divided into groups of minterms having the same index value.

Example 1
A function is given by $F(D, C, B, A) = \Sigma\ 6, 7, 9, 12$. We first evaluate the index values: 6 (0110, index 2), 7 (0111, index 3), 9 (1001, index 2), 11 (1011, index 3), 12 (1100, index 2). The list of minterms grouped according to their index is shown in Figure 2.12

Index	Minterms
0	—
1	—
2	6
	9
	12
3	7
	11
4	—

Figure 2.12 *Minterms grouped according to index value*

x	y	y – x	Result
6	7	$1 = 2^0$	6 and 7 merge
6	11	5	
9	7	–ve	
9	11	$2 = 2^1$	9 and 11 merge
12	7	–ve	
12	11	–ve	

Figure 2.13 *Comparison of the minterms shown in Figure 2.12*

The comparisons are shown in Figure 2.13 where each minterm in one index group is compared with every minterm in the next higher index group. If we are doing this by hand, a convenient way of writing this is shown in Figure 2.14. When minterms 6 and 7 are compared, and found to merge, mark both minterms in Column 1, and write 6(1) in Column 2, where the number in brackets is the numerical difference. Similarly, the comparison of minterms 9 and 11 gives marks against 9 and 11 in Column 1 and 9(2) in Column 2. When all comparisons have been made, the unmarked minterms in Column 1 do not merge while Column 2 indicates pairs of minterms. Thus, we have found prime implicants 12, 6(1), and 9(2). Since this example uses only four variables, we can verify that on the KV map, these prime implicants correspond to loops around 12, pair 6 and 7, and pair 9 and 11.

How do we turn these numbers – 12, 6(1), 9(2) – back into logical expressions using the variable names? Clearly, prime implicant 12, 1100 in binary, means minterm D.C./B./A. Prime implicant 6(1) means the logical OR of minterms 6 and 7; that is /D.C.B./A + /D.C.B.A = /D.C.B.(/A + A) = /D.C.B. A simple way of arriving at this result is to write minterm 6 as /D.C.B./A and then to strike out the variable that has a weight of 1, that is variable A. This leaves /D.C.B. Similarly, implicant 9(2) is written as D./C./B.A and then variable B is struck out, leaving D./C.A. The simplified function is thus: F = D.C./B./A + /D.C.B + D./C.A.

Index	Column 1	Column 2
0	—	—
1	—	—
2	6✓	6(1)
	9✓	9(2)
	12	
3	7✓	—
	11✓	
4	—	—

Figure 2.14 *Tabular reduction of minterms 6, 7, 9, 11, 12*

2.7.2 Finding larger groups of minterms

The procedure for finding pairs of minterms can be extended to detect larger groups.

Example 2
A function is given by F(D, C, B, A) = Σ 1, 4, 10, 11, 12, 14, 15. We begin with the table shown in Figure 2.15. In Column 1, the minterms have been grouped according to their index. In Column 2, minterms 4 and 12 are merged to form pair 4(8), 10 and 11 form pair 10(1), 10 and 14 form pair 10(4), 12 and 14 form pair 12(2), 11 and 15 form pair 11(4), and 14 and 15 form pair 14(1). All these merged minterms are marked in Column 1.

Figure 2.16 shows Column 3 filled; the marks in Column 2 now indicate adjacent pairs of squares that have been merged into the groups of four shown

Index	Column 1	Column 2	Column 3
0	—	—	
1	1		
	4✓	4(8)	
2	10✓	10(1)	
	12✓	10(4)	
		12(2)	
3	11✓	11(4)	
	14✓	14(1)	
4	15✓	—	

Figure 2.15 *Filling Columns 1 and 2*

Index	Column 1	Column 2	Column 3
0	—	—	—
1	1		—
	4✓	4(8)	
2	10✓	10(1)✓	10(1,4)
	12✓	10(4)✓	10(4,1)
		12(2)	
3	11✓	11(4)✓	—
	14✓	14(1)✓	
4	15✓	—	—

Figure 2.16 *Filling Column 3*

in Column 3. As before, this has been achieved by comparing each implicant in each index group in Column 2 with each implicant in the next higher index group. The added requirement is that implicants can merge only if they have the same number in brackets. Thus, 10(1) and 14(1) merge into 10(1,4) and 10(4) and 11(4) merge into 10(4,1). The implicants 10(1,4) and 10(4,1) are in fact the same group of four minterms; both describe the group of minterms 10 + 0, 10 + 1, 10 + 4, and 10 + 1 + 4, that is, 10, 11, 14, and 15. No further simplification is possible since there are no possible comparisons in Column 3. The implicants are thus 1, which is unmarked in Column 1, 4(8) and 12(2), which are unmarked in Column 2, and 10(1, 4), which is unmarked in Column 3. A prime implicant selection table, as described in an earlier section, must now be used to select which of the prime implicants are required for the function. In this example, prime implicants 1, 4(8), and 10(1, 4) are essential, and prime implicant 12(2) is not required. The required function is thus F(D, C, B, A) = Σ 1, 4(8), 10(1,4) = /D./C./B.A + ~~D~~.C./B./A + D.~~C~~.B.~~A~~ = /D./C./B.A + C./B./A + D.B.

Example 3
We require the simplification of the function G(F, E, D, C, B, A) = Σ 0, 8, 16, 24, 32, 40, 48, 56. The simplification is shown in Figure 2.17. The algorithm extends to four columns, and all minterms and implicants merge into the single prime implicant 0(8, 16, 32). The first three entries in Column 3 have been produced by detecting that 0(8) and 16(8) merge to form 0(8, 16). Also, 0(8) and 32(8) merge to form 0(8, 32). Also, 0(16) and 8(16) merge to form 0(16, 8), which is the same as the previously detected 0(8, 16). To form Column 4, 0(8, 16) and 32(8, 16) have been merged into 0(8, 16, 32), since these implicants have the same numbers in brackets and differ by a power of 2. Similarly, 0(8, 32) and 16(8, 32) merge into 0(8, 32, 16) which is the same as 0(8, 16, 32). Also, 0(16, 32) and 8(16, 32) merge into 0(16,

Index	Column 1	Column 2	Column 3	Column 4
0	0✓	0(8)✓	0(8, 16)✓	0(8,16,32)
		0(16)✓	0(8, 32)✓	
		0(32)✓	0(16, 32)✓	
1	8✓	8(16)✓	8(16, 32)✓	—
		8(32)✓		
	16✓	16(8)✓	16(8,32)✓	
		16(32)✓		
	32✓	32(8)✓	32(8, 16)✓	
		32(16)✓		
2	24✓	24(32)✓	—	—
	40✓	40(16)✓		
	48✓	48(8)✓		
3	56✓		—	—
4	—	—	—	—
5	—			
6	—			

Figure 2.17 *Simplification of Example 3*

32, 8) which is the same as 0(8, 16, 32). The only prime implicant that is unmarked in the table is 0(8, 16, 32). This is ~~/F./E./D.~~/C./B./A or /C./B./A[6].

Example 4

We require the simplification of the function H(E, D, C, B, A) = Σ 0, 1, 2, 3, 10, 16, 17, 18, 19, 28, 29. The simplification is shown in Figure 2.18. The first few entries in Column 3 have been produced by detecting the following merges. Implicants 0(1) and 2(1) merge to form 0(1, 2). Implicants 0(1) and 16(1) merge to form 0(1, 16). Implicants 0(2) and 1(2) merge to form 0(1, 2). Implicants 0(2) and 16(2) merge to form 0(2, 16). Implicants 0(16) and 1(16) merge to form 0(1, 16), which has previously been detected.

To form Column 4, 0(1, 2) and 16(1, 2), merge into 0(1, 2, 16), since these implicants have the same numbers in brackets and differ by a power of 2. Similarly, 0(1, 16) and 2(1, 16) merge into 0(1, 2, 16). Also, 0(2, 16) merges with 1(2, 16) to form 0(1, 2, 16). The unmarked prime implicants are 2(8), 28(1) and 0(1, 2, 16).

---

[6] We might have written this result down immediately since the minterm list is all the multiples of 8 that can be accommodated in 6 bits. All multiples of 8 end in ...000.

Index	Column 1	Column 2	Column 3	Column 4
0	0✓	0(1)✓	0(1, 2)✓	0(1, 2, 16)
		0(2)✓	0(1, 16)✓	
		0(16)✓	0(2, 16)✓	
1	1✓	1(2)✓		—
		1(16)✓		
	2✓	2(1)✓	2(1, 16)✓	
		2(8)		
	16✓	2(16)✓	16(1, 2)✓	
		16(1)✓		
		16(2)✓		
2	3✓		—	—
	10✓			
	17✓			
	18✓	18(1)✓		
3	19✓		—	—
	28✓	28(1)		
4	29✓	—	—	—
5	—			

Figure 2.18 *Simplification of Example 4*

Implicant 2(8) covers minterms 2 and 10, prime implicant 28(1) covers minterms 29 and 29, while implicant 0(1, 2, 16) covers the eight minterms 0, 1, 2, 3, 16, 17, 18, 19. The prime implicant selection table shows that all these are essential prime implicants. The simplified function is thus H = 2(8) + 28(1) + 0(1, 2, 16) = /E.~~D~~./C.B./A + E.D.C./B.~~A~~ + ~~E~~./D./C.~~B~~.~~A~~, that is, H = /E./C.B./A + E.D.C./B + /D./C.

2.8 Problems

1   Given C = 1, B = 0, and A = 1, and F = /C.B./A + C./B.A + C.B./A + C.B.A, what is the value of F?

2   Given C = 1, B = 0, and A = 1, and G = /C./B./A + /C.B.A + C./B./A, what is the value of G?

3   Construct the truth table for F = /C.B./A + C./B.A + C.B./A + C.B.A.

4   Construct the truth table for G = /C./B./A + /C.B.A + C./B./A.

5   In Figure 2.6, in which squares are the orchestra members that play strings AND wind?

6   In Figure 2.6, in which squares are the orchestra members that play strings OR wind?

7   In Figure 2.6, in which squares are the orchestra members that do NOT play strings AND play wind?

8   In Figure 2.6, in which squares are the orchestra members that play strings OR percussion OR wind?

9   In Figure 2.6, in which squares are the orchestra members that do NOT play strings AND do NOT play percussion AND do NOT play wind?

10   In Figure 2.6, do the orchestra members in square 2 play strings?

11   In Figure 2.6, how can the members in squares 6, 7 be described?

12   Using a map, show that F = C./B.A + C.B.A. = C.A.

13   Using a map, show that F = BA + /C./B.A + C.B./A. = /C.A + C.B.

14   Using a map, show that F = BA + C.B + /B./A + /C./B = /C./B + B.A + C./A.

15   Using a map, show that F = BA + C.B + /B./A + /C./B = /B./A + /C.A + C.B.

16   Using a map, show that:

   (i)   Z = C.B./A + /C./B + /B.A
   (ii) Y = /B.A + C./B + C.A
   (iii) X = B./A + C.A + C.B

where the functions are defined by the following truth table.

C	B	A	Z	Y	X
0	0	0	1	0	0
0	0	1	1	1	0
0	1	0	0	0	1
0	1	1	0	0	0
1	0	0	0	1	0
1	0	1	1	1	1
1	1	0	1	0	1
1	1	1	0	1	1

17 Using a KV map, show that /D./C.B.A + /D.C./B.A + /D.C.B.A + D./C.B.A = /D.C.A + /C./B.A.

18 Using a KV map, show that /D./C./B./A + /D./C./B.A + D.C.B./A + D.C.B.A + /D.C = /D./B + C.B.

19 Solve Problem 12 using the Quine–McCluskey method.

20 Solve Problem 13 using the Quine–McCluskey method.

21 Solve Problem 14 using the Quine–McCluskey method.

22 Solve Problem 15 using the Quine–McCluskey method.

23 Solve Problem 16 using the Quine–McCluskey method.

24 Solve Problem 17 using the Quine–McCluskey method.

25 Solve Problem 18 using the Quine–McCluskey method.

26 Using the Quine–McCluskey method, simplify H(E, D, C, B, A) = Σ 0, 4, 9, 14, 25, 30.

3 Electronic logic circuits

3.1 Electronic controller

We want an electronic circuit that automatically performs the function of the bank vault access controller discussed in Chapter 2. In this chapter, we see how electronic circuits, called **gates**, can be made to perform the basic logical functions, AND, OR, and NOT. Using these, we design two commonly used devices, the **decoder** and the **multiplexer**. We also see how circuits made from gates can be made to store binary values and how these **flip-flops** are used to make **state machines**.

3.2 Development of the bank vault controller design

In Chapter 2 we arrived at the logic expression for a device that will control access to a bank vault. To develop this algebraic expression into functioning hardware, we decide that we will have on/off switches to represent whether a particular bank employee is present or not. (In practice, these might be on/off switches that can be operated only by a conventional key held by the Manager, Assistant Manager, and Chief Cashier.) We assume that the bank vault lock is an electromechanical device that opens only if a control signal to the lock, named 'Allow_access', has the logical value 1. Each switch circuit is required to generate a binary signal having a logical value of 0 or 1. We let logical value 1 be represented by 5 volts and let logical value 0 be represented by 0 volts. A simple circuit, Figure 3.1 will do this. Using three of these, the outline of the design is as shown in Figure 3.2. The combinational logic box has three inputs, M, A, C, and one output, Allow_access.

The combinational logic box is required to generate the signal Allow_access according to either of the expressions derived in Chapter 1:

Allow_access = /M.A.C + M./A.C + M.A./C + M.A.C
Allow_access = M.A + M.C + A.C

Figure 3.1 (a) *Circuit to generate a 5 V or 0 V signal from a toggle switch;* (b) *schematic representation of the switch that generates signal M*

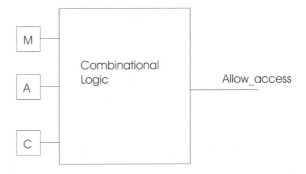

Figure 3.2 *Overall design concept*

We choose to implement the second of these expressions since it is simpler. Now we need electronic circuits that perform the AND, OR, and NOT operations.

3.3 Gates – electronic circuits that perform logical operations

With a little ingenuity we can design simple circuits[1] that make use of the properties of the diode to perform the logical operations AND and OR. We shall assume that when a diode conducts current, it has 0 volts across its terminals. Then, in the circuit, Figure 3.3(a), if both inputs A and B are at

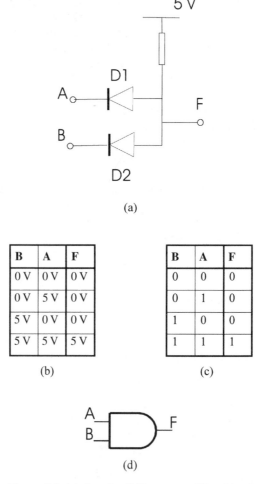

(a)

B	A	F
0 V	0 V	0 V
0 V	5 V	0 V
5 V	0 V	0 V
5 V	5 V	5 V

(b)

B	A	F
0	0	0
0	1	0
1	0	0
1	1	1

(c)

(d)

Figure 3.3 (a) *Simple AND circuit;* (b) *table showing all possible inputs and corresponding output;* (c) *truth table;* (d) *symbol*

---

[1] These circuits work quite well when used on their own. However, problems arise when the output of one gate is connected to the input of other gates. This is due primarily to the fact that a real diode, when conducting, does not have zero voltage across it. Practical gates are made with more sophisticated circuits using transistors.

0 volts, both diodes conduct current and the voltage at F is zero. If input A is at zero volts while input B is at 5 volts, diode D1 will conduct so pulling F down to zero volts; diode D2 is not conducting. Only when both inputs are at 5 volts will the output F be at 5 volts. A table showing these voltages is shown in Figure 3.3(b). Remembering that 5 volts represent a logical 1, and 0 volts represent a logical 0, we have the truth table of the AND circuit, Figure 3.3(c).

Similarly, in the circuit of the OR gate, Figure 3.4(a), if either or both of the inputs are at 5 volts, a conducting diode brings F to 5 volts. The output F is at 0 volts only when both inputs are at 0 volts.

The NOT circuit, Figure 3.5(a), uses a transistor that acts like an on/off switch. When input A is at 5 volts, the transistor is switched on and output F is at zero volts; when input A is at zero volts, the transistor is switched off and output F is at 5 volts.

To avoid drawing the detail of these gates every time we need them, we give the gates the graphical symbols shown in the figures. Using these symbols, the **logic circuit** of the vault-access controller is shown in Figure 3.6. This shows the appearance of program `Boo11.exe` when this function has been selected. In `Boo11.exe`, a wire that carries a logical 1 signal is

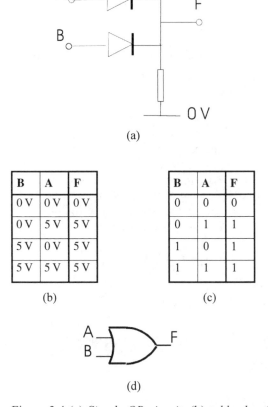

(a)

B	A	F
0 V	0 V	0 V
0 V	5 V	5 V
5 V	0 V	5 V
5 V	5 V	5 V

(b)

B	A	F
0	0	0
0	1	1
1	0	1
1	1	1

(c)

(d)

Figure 3.4 (a) *Simple OR circuit;* (b) *table showing all possible inputs and corresponding output;* (c) *truth table;* (d) *symbol*

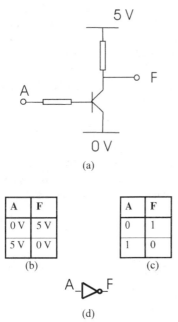

(a)

A	F
0 V	5 V
5 V	0 V

(b)

A	F
0	1
1	0

(c)

(d)

Figure 3.5 (a) *Simple NOT circuit;* (b) *table showing all possible inputs and corresponding output;* (c) *truth table;* (d) *symbol*

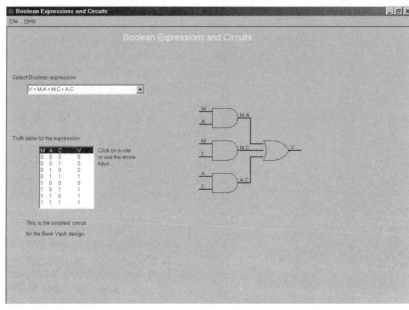

Figure 3.6 *Logic circuit for Allow_access, V = M.A + M.C + A.C*

shown in red, otherwise, it is green. Select a row of the truth table by clicking on it and observe the inputs and outputs of all the gates.

Select the other logic circuits in `Bool1.exe` and see them in operation.

This is a good time to try Problems 1 to 9.

3.4 Decoder circuit

Sometimes we wish to convert a pattern of bits that represent a number into several outputs, each of which identifies the input number. Thus, in Figure 3.7, we regard inputs W1 and W0 as a 2-bit number, <W1, W0>. This number is decimal 0 to 3. Only one of the outputs, Y0 to Y3, will be a logical 1, that output indicating the value of the 2-bit number at the input. The logic expressions for the four outputs are simply:

$$Y0 = /W1./W0$$
$$Y1 = /W1.W0$$
$$Y2 = W1./W0$$
$$Y3 = W1.W0$$

One use of a decoder circuit is in the device we consider next, the multiplexer.

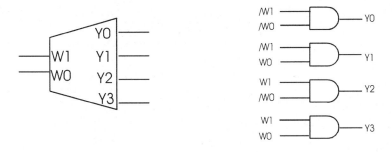

(a)

W1	W0	Y0	Y1	Y2	Y3
0	0	1	0	0	0
0	1	0	1	0	0
1	0	0	0	1	0
1	1	0	0	0	1

(b)

Figure 3.7 (a) *Diagram of a two-line to four-line decoder;* (b) *function table*

3.5 Multiplexer circuit The multiplexer is the logical equivalent of a mechanical multiway switch. A mechanical multiway switch is positioned by hand to select one of a number of inputs to the output. The multiplexer performs the same function but allows the required input to be selected by binary signals. A four-way multiplexer is shown in Figure 3.8(a); any of the four inputs can be connected to the output. The particular input is selected according to the numerical value of the two inputs, S1 and S0, which are regarded as the number <S1, S0>. We *could* design the multiplexer logic circuit by regarding it as a circuit with six inputs, four of which are the data inputs and the other two are the select signals, S1 and S0. Instead, we design it more intuitively.

The basis of our approach to the design of the circuit is the concept of **enabling** an AND gate. Consider an AND gate with two inputs, X and Y. If $Y == 0$, the gate output is $X.Y = X.0 = 0$. However, if $Y == 1$, the gate output is $X.1 = X$. We can regard Y as a signal that enables the AND gate. If $Y == 1$, the gate is **enabled** and its output is the same as X; if $Y == 0$, the gate is **disabled** and its output is 0 whatever the value of X.

In Figure 3.8(b), each of the four AND gates is enabled by a signal from the decoder. Since only one of the decoder outputs is a logical 1, only one of the AND gates is enabled. The enabled AND gate passes its input, Xn, to its output and to the OR gate. All the other inputs to the OR gate are logical 0 so that Z is the same as the selected Xn input. For example, assume

<S1, S0> = = <1, 0>, then only Y2 is a logical 1 and X2 is effectively connected to Z.

We can merge the logic of the decoder with the AND gates connected to the X inputs, giving the circuit of Figure 3.8(c). A more sophisticated approach to the design of this device would be to begin by considering its required function as defined in Figure 3.8(d). From this we can immediately write Z = /S1./S0.X0 + /S1.S0.X1 + S1./S0.X2 + S1.S0.X3, which is the logical expression implemented in Figure 3.8(c).

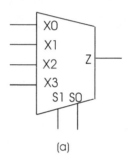

(a)

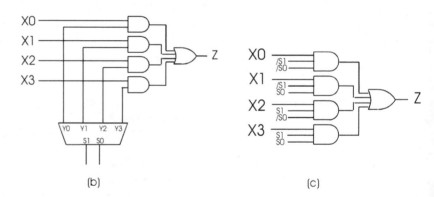

(b)

(c)

S1	S0	Z
0	0	X0
0	1	X1
1	0	X2
1	1	X3

(d)

Figure 3.8 *Four-way multiplexer*

3.6 Flip-flops   Flip-flops are produced from combinational logic circuits in which an output is connected so as to form one of its inputs. This **feedback** connection gives rise to devices that **store** a single bit.

3.6.1 Basic flip-flop[2]

Consider the logic circuit in Figure 3.9. Both drawings represent the same circuit.

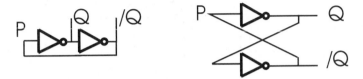

Figure 3.9 *Logic circuit for the basic flip-flop*

Here the output of the logic circuit is fed back to become an input to the circuit. Suppose $Q = = 1$ then $/Q = = 0$, which feeds back to point P so making $Q = = 1$. The circuit is thus in a stable state with $Q = = 1$ and $/Q = = 0$. Alternatively, suppose $Q = = 0$ then $/Q = = 1$, which feeds back to point P so making $Q = = 0$. The circuit is again in a stable state with $Q = = 0$ and $/Q = = 1$. Hence, the circuit has two states, one with $Q = = 0$ and the other with $Q = = 1$.

Taking the output of this circuit as Q, the circuit may be regarded as a store for a single bit. To make the circuit useful we must be able to set Q to the value we wish to store. We can do this by incorporating OR gates at the inputs to the inverters, as shown in Figure 3.10.

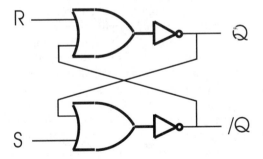

Figure 3.10 *Logic circuit for the RS flip-flop*

The inputs R and S are normally at 0 but may be pulsed, that is, taken to a 1 and then back to 0. When S is pulsed, it makes $Q = 1$; when R is pulsed, $Q = 0$. Thus we can force the circuit into either of its two states, and we have a useful device that can store a 0 or a 1. This circuit is called the RS

---

[2] The behaviour of this circuit was first reported by Eccles and Jordan as long ago as 1919.

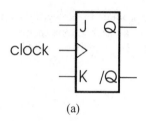

(a)

J	K	Q+	
0	0	Q	No change
0	1	0	Store 0
1	0	1	Store 1
1	1	/Q	Toggle

(b)

Figure 3.11 *JK flip-flop:* (a) *schematic;* (b) *function table*

flip-flop, the Reset/Set flip-flop, or simply, the basic flip-flop. The RS flip-flop forms the basis of more useful types of flip-flop, those that change their state only when a clock signal is active. The most important of these flip-flops are the JK flip-flop and the D flip-flop.

3.6.2 Edge-triggered JK flip-flop

The schematic symbol and function table of the edge-triggered JK flip-flop are shown in Figure 3.11. The signals J and K are the inputs that determine what value the output will take after the rising edge of the clock pulse. The output of the flip-flop before the rising edge of the clock pulse is called Q; the output after the rising edge is called Q^+. The function table shows that if we wish to store a 0 in the flip-flop, we can set <JK> = = <01>, then after the next rising edge of the clock, Q will have the value 0. Similarly, by setting <JK> = = <10>, we can store a 1. If <JK> = = <00>, the output of the flip-flop will not change even after a rising edge of the clock. Finally, if <JK> = = <11>, the output of the flip-flop will change to its alternative value after a rising edge of the clock; this is called **toggling**.

3.6.3 Edge-triggered D flip-flop

The schematic symbol and function table for the edge-triggered D flip-flop are shown in Figure 3.12. Its behaviour is very simple: after a rising edge of the clock pulse, the output of the flip-flop becomes whatever it was on the D input just before the rising edge.

(a)

D	Q+	
0	0	Store 0
1	1	Store 1

(b)

Figure 3.12 *D flip-flop:* (a) *schematic;* (b) *function table*

3.7 Storage registers

In our later study of computing machines we shall use flip-flops to store patterns of 0s and 1s. For example, to store a 4-bit number, we shall use four D flip-flops, Figure 3.13. To store a number that is currently on the wires B_3, B_2, B_1, and B_0, all the computing machine will have to do is to produce a rising edge on the wire labelled *load_Register*. The output wires Q will then continue to hold the number even when the inputs B_i change.

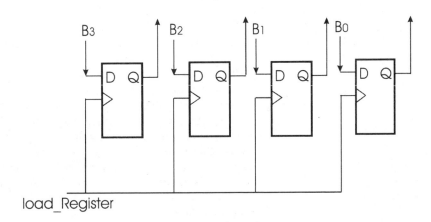

load_Register

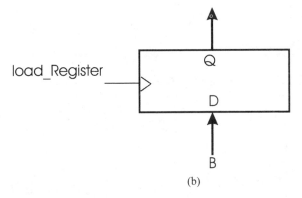

(b)

Figure 3.13 *Four-bit register:* (a) *four individual flip-flops;* (b) *schematic*

3.8 State machines*

Combinational logic circuits have outputs that depend *only* on the current inputs. State machines on the other hand are digital circuits whose outputs depend not only on their current inputs but also on the previous **state** of the circuit. At any time, the state of a state machine is the contents of all its flip-flops together with the value of all its input signals. A clock pulse causes a state machine to change its state.

   A simple example of a state machine is a counter circuit in which we want the next output of the counter, which is generated after a clock pulse, to depend on its previous output. A counter that is able to count up and down must have an input signal that indicates the direction of the count; in general, state machines may have any number of input signals. Very often we use state machines to generate arbitrary sequences of 0s and 1s, that is, binary waveforms. In such cases we might allocate a flip-flop in the machine to each output and we design the state machine so that the flip-flops change according to the required sequence of outputs. We begin with an example of such a machine. Because state machines go through a sequence of states, they are a type of **sequential machine**.

3.8.1 State Machine 1 using D type flip-flops

This example of a state machine has no external inputs. The machine is to go through the sequence shown in the **state diagram**, Figure 3.14. That is, when a clock pulse occurs, the machine will go from its present state to the state pointed to by the arrow. The design of a circuit that behaves in this way begins by transferring the information from the state diagram to the **state transition table**, Figure 3.15. The column headed 'Present State' simply lists all the possible states of the three flip-flops in numerical order. Now we choose a row in the table and write down what the next state is to be; this is simply the state at the head of the arrow that starts at the present state in the state diagram. We do this for all the rows in the table.

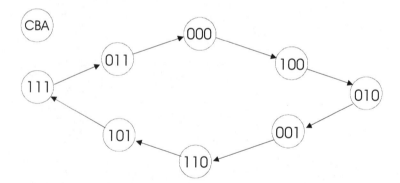

Figure 3.14 *State diagram of Machine 1*

The required flip-flop inputs must now be determined. If we choose to use D type flip-flops all we have to do is copy the C^+ column to the D_c column, copy the B^+ column to the D_b column, and copy the A^+ column to the D_a column. The reason for this simplicity is that D type flip-flops simply store the data on their D input when a clock pulse occurs. Thus, for example, if the next state of the machine is to be <110> the circuit must make <D_c, D_b, D_a> = <110>. Then, after a clock pulse these data are stored in the flip-flops and the machine has moved to state <110>.

Now regard the signals C, B, and A as the inputs to combinational logic that produces outputs D_c, D_b, and D_a. That is, regard columns C, B, A, and D_c, D_b, D_a as a truth table for the required combinational logic. All that remains is to simplify this combinational logic and the design is done. This

Present state			Next state			Inputs to flip-flops		
C	B	A	C+	B+	A+	D_c	D_b	D_a
0	0	0	1	0	0	1	0	0
0	0	1	1	1	0	1	1	0
0	1	0	0	0	1	0	0	1
0	1	1	0	0	0	0	0	0
1	0	0	0	1	0	0	1	0
1	0	1	1	1	1	1	1	1
1	1	0	1	0	1	1	0	1
1	1	1	0	1	1	0	1	1

Figure 3.15 *State transition table for Machine 1, with required inputs to flip-flops*

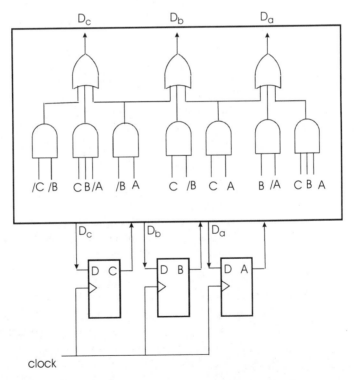

Figure 3.16 *Circuit for Machine 1 using D type flip-flops*

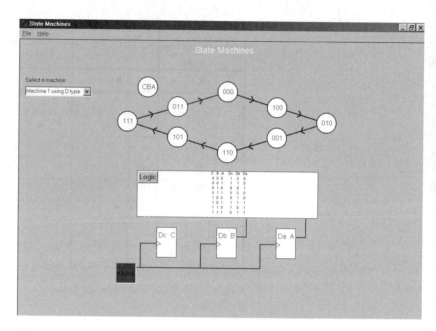

Figure 3.17 *Program Seq1.exe when showing Machine 1 using D type flip-flops*

combinational logic, whose outputs are connected to the flip-flop inputs, is usually called the **next state logic**.

After simplifying, the next state logic is:
$$D_c = /C./B + /B.A + C.B./A$$
$$D_b = C./B + /B.A + C.A$$
$$D_a = B./A + C.B.A + C.A$$

Figure 3.16 shows the complete circuit diagram for this state machine. (We will not draw the complete circuit diagram for subsequent examples since the next state logic can be adequately expressed by Boolean expressions.) You can see this machine in operation by running program Seq1.exe and selecting 'Machine 1 using D type' in the selection box, Figure 3.17. Click on the toggle switch that generates the clock signals for the flip-flops, and observe the operation of this state machine. In particular, observe that the next state logic generates the inputs to the flip-flops that are required to move it to the next state when the clock signal is a rising edge. Note too that a falling edge on the clock signal has no effect.

3.8.2 State Machine 2 using D type flip-flops

This example of a state machine has a single external input, P. Thus, the next state of this machine depends on P as well as the present state. Its state diagram can be seen when you run program Seq1.exe and select 'Machine 2 using D type' in the selection box. Observe that, in any given present state,

Present state				Next state		
P	**C**	**B**	**A**	**C+**	**B+**	**A+**
0	0	0	0	1	0	0
0	0	0	1	1	1	0
0	0	1	0	0	0	1
0	0	1	1	0	0	0
0	1	0	0	0	1	0
0	1	0	1	1	1	1
0	1	1	0	1	0	1
0	1	1	1	0	1	1
1	0	0	0	1	0	0
1	0	0	1	1	1	0
1	0	1	0	1	1	1
1	0	1	1	0	0	0
1	1	0	0	0	1	0
1	1	0	1	1	1	1
1	1	1	0	0	0	0
1	1	1	1	0	1	1

Figure 3.18 *State transition table for Machine 2*

the next state depends on the state of the switch that generates signal P. (In some present states, the next state is the same irrespective of the value of P.) In the state transition table, Figure 3.18, the present state columns have an additional column for P. We have omitted the columns D_c, D_b, and D_a because these are the same as C^+, B^+, and A^+ respectively. The design process follows that described for Machine 1 but here there are four inputs (P, C, B, A) to the next state logic. Thus we draw a four-variable map for D_c, a second map for D_b, and a third map for D_a. The simplified next state logic can be seen by clicking on the **Next-state Logic** button when running program Seq1.exe.

3.8.3 State Machine 1 using JK flip-flops

If we choose to use JK flip-flops to make a state machine, the next state logic must produce a J and a K input for each flip-flop. The immediate question is – what must these J and K inputs be in order to cause the JK flip-flop to go to the required state after a clock pulse? Suppose the flip-flop is currently storing 1 (Q = = 1) and, after a clock pulse, we wish it to store 0 (Q^+ = = 0). This is the transition, $1 \rightarrow 0$. From the table given earlier, Figure 3.11, we see that <JK> = = <01> causes the flip-flop to store 0. We also see that

Q	→	Q+	J	K
0	→	0	0	X
0	→	1	1	X
1	→	0	X	1
1	→	1	X	0

Figure 3.19 *Table showing required values of JK in order to obtain a particular transition*

$<JK> = = <11>$ causes the flip-flop to toggle. Thus both $<JK> = = <01>$ and $<JK> = = <11>$ will cause the transition $1 \to 0$. Hence, to cause the transition $1 \to 0$ requires that $K = 1$ and the signal level on the J input is irrelevant. In the table, Figure 3.17, the transition $1 \to 0$ is shown as requiring $<JK> = <X1>$, where the X indicates an irrelevant value that can be either 0 or 1. Irrelevant values are often called **don't care** values. It is a good idea for you to check how the other entries in this table have been obtained.

We are now able to define the next state logic that determines the next state of Machine 1 using JK flip-flops. First we draw the outline of the state transition table, Figure 3.20. All possible present states are then added in numerical order, and the required next state entered into the next state columns. Then, rather tediously, we look at the present state and the next state of each flip-flop for every possible present state and determine the required values of the J and K inputs by referring to Figure 3.19.

To simplify the next state logic we must draw six maps, one each for J_c, K_c, J_b, K_b, J_a, and K_a. (You can use KVMap.exe to help with this.) Each of these maps is a three-variable map and each is littered with the don't care symbol, X. How are we to deal with them? Remember that to obtain the simplest logic expression we must place all squares marked with 1 in the largest possible group. If any adjacent squares marked with X allow us to draw a larger group, then we *must* regard those Xs as 1s and include them in the larger group. Any X that does not help us to identify a larger group is regarded as a 0 and not placed in a group. You should try to do this; the best solution can be seen by clicking on the **Next-state Logic** button when running program Seq1.exe, having selected 'Machine 1 using JK'. Incidentally, this logic is considerably simpler than that required when using D type flip-flops. Alas, we do not know which type of flip-flop requires simpler next state logic until we have carried out the design for both types of flip-flop.

Present state			Next state			Inputs to flip-flops					
C	B	A	C+	B+	A+	J_c	K_c	J_b	K_b	J_a	K_a
0	0	0	1	0	0	1	X	0	X	0	X
0	0	1	1	1	0	1	X	1	X	X	1
0	1	0	0	0	1	0	X	X	1	1	X
0	1	1	0	0	0	0	X	X	1	X	1
1	0	0	0	1	0	X	1	1	X	0	X
1·	0	1	1	1	1	X	0	1	X	X	0
1	1	0	1	0	1	X	0	X	1	1	X
1	1	1	0	1	1	X	1	X	0	X	0

Figure 3.20 *State transition table for Machine 1 with required JK values*

3.8.4 State Machine 2 using JK flip-flops

The design of this machine follows the steps in the previous section. However, the present state is now determined by the four variables P, C, B, and A giving 16 rows in the state transition table. (The design process is becoming rather laborious! Fortunately, practising engineers have the benefit of computer-based design tools to do this task more quickly and more reliably.) Check your design of the next state logic with that seen by clicking on the Next-state Logic button when running program Seq1.exe having selected 'Machine 2 using JK'.

3.9 Programmable logic devices*

There is a similarity in all the combinational logic expressions and their circuits that we have considered. All the expressions are of the form:

$$output = AND\ of\ some\ inputs\ +\ AND\ of\ some\ inputs\ +\ ... \\ +\ AND\ of\ some\ inputs,$$

where some of the inputs may be inverted. This leads directly to circuits that comprise a layer of AND gates, each of which performs the logical AND of some inputs, the outputs of which are connected to a single OR gate that produces the required output signal. Revisit the Bool1.exe examples if you have not noticed this similarity.

In the early 1980s, it was recognized that it was possible to make use of this similarity by making a circuit on silicon, containing a number of AND gates whose outputs are connected to an OR gate. All the inputs, and their complements, are connected to all the AND gate inputs using connections that are **fuses** and so can be removed. Additional circuits allow individual fuses to be broken or 'blown'. By blowing the appropriate fuses, we are left with the logic circuit we require. These devices are called programmable logic devices, **PLD**s. The fuses are blown using an apparatus called a '**PLD programmer**'.

Manufacturers of PLDs distribute computer software that allows the user to type in the required logical function and the software generates a data file containing the information that the PLD programming apparatus needs to blow the appropriate fuses. Using a connection between the user's computer and the PLD programmer apparatus, this data is sent to the PLD programmer that then blows the appropriate fuses to leave intact only the fuses that produce the required logic function. Subsequently, the designers of these circuits have added flip-flops into PLDs so that state machines can also be constructed on a single chip. Consequently, modern logic circuits are usually made from PLDs rather than from individual gates and flip-flops.

3.10 Problems

1   Devise a logic circuit to perform the function $F = C.A + B.C$.

2   Devise a logic circuit to perform the function $G = C./A + /B./C$.

3   Devise a logic circuit to perform the function $H = D.C.B.A + B.C./A$.

4   The diagram, Figure P3.1, shows two identical circuits connected to a long wire called 'Bus'. The Bus wire is pulled up to 5 volts by the resistor connected to 5 volts.

   (i) Determine the voltage level of Bus for all four combinations of voltage on B and A.

   (ii) Assuming the usual convention (5 V = logical 1, 0 V = logical 0), complete the expression: Bus = _____ .

   (iii) Assuming the usual convention (5 V = logical 1, 0 V = logical 0), complete the expression: /Bus = _____ .

   (iv) If many transistors were to be connected to the Bus wire, describe in English what input signals make Bus = 0.

This sort of circuit is widely used in computers where the Bus wire is on the motherboard or backplane and connects to several printed circuit boards.

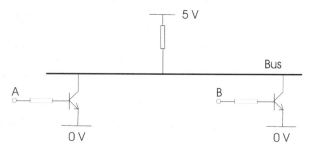

Figure P3.1

You can use program KVMap.exe to check your solutions for the following problems.

5   A circuit is required to accept two 2-bit unsigned integers, <X1, X0> and <Y1, Y0>, and output their product. Construct the truth table for the circuit, obtain minimal logic expressions for the outputs, and sketch a logic diagram.

6   A circuit is required to accept two 2-bit unsigned integers, <X1, X0> and <Y1, Y0>, and output the signals G, E, and L defined as follows.

   When <X1, X0> is greater than <Y1, Y0>, G = 1, else G = 0.
   When <X1, X0> is equal to <Y1, Y0>, E = 1, else E = 0.
   When <X1, X0> is less than <Y1, Y0>, L = 1, else L = 0.

   (i) Construct a truth table to completely specify the circuit.

   (ii) Derive minimal Boolean expressions for each output G, E, and L.

   (iii) Sketch a logic circuit using AND, OR, and NOT gates.

7   A four-segment display device is shown below. The segments are labelled A, B, C, and D. It is required to display the characters shown in response to the three inputs X, Y, and Z. Obtain the simplified logical expressions for the four outputs of an encoder that is to drive the display. Assume that a logical 1 to a display segment causes that segment to illuminate.

A\ /B

C/ \D Segment disposition and labels.

X, Y, Z	Display
0 0 0	Blank
0 0 1	\ /
0 1 0	/ \
0 1 1	/ /
1 0 0	\ \
1 0 1	/\
1 1 0	\ /
1 1 1	\ / /\

8   Design a state machine using D type flip-flops having the following state transition table. This device is a **self-starting ring counter**.

Present state			Next state		
C	B	A	C+	B+	A+
0	0	0	1	0	0
0	0	1	1	0	0
0	1	0	0	0	1
0	1	1	0	0	1
1	0	0	0	1	0
1	0	1	0	1	0
1	1	0	0	1	1
1	1	1	0	1	1

9　Design a state machine using D type flip-flops having the following state transition table. This is a **3-bit Gray-code counter**.

Present state			Next state		
C	B	A	C+	B+	A+
0	0	0	0	0	1
0	0	1	0	1	1
0	1	0	1	1	0
0	1	1	0	1	0
1	0	0	0	0	0
1	0	1	1	0	0
1	1	0	1	1	1
1	1	1	1	0	1

10　Design a **4-bit right-shift register** using D flip-flops. On each clock pulse, the data in the register moves one place to the right and flip-flop D becomes 0. For example, <DCBA> = <1011> becomes <DCBA> = <0101>.

11　Design a **3-bit pure binary up-counter** using JK flip-flops. When the counter reaches state <111> its next state is to be <000>.

12　Design a **3-bit pure binary up–down counter** using JK flip-flops. When input U == 1, the counter counts up, when U == 0, the counter counts down.

13　The behaviour of a particular sequential circuit is described by the state diagram shown in Figure P3.2.

(i)　Obtain the required logic, assuming the use of D type flip-flops.
(ii)　Obtain the required logic, assuming the use of JK type flip-flops.
(iii)　Sketch the circuit of the simpler of your two designs.

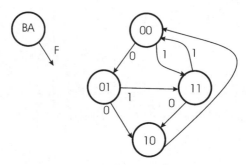

Figure P3.2

14 The behaviour of a particular sequential circuit is described by the state diagram shown in Figure P3.3.

(i) Obtain the required logic, assuming the use of D type flip-flops.
(ii) Obtain the required logic, assuming the use of JK type flip-flops.
(iii) Sketch the circuit of the simpler of your two designs.

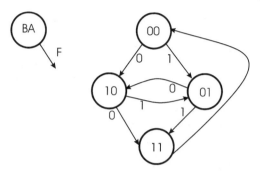

Figure P3.3

15 Using D type flip-flops, design and sketch the circuit of the state machine whose behaviour is shown in Figure P3.4.

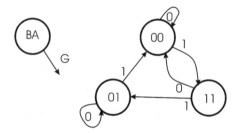

Figure P3.4

Determine the behaviour of your circuit should it erroneously get into the unspecified state and draw the full state diagram.

16 Design a synchronous counter using JK flip-flops having the state sequence shown in Figure P3.5. The decimal numbers indicate the binary number <DCBA>.

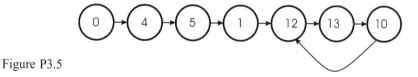

Figure P3.5

4 Computer arithmetic

A result of our choosing to represent numbers in binary notation is that we can devise logic circuits to process the numbers. In this chapter, we design a simple adder circuit and develop it into a more useful **ALU** (arithmetic and logic unit). We see how the simple adder can be made to operate faster by using the **carry-look-ahead** technique. Finally, we look at how **floating-point numbers** are represented and how arithmetic is performed on them.

4.1 Circuit to add numbers

We wish to construct a circuit that will form the sum of two 4-bit numbers. Let these numbers be $A = = <A_3 A_2 A_1 A_0>$ and $T = = <T_3 T_2 T_1 T_0>$ while the sum of A and T is $S = = <S_4 S_0 S_2 S_1 S_0>$.

$$
\begin{array}{cccc}
A_3 & A_2 & A_1 & A_0 \\
T_3 & T_2 & T_1 & T_0 \\
\hline
S_4 \quad S_3 & S_2 & S_1 & S_0
\end{array} \quad \text{ADD}
$$

The notation Y_i refers to bit i of number Y. As noted in Chapter 1, the sum, S, has one more bit than A and T. Our aim is to make the device shown in Figure 4.1. This device has eight inputs and five outputs.

We *could* draw the truth table for this device and derive the logic expressions in a way similar to that used in Chapter 1. Since there are eight inputs, the truth table would have 2^8 (256) rows. However, if we want an adder to add two 8-bit numbers, there will be 16 inputs, giving 2^{16} (65 536) rows! We will take another approach; we shall copy the way humans perform addition. Humans proceed by first adding A_0 and T_0 using the rules for adding two 1-bit numbers to produce a 2-bit sum:

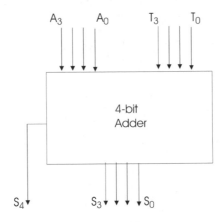

Figure 4.1 *Four-bit adder*

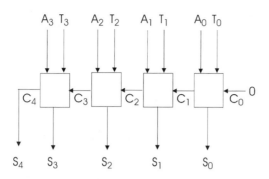

Figure 4.2 *Four-bit adder using four full adders*

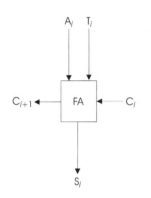

Figure 4.3 *Full adder:*
(a) *connections;* (b) *truth table*

A_i	T_i	C_i	C_{i+1}	S_i
0	0	0	0	0
0	0	1	0	1
0	1	0	0	1
0	1	1	1	0
1	0	0	0	1
1	0	1	1	0
1	1	0	1	0
1	1	1	1	1

0 plus 0 = 00   0 plus 1 = 01
1 plus 0 = 01   1 plus 1 = 10

We write down the right-hand bit of the 2-bit sum as part of the answer and carry the left-hand bit into the column to the left. Now when we add bits A_1 and T_1 we also add the carry from the previous column. We continue in this way until all the 4 bits in the numbers have been added. Using this method, the adder design becomes as shown in Figure 4.2, which shows how the 4-bit adder can be made from four identical 1-bit adders. The 1-bit adder is traditionally called a **full adder**.

We can easily design the circuit of the full adder using the truth-table method from Chapter 2. The truth table of the required logic is given in Figure 4.3. After simplification we obtain the expressions for the logic of the full adder:

$$S_i = /C_i./A_i.T_i + /C_i.A_i./T_i + C_i./A_i./T_i + C_i.A_i.T_i$$
$$C_{i+1} = A_i.T_i + A_i.C_i + T_i.C_i$$

Connecting four of these devices as in Figure 4.2 results in the required 4-bit adder. This adder has a width of 4 bits; it can readily be extended to produce an adder of any width. This form of adder circuit is called a **ripple carry** adder, a name which indicates its main weakness; that C_4 cannot be generated until C_3 has been generated, but C_3 cannot be generated until C_2 has been generated, and so on. The ripple-carry adder is therefore quite slow. Later, we will investigate a faster circuit.

4.2 Adder/Subtractor

We can extend the adder to make it perform subtraction as well as addition. Recall from Chapter 1 that subtraction may be performed by 'change the sign and add'. Changing the sign of a two's complement number, or multiplying it by -1, simply requires inversion of all the bits and adding 1. The inversion can be implemented by using an exclusive-OR, XOR, gate. The truth table and symbol for this gate are shown in Figure 4.4. Note that if input B = = 1, the output is the complement of A while if B = = 0, the output is the same as A. Thus, we have a device that can be made to behave both like

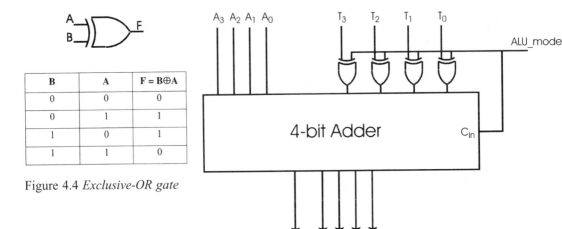

B	A	F = B⊕A
0	0	0
0	1	1
1	0	1
1	1	0

Figure 4.4 *Exclusive-OR gate*

Figure 4.5 *Adder/Subtractor circuit*

a NOT gate or a direct connection according to input signal B. We place these gates at one of the inputs to an adder circuit, Figure 4.5. When control signal *ALU_mode* is set to 1, the XOR gates behave as inverters and the carry into the first stage of the adder is forced to 1. The output from the adder is thus $A + (-T)$, or $A - T$. When control signal *ALU_mode* is set to 0, the XOR gates behave as direct connections and the carry into the adder is forced to 0, so that the output is A plus B. We now have an adder/subtractor circuit whose function is determined by the control signal, *ALU_mode*.

4.3 Arithmetic and logic unit

As well as addition and subtraction, a programmer is likely to want to perform logical operations such as AND and OR. We can include these functions in a variety of ways. The most straightforward way to incorporate these functions is to include an AND gate and an OR gate into the circuit and use a multiplexer to select the required output signal, Figure 4.6. Because the device can now perform four functions, it requires two[1] control signals, *ALU_mode0* and *ALU_mode1*, in order to select a particular function. These signals are connected to the select inputs of the multiplexer, and *ALU_mode0* is also connected to C_0, the carry-in of the first stage of the complete circuit. You should verify that when the *ALU_mode* signals are set to the values shown in the function table, the indicated functions are performed. Since the device performs arithmetic as well as logical operations, it is called an arithmetic and logic unit, or ALU.

Figure 4.7 shows an 8-bit ALU together with its associated registers, A and T. The registers hold 8 bits and the broad lines represent eight individual wires, one for each bit. Since the registers are edge triggered flip-flops, when control signal *load_T* changes from low to high it causes the data present at the input of register T to be stored in the register. Similarly, a rising edge

---

[1] Remember that there are 2^N different patterns of N binary signals.

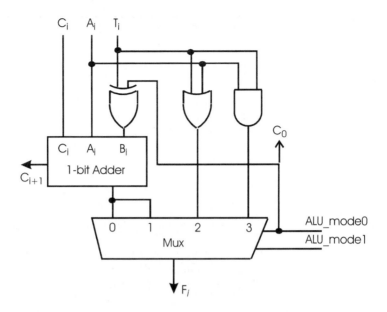

ALU_mode1	ALU_mode0	Function
0	0	F = A plus T
0	1	F = A minus T
1	0	F = A OR T
1	1	F = A AND T

Figure 4.6 *One bit of ALU having four functions*

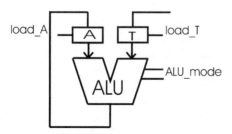

Figure 4.7 *Simple ALU*

on *load_A* loads register A with the number at the output of the ALU. The inputs to the ALU are thus the numbers stored in registers A and T. For example, to add a number, *num2*, to the number *num1*, which is currently in register A, we must perform the sequence of operations in Figure 4.8.

We shall see the ALU in operation when we execute programs on the G80. For example, we shall see that in order to perform an instruction to

Required action	Effect of the action	Shorthand description
(Register A holds *num1*.)		(A = *num1*)
Connect the source of *num2* to the input of register T.		
Set ALU_mode to ADD.	ALU becomes an adder.	ALU_mode = ADD
Pulse load_T.	Loads *num2* into register T.	T ← *num2*
Short delay.	ALU forms the sum of *num1* and *num2* at its output.	
Pulse load_A.	Stores ALU output in register A.	A ← ALU

Figure 4.8 *Sequence of operations to add* num2 *to the contents of register A*

subtract the number stored in register T from the number currently stored in the accumulator, the control unit sets the *ALU_mode* signals to the pattern that makes the ALU into a subtractor. After a very short delay (even electricity takes time to flow!), the output of the ALU becomes the current contents of the accumulator minus the contents of register T. This number is then loaded into the accumulator, replacing the original contents.

The ALU developed in this chapter does not provide for multiplication and division. We shall perform these operations in software; these programs will require that data can be shifted, an operation that we consider next.

4.4 Shifting data

It is often convenient to be able to **shift** a pattern of bits to the left or right. More generally, we may wish to **shift circularly** or **rotate** data. In this type of shift, the bits that reach the end of the bit pattern when shifted are fed into the other end. Thus, the bits, $<b_7 \ b_6 \ b_5 \ b_4 \ b_3 \ b_2 \ b_1 \ b_0>$, when rotated 2 bits to the right, become $<b_1 \ b_0 \ b_7 \ b_6 \ b_5 \ b_4 \ b_3 \ b_2>$. This *could* be achieved by placing the data into a shift register and generating two shift pulses. Rotations to the left might be achieved by making the shift register bi-directional, or by obtaining an N-bit rotate to the left by rotating right 8-N places. However, this implementation will be very slow, particularly if the data were, say, 32 bits and a rotation by many bits is required. We seek a faster way of rotating data.

Eight two-way multiplexers, Figure 4.9, are connected so that they rotate the data right 2 bits. The multiplexer control signal is labelled *Rotate2* since, when it is asserted, the device rotates the data two places while if not asserted the data passes through the device unchanged. We can make similar circuits that rotate one place and four places. When these are connected as shown in Figure 4.10, we have a device that is called a **barrel shifter**. The control register holds the number of places to rotate. For example, if this register is loaded with the number 5, the 4-bit shifter and the 1-bit shifter will actually shift the data while the 2-bit shifter passes its input unchanged to its output. The output data is thus rotated by the required 5 bits.

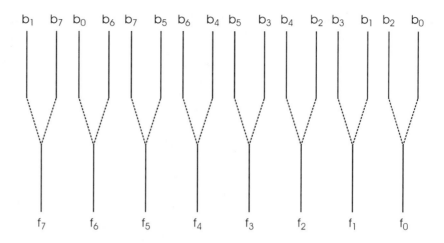

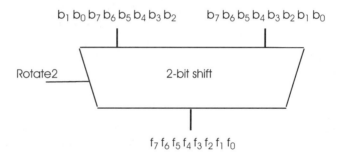

Figure 4.9 (a) *Multiplexers connected to rotate right two bits;* (b) *block diagram*

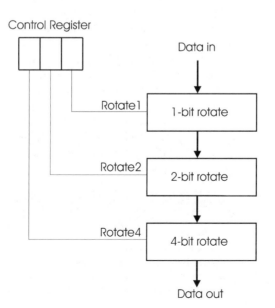

Figure 4.10 *Barrel shifter*

4.4 Fast adders*

A great deal of effort has gone into the design of ALU circuits that operate faster than those based on the ripple carry adder. We have noted earlier that the ripple carry adder is slow because each adder stage can form its outputs only when all the earlier stages have produced theirs[2]. Since stage i produces a carry-out bit, C_{i+1}, that depends on the inputs A_i, T_i, and C_i, it is possible to obtain logic equations for the carry-out from each stage.

Our first attempt is to use the relationship derived earlier:

$$C_{i+1} = A_i.T_i + A_i.C_i + T_i.C_i$$

Putting $i = 0$, we have:

$$C_1 = A_0.T_0 + A_0.C_0 + T_0.C_0$$

Putting $i = 1$, we have:

$$
\begin{aligned}
C_2 &= A_1.T_1 + A_1.C_1 + T_1.C_1 \\
&= A_1.T_1 + A_1.(A_0.T_0 + A_0.C_0 + T_0.C_0) + T_1.(A_0.T_0 + A_0.C_0 \\
&\quad + T_0.C_0) \\
&= A_1.T_1 + A_1.A_0.T_0 + A_1.A_0.C_0 + A_1.T_0.C_0 + T_1.A_0.T_0 \\
&\quad + T_1.A_0.C_0 + T_1.T_0.C_0
\end{aligned}
$$

Similarly, we can write expressions for C_3, C_4, and so on. Theoretically, these expressions allow us to design a logic circuit to produce all the carry signals at the same time using two layers of gates. Unfortunately, the expressions become extremely long; give a thought to how the expression for C_{31} would look! We do not pursue this possible solution any further because the number of gates becomes extremely large.

Our second attempt at a solution will result in a practical fast adder. The so-called **carry-look-ahead**[3] ALU generates all the carry signals at the same time, although not as quickly as our first attempt would have done. Reconsider the truth table for the adder, Figure 4.3. Note that when A_i and T_i have different values, the carry-out from the adder stage is the same as the carry-in. That is, when $A_i./T_i + /A_i.T_1 == 1$, then $C_{i+1} = C_i$; we regard this as the carry-in 'propagating' to the carry-out. Also, when A_i and T_i are both 1, $C_{i+1} = 1$, that is, when $A_i.T_i == 1$, then $C_{i+1} = 1$; we regard this as the carry-out being 'generated' by the adder stage. Putting these expressions together, we have:

$$C_{i+1} = (A_i./T_i + /A_i.T_i).C_i + A_i.T_i.$$

---

[2] Charles Babbage recognized this problem and produced a mechanism for high speed carries for his decimal computer, in the 1830s.

[3] The carry-look-ahead solution described here was devised by O. L. MacSorley in 1961.

This can be simplified to:

$$C_{i+1} = (A_i + T_i).C_i + A_i.T_i.$$

For brevity, let $P_i = A_i + T_i$ and let $G_i = A_i.T_i$.

Then $\quad C_{i+1} = P_i.C_i + G_i.$

This is really a formal statement of common sense. The carry-out, C_{i+1}, is 1 if the carry-in, C_i, is a 1 AND the stage propagates the carry through the stage OR if the carry-out is set to 1 by the adder stage itself. At first sight, this does not appear to be an improvement over the ripple-carry adder. However, we persevere with the analysis; putting i = 0, 1, 2, 3, ..., we obtain:

$$C_1 = P_0.C_0 + G_0$$

$$C_2 = P_1.C_1 + G_1 = P_1.(P_0.C_0 + G_0) + G_1 = P_1.P_0.C_0 + P_1.G_0 + G_1$$

$$C_3 = P_2.C_2 + G_2 = P_2.(P_1.P_0.C_0 + P_1.G_0 + G_1) + G_2$$
$$= P_2.P_1.P_0.C_0 + P_2.P_1.G_0 + P_2.G_1 + G_2$$

$$C_4 = P_3.C_3 + G_3 = P_3.(P_2.P_1.P_0.C_0 + P_2.P_1.G_0 + P_2.G_1 + G_2) + G_3$$
$$= P_3.P_2.P_1.P_0.C_0 + P_3.P_2.P_1.G_0 + P_3.P_2.G_1 + P_3.G_2 + G_3$$

We can readily make a 4-bit adder from these equations. However, the equations are becoming rather large, implying that a large number of gates will be required to produce C_{31}. To overcome this difficulty, let us regard a 4-bit adder as a building block, and use four of them to make a 16-bit adder. We *could* simply connect the carry-out of each 4-bit adder to the carry-in of the next 4-bit adder, as shown in Figure 4.11(a). In this case, we are using a ripple-carry between the 4-bit blocks. Alternatively, we can regard each 4-bit block as either generating or propagating a carry, just as we did for the

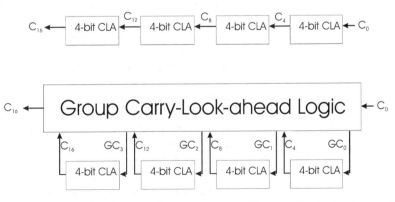

Figure 4.11 (a) *Ripple-carry between groups;* (b) *carry look-ahead over the groups*

1-bit adders. This allows us to devise carry-look-ahead logic for the carry-in signals to each 4-bit adder block, as shown in Figure 4.11(b). (The logic equations turn out to be the same as that for the 1-bit adders.) We now have a 16-bit adder made from four blocks of 4-bit adders with carry-look-ahead logic. Wider adders can be made by regarding the 16-bit adder as a building block and, again, similar logic allows us to produce carry-look-ahead circuits for groups of 16-bit adders. Even though there are now several layers of look-ahead logic, this adder has a substantial advantage in speed of operation when compared with the ripple-carry-adder. As is often the case, this speed advantage is at the expense of a more complex circuit.

4.5 Floating-point numbers*

An 8-bit number allows us to represent unsigned integers in the range 0 to 2^8-1 (255). If we choose to regard the bits as a signed integer, the range becomes -2^7 (-128) to $+2^7-1$ ($+127$). In either case, there are 256 different numbers. Numbers with 16 bits extend these ranges to 0 to $2^{16}-1$ (65 535) and -2^{15} ($-32\,768$) to $+2^{15}-1$ ($+32\,767$); in both cases 2^{16} different numbers are represented. If we wish to use larger integers, we simply use more bits in the number. For example, using 32-bit numbers gives us 2^{32} (approximately 4 000 000 000) different numbers, which we can regard as unsigned integers in the range 0 to $2^{32}-1$ and signed integers -2^{31} to $+2^{31}-1$. Whatever the number of bits, these integer numbers effectively have the binary point at the right-hand end of the number. If we regard the binary point as being two places from the right-hand end, we have a binary fraction. Thus, the 8-bit number 000101.11 has the decimal value 5.75, since the bits after the binary point have weights of 2^{-1} (0.5) and 2^{-2} (0.25). All these numbers are called **fixed point** numbers, because the binary point is always at the same, fixed, position in every number.

Suppose we wish to cope with very large and very small numbers, such as the decimal numbers 5 432 678 123 456 and 0.000 000 000 000 432 196. If the sum of these two numbers must be *exactly* 5 432 678 123 456.000 000 000 000 432 196, a number must be represented by a very large number of bits. Usually this amount of precision is not required and some approximation of the number is acceptable. In such cases, we can use **floating-point** numbers.

The decimal number 5 432 678 123 456 may be represented in floating-point format as $5.432\,678\,123\,456 \times 10^{12}$ and 0.000 000 000 000 432 196 as $4.32\,196 \times 10^{-13}$. This number representation actually uses two numbers, the **mantissa**[4], and the **exponent**. Thus, $4.32\,196 \times 10^{-13}$ has a mantissa of 4.32 196 and an exponent of -13, so may be represented by the two numbers 4.32 196 and -13.

Clearly, we may choose to store the mantissa and exponent in any number of bits. Manufacturers of early computers used different ways of representing these numbers, which caused difficulties when transferring programs and data between different computers. A committee of the IEEE[5] agreed a standard for floating-point numbers in 1985, called IEEE standard 754 (1985). We will adhere to this standard in our discussion.

---

[4] The mantissa is sometimes called the significand.
[5] The IEEE is the Institution of Electrical and Electronic Engineers, based in the USA.

For binary numbers, we may write:

$$11011100.0 \text{ as } 1.1011100 \times 2^7$$
$$00011100.0 \text{ as } 1.1100000 \times 2^4$$
$$0.00111010 \text{ as } 1.1101000 \times 2^{-3}$$

The floating-point representations of these numbers are written in the form $1.xxxx \times 2^E$, that is the first bit of the number is always 1. This is called the **normalized** representation. Since the first bit of a normalized number is always 1, there is no need to store it. Thus, number $1.bb..bbbb \times 2^E$ will be stored as the two quantities F and E, where F = 0.bb..bbbb, it being assumed that the first bit of F is 1. We now have: number $= (1 + F) \times 2^E$.

To accommodate signed numbers, we add a sign bit, S, such that if S = = 0, the number is positive.

We now have: number $= (-1)^S \times (1 + F) \times 2^E$.

The IEEE 754 provides for floating-point numbers of various lengths; the most popular of these have the formats shown in Figure 4.12.

Description	S	E	F
Single precision, 32 bit	1 bit	8 bits	23 bits
Double precision, 64 bit	1 bit	11 bits	52 bits
Double extended, 80 bit	1 bit	15 bits	64 bits

Figure 4.12 *Popular IEEE floating-point formats*

The exponent, E, is stored as a biased number, so that the 8-bit exponent of single precision numbers is written:

Largest: $11111111 = 255$ in pure binary $= +128$ biased
Smallest: $00000000 = 0$ in pure binary $= -127$ biased.

That is, E is biased by 127; the value of E is obtained by subtracting 127 from its pure binary value. Thus, number $= (-1)^S \times (1 + F) \times 2^{E-127}$. The 11-bit exponent used in double precision numbers is biased by 1023. This apparently strange representation simplifies the comparison of the exponents in two numbers during addition and subtraction of floating-point numbers.

4.5.1 Special quantities

Let us look closely at the representation of zero. When we write the smallest magnitude by setting E = 0 and F = 0, the formula for single precision numbers gives $(-1)^0 \times (1 + 0) \times 2^{0-127} = +1 \times 2^{-127}$, which is very small, but not exactly zero. However, the IEEE 754 standard *defines* the all 0s number as zero. This is not only logically pleasing but it also facilitates

---

[6] This is also called 'excess-127' format.

E	F	Object represented
$0 < E < E_{max}$	anything	Normalized number, $(-1)^s \times (1 + F) \times 2^{E-127}$
0	0	Zero, $(-1)^s \times 0$
0	$\neq 0$	Denormalized number, $(-1)^s \times (0 + F) \times 2^{-126}$
E_{max}	0	Infinity, $(-1)^s \times \infty$
E_{max}	$\neq 0$	Not a Number, NaN

Figure 4.13 *IEEE 754 definitions, for single precision numbers; $E_{max} = 255$*

checking to see if a number is zero, for example to prevent division by zero. The IEEE standard also defines the extreme values of E to signify infinity, and other objects, as shown in Figure 4.13. The table shows that the result of some arithmetic operations should return with E = 255 and F > 0, which indicates that it is not a number, NaN. For example, the result should be NaN after attempting to perform $\infty + \infty$, $\infty - \infty$, $0 \times \infty$, $0/0$, and ∞/∞.

4.5.2 Smallest and largest numbers

What is the smallest number that can be represented in single precision? Since numbers may be positive or negative, we will concern ourselves only with the magnitude of the numbers.

Clearly, the smallest number is zero, which is defined as having E = 0, F = 0.
However, the smallest non-zero number has E = 1, F = 0, giving a magnitude of:

$$1.00000000000000000000000 \times 2^{1-127}$$

$$= (1.0) \times 2^{-126} \approx 1.2 \times 10^{-38}$$

The largest value for E is 254, since 255 is used to represent infinity or NaN. The largest value of F is 11111111111111111111111 (23 bits), so the number with the largest magnitude is:

$$1.11111111111111111111111 \times 2^{254-127}$$

$$= (2 - 2^{-23}) \times 2^{127}$$

$$\approx 2^{128} \approx 3.4 \times 10^{38}$$

If the result of floating-point arithmetic is a number larger than this, the number is said to **overflow** and the result should be set to E = 255, F > 0, which indicates that the result is not a number, NaN.

4.5.3 Denormalized numbers

Considering single precision numbers only, we have seen that the smallest non-zero number has a magnitude of 1.0×2^{-126}. Tiny numbers, those between zero and 1.0×2^{-126} are too small to be represented as normalized numbers, which are evaluated according to the formula, $(-1)^S \times (1 + F) \times 2^{E-127}$. Instead, these tiny, denormalized, numbers are stored as E = 0, F > 0, but are evaluated by $(-1)^S \times (0 + F) \times 2^{-126}$, that is, a 1 is not added to F and the exponent is always -126.

The largest denormalized number is stored as:

E = 0   F = 11111111111111111111111 (23 bits) and evaluated as:

$$\text{number} = 0.11111111111111111111111 \times 2^{-126}$$

$$= (1 - 2^{-23}) \times 2^{-126}$$

$$\approx 2^{-126}$$

The smallest denormalized number is stored as:

E = 0   F = 00000000000000000000001 (23 bits) and evaluated as:

$$\text{number} = 0.00000000000000000000001 \times 2^{-126}$$

$$= (2^{-23}) \times 2^{-126}$$

$$= 2^{-149}$$

If the result of floating-point arithmetic is a number smaller than this, the number is said to **underflow** and the result should be set to E = 255, F > 0,

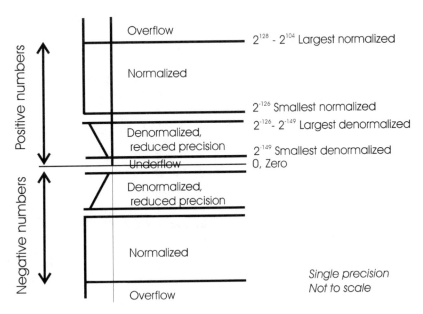

Figure 4.14 *Number range for single precision floating-point numbers*

which indicates that the result is not a number, NaN. Since denormalized numbers may have leading 0s in them, their precision is less than that of normalized numbers.

The whole number range is represented in Figure 4.14.

4.5.4 Multiplication and division

Floating-point multiplication and division are based on the rules:

Given $X = a \times 2^p$ and $Y = b \times 2^q$,

then $X \times Y = a \times b \times 2^{p+q}$.

and $X/Y = a/b \times 2^{p-q}$

The steps for multiplication are thus:

Step 1   Check for zeros. If X or Y is zero, result is zero.
Step 2   Add exponents.
Step 3   Multiply the mantissae.
Step 4   Normalize the result.
Step 5   Round the result.
Step 6   Determine sign.

We shall use decimal numbers to illustrate these steps for multiplication and assume that the computer stores four decimal digits in the mantissa and two decimal digits in the exponent.

$0.1112 \times 10^7 \times 0.4200 \times 10^{-4}$

Step 1:   Neither operand is zero, so continue.

Step 2:   Add the exponents. $7 + (-4) = 3$
(If the exponents are biased, we must subtract the bias.)

Step 3:   Multiply the mantissae.

```
        1112
        4200
   _____
   00000000
   0000000.
   002224..
   04448...
   _____
   04670400        Product is 0.04670400 × 10³
```

Step 4: Normalize

$$0.04670400 \times 10^3 = 0.4670400 \times 10^2$$

(Check that exponent has not overflowed or underflowed.)

Step 5: Round to nearest.
0.4670400×10^2 rounds to 0.4670×10^2

Step 6: Determine sign.
If the operands have the same sign, the result is positive, otherwise it is negative. Here, the result is positive.

4.5.5 Addition and subtraction

Steps:
Step 1   Check for zeros.
Step 2   Align the mantissae.
Step 3   Add or subtract the mantissae.
Step 4   Normalize the result.
Step 5   Round the result.

Example:
$0.9992 \times 10^3 + 0.1321 \times 10^1$

Step 1: Neither operand is zero, so continue.

Step 2: Shift the smaller number until its exponent is the same as that of the larger number. $0.1321 \ 10^1 = 0.001321 \times 10^3$, which becomes 0.0013×10^3 because the machine can hold only four digits.

Step 3: Add significands.

```
0.9992
0.0013
──────
1.0005
```
          Sum is 1.0005×10^3

Step 4: Normalize $1.0005 \times 10^3 = 0.10005 \times 10^4$.
(Check that exponent has not overflowed or underflowed.)

Step 5: Round to nearest.
0.10005×10^4 becomes 0.1001×10^4

4.5.6 Rounding

The IEEE standard requires that 'all operations ... shall be performed as if correct to infinite precision, then rounded'. If intermediate results are rounded to fit the number of bits available, then precision is lost. To meet this requirement, 2 additional bits, called **guard** and **round**, are saved at the right hand of the number.

The standard actually defines four rounding methods:

(i)   Round towards zero – truncate
      Simply ignore any extra bits. The rounded result is nearer to zero than the unrounded number.

(ii) Round towards + ∞
      The rounded result is nearer to + ∞ than the unrounded number.

(iii) Round towards − ∞
      The rounded result is nearer to − ∞ than the unrounded number.

(iv) Round to nearest even
      This determines what to do if the number is at the halfway value. Instead of always rounding a number such as 0.72185 to 0.7219, this is done only half the time. For example, 3.25 rounds to 3.2 while 3.75 rounds to 3.8. Thus, the last digit is always even, which gives the method its name. For a large array of numbers, this method tends to 'average out' the error due to rounding.

      In binary, if the bit in the least significant position (not including guard and round bits) is 1, add 1 in this position, else, truncate. This requires an extra bit, the **sticky** bit. This bit is set whenever there are non-zero bits to the right of the round bit. For example, in decimal, 0.500 ... 0001 will set the sticky bit. When the number is shifted to the right, so that the least significant digit gets lost, **sticky** indicates that the number is truly greater than 0.5 so the machine can round accordingly.

4.5.7 Precision

It should not be forgotten that there are only 2^{32} different bit patterns in the 32-bit single precision representation of floating-point numbers so there are at most only 2^{32} different floating-point numbers. Since there is an infinity of real numbers, a floating-point number can only approximate a real number. One result of this is that the addition of two numbers of very different magnitudes may result in the smaller number being effectively zero. Care must be exercised in the design of complicated numerical algorithms in order to preserve their accuracy. Consider the computation of $x + y + z$, where $x = 1.5 \times 10^{30}$, $y = -1.5 \times 10^{30}$, and $z = 1.0 \times 10^{-9}$ Computing $(x + y) + z$ gives:

$$(1.5 \times 10^{30} - 1.5 \times 10^{30}) + 1.0 \times 10^{-9}$$

$$= (0.0) + 1.0 \times 10^{-9}$$

$$= 1.0 \times 10^{-9}$$

Computing $x + (y + z)$ gives:

$$1.5 \times 10^{30} + (-1.5 \times 10^{30} + 1.0 \times 10^{-9})$$

$$= 1.5 \times 10^{30} + (-1.5 \times 10^{30}), \text{ since the } 1.0 \times 10^{-9} \text{ gets lost}$$

$$= 0.0$$

Thus, we have that $(x + y) + z \neq x + (y + z)$.

Large computers usually incorporate a hardware floating-point unit, FPU, which performs the arithmetic operations according to the IEE 754 standard. These FPUs also compute square roots and functions such as sin(), cos(), and log(). If we wish to use floating point in a small computer without an FPU, we shall have to write program code to perform the operations.

We can now design a computing machine using the concepts and digital devices we have considered.

4.6 Problems

1   Two methods of generating the carry-out from an adder stage were considered under the heading 'Fast Adders'.

    (i)   The first method was said to be impractical because the length of the logical expression for C_n becomes extremely large for a large n. How many product terms are there in the expression for C_n? Assuming a 16-bit adder, how many product terms are there in the expression for C_{16}?

    (ii) The second method, carry-look-ahead, gives C_n in terms of P and G. How many product terms are there in the expression for C_n? How many product terms for C_{16}?

2   What decimal number does the IEEE 32-bit standard number 11000000011000000000000000000000 represent?

3   Convert the decimal number $+10.75$ to the IEEE 32-bit standard floating-point representation.

4   Convert $+1.0 \times 2^{125}$ to the IEEE 32-bit standard floating-point representation.

5   Convert $+1.0 \times 2^{-125}$ to the IEEE 32-bit standard floating-point representation.

6   It is required to evaluate the sum $(+2^{125}) + (+2^{-125})$, assuming IEEE 32-bit standard floating point representation. What will be the result?

PART 2

Computing Machines

5 Computer design

In this chapter we look at manual computation and ask how it can be automated. We shall identify the main components of an automatic computing machine and decide how to replicate their function using digital components. This leads to the design of a machine called Simple Machine. We develop the design of Simple Machine by adding a few data storage registers and including logic to control three **flags**. These flags allow the machine to perform **conditional branch** instructions. The resulting computer is called G80. We shall add further improvements to G80 as the need arises in subsequent chapters.

5.1 A manual computing system

Consider a manual computing system of the sort that was common until the 1960s, Figure 5.1. Here the computer (a person) is given a calculator, on which to perform arithmetic, and a list of instructions, called the 'program'. The person has to read the first line of the program, perform the required instruction, then read the next line, and so on until the end of the program is reached[1].

line 0:	Enter the number given in line 6.
line 1:	Add the number given in line 7.
line 2:	Multiply by the number given in line 5.
line 3:	Write result into line 8.
line 4:	Halt
line 5:	4
line 6:	12
line 7:	3
line 8:	..

Figure 5.1 *A manual computing system*

---

[1] This type of computing system was in common use until the 1960s for tasks such as working out actuarial tables and payroll.

There are three major components in the system:

- the program and data store (here a sheet of paper), which is capable of being read from and written to;
- the calculator, on which the basic arithmetical operations are performed. Until the 1960s, the calculator would be a mechanical device which represented numbers by the position of ten-toothed cogs, in a similar way that a car mileage meter stores and displays the distance travelled;
- the human controller, who first reads an instruction from the program store, then interprets what has to be done in order to carry out the instruction (that is, determines which buttons on the calculator are to be pressed), and finally presses the required buttons.

The most obvious way to automate this system is to replace each of the three major components with devices that perform their function[2]. An outline of such a computing machine is shown in Figure 5.2. The 'Memory' performs the functions of the program and data store, and the 'Arithmetic and Logic Unit', ALU, performs the functions of the calculator. The 'Control Unit' replaces the human operator. The 'Accumulator' attached to the ALU is a register for storing the current output of the ALU.

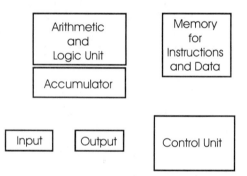

Figure 5.2 *Block diagram of a computer*

5.2 Storing data and program instructions

In the design of the G80 we let each number, or any other form of data, have 8 bits[3]. We store each of these bits in a flip-flop and call the collection of flip-flops a **register**. Instructions are also stored in our binary computer as patterns of bits.

The purpose of the memory is to store program instructions and data. We can construct a memory from registers. Since our numbers require 8 bits, we will design the memory such that each storage **location** in the memory stores 8 bits. The memory may be regarded as a collection of 8-bit registers as shown in Figure 5.3. We shall make provision for 65 536 (2^{16}) locations in the memory[4].

---

[2] Charles Babbage incorporated these components into his design of the 'Analytical Engine' during the 1830s.

[3] A collection of 8 bits is called a 'byte'.

[4] Large computers have many millions of memory locations. In order to reduce the financial cost, these use a cheaper form of memory circuit, called dynamic RAM or DRAM. For even greater storage at reasonable cost, magnetic disks and optical disks are used.

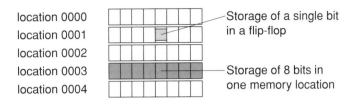

Figure 5.3 *Eight-bit wide memory*

The position of a particular storage location in the memory is called its **address**. To use the memory chip shown in Figure 5.4, the address of the storage location to be accessed is placed on the 16 address pins of the memory chip. Since the address is a 16-bit number, 2^{16} (65 536) different addresses are possible. If new data is to be written to the addressed location, the data must be connected to the DataIn pins of the memory and the control signal, WriteEnable, must be asserted. If existing data is to be read from the location, WriteEnable must be de-asserted and the memory will connect the addressed location to the DataOut pins.

For example, to read the data stored in memory location 0x49C8, the address wires must carry the pattern 0100 1001 1100 1000 (0x49C8) and the WriteEnable control signal must be de-asserted; then, after a short delay[5], the contents of storage location 0x49C8 will appear on the DataOut wires. Similarly, to write, say, 0x42 to location 0x49C8, the address lines must carry 0100 1001 1100 1000 (0x49C8), the DataIn lines must carry 0100 0010 (0x42), and the WriteEnable signal must be asserted. The data 0x42 will then be written into memory location 0x49C8.

Many semiconductor memory devices have only one set of data pins that are used both for DataIn and DataOut[6]. We shall use such devices.

While all the wires in our design carry binary signals, a particular wire will carry only either a data bit, an address bit, or a control signal. Thus, a data wire will carry a binary signal that forms 1 bit of data, an address wire will carry 1 bit of an address, and a wire carrying a control signal goes to logic circuits in the computer that control what the circuits do.

Whatever the technology used for the various forms of memory, the size of the memory is usually given as a number of bytes.

[5] All storage devices take a finite time to access the addressed memory location. This is called the **access time** of the memory. Generally, memory devices with short access times are financially more costly than devices with longer access times.

[6] This reduces the number of pins required on the package that contains the silicon chip and so reduces its manufacturing cost.

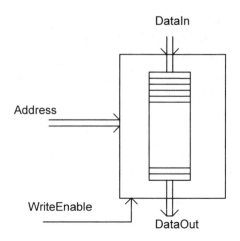

Dataln

Address

WriteEnable

DataOut

Figure 5.4 *Connections to the memory*

5.3 Connecting the machine components

The various components have to be connected so that they can work together. Our machine has to be able to move data between the memory and a register and from one register to another. Thus, we saw in Chapter 4, that in order to add a number to the contents of the accumulator register, the required number has first to be transferred into register T.

In general, we seek a solution to the following problem. Given a number of registers, how do we make a circuit that can copy data from any one of them to any other? Clearly, there has to be a **data path** from the source register, which contains the data, to the destination register, to which the source data is to be copied. We shall use a widely used technique, which is to connect all the inputs and all the outputs of all the registers to a **bus**, Figure 5.5. This shows how three 4-bit registers may be connected to each other. Each of the four long wires in the figure is a bus wire – a bus wire goes to many places.

Any data present on the bus may be loaded into any register by a rising edge on the appropriate **load_Rx** control signal. Although we can connect all the register inputs to the bus, we cannot connect register outputs directly to the bus, since some flip-flops would be attempting to drive the bus wire to a 1 while others may be attempting to drive it to a 0. This problem is

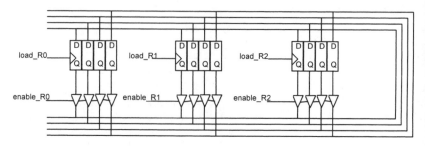

Figure 5.5 *Three 4-bit registers connected to each other via a bus*

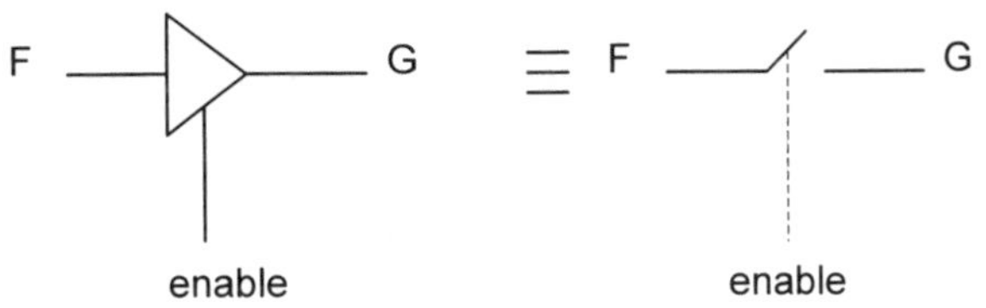

Figure 5.6 *Three-state buffer*

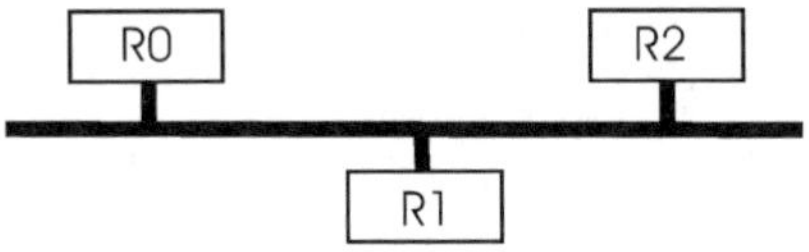

enable   enable

Figure 5.7 *Three registers connected to each other via a bus*

overcome by connecting the output of each flip-flop to the bus via **three-state buffers**. These circuits behave like an open/closed contact, Figure 5.6. When the buffer is enabled, it behaves as a closed contact; when not enabled, it behaves as an open contact. The detail of Figure 5.5 may be hidden, so as to make its function more clear, as shown in Figure 5.7.

To transfer data from R0 to R2, the Control Unit of the machine must generate the following sequence of control signals; each control signal follows the previous one after a short interval of time.

Control signal	Effect
Assert *enable_R0*	Place the data in R0 on the bus
Produce rising edge on *load_R2*	Load R2 from the bus
De-assert *enable_R0*	Remove the data in R0 from the bus
Produce falling edge on *load_R2*	Bring *load_R2* back to normal level

We can connect the Data pins of a memory device to the bus so allowing us to transfer data between a register and the memory. The data transfer will be accomplished by a similar sequence of control signals to that given above for a register to register transfer.

5.4 Architecture of Simple Machine

We can now assemble the various components into a computing machine, Figure 5.8. This diagram shows the components and the data paths between them. It does not show the control signals to the registers nor the three-state buffers that connect the output of the devices to a bus because that would require a very complex diagram that obscures the general concept.

5.4.1 Data paths

The ALU and its associated registers A and T together form the part of the machine that processes data[7]. Because we will want to transfer data from memory to registers A and T, a data path from the memory Data connections to these registers is provided. This path is along the Data Bus. Since

---

[7] This is the part of the computer that does the real work of processing the data. Other parts of computer manage the flow of the data that is presented to the ALU for processing.

we shall also need to store the contents of register A in memory, we make the data path between the memory and register A bi-directional.

5.4.2 Program Counter

An obvious way of storing program instructions is to store them in sequential locations in the memory, so we provide a 16-bit counter circuit to hold the address of the storage location from where the next instruction is to be read. This counter is called the **Program Counter**, PC, or **Instruction Pointer**, IP, since it points to the memory location that holds the next instruction. We will arrange for the Program Counter to be automatically incremented each time an instruction is read. The PC is connected to the address pins of the memory via the address bus.

5.4.3 Operation of Simple Machine

The machine is designed to operate by repeating the following two phases for every instruction in the program.

Phase 1 – Instruction fetch
> The Control Unit generates the control signals that copy an instruction byte from the memory into the **Instruction Register**, IR. The address of this instruction is in the **Program Counter**, PC.

Phase 2 – Instruction execute
> The 8 bits in the IR are connected to the Control Unit. These 8 bits determine the sequence of control signals that the Control Unit generates. The sequence of control signals generated by the Control Unit causes the execution of the instruction. The sequence finishes by starting Phase 1, so fetching the next instruction into the IR.

The Control Unit is a complex sequential circuit having inputs from the IR that determine the sequence of control signals that the Control Unit generates. The system clock signal determines the timing of all these control signals. There are a large number of control signals. Thus there will be a control signal that is connected to the enable input of a three-state buffer that connects a register to a bus. There will be other signals that are connected to the load input of every register so causing that register to be loaded from the bus. Yet other signals will go to the ALU_mode control signals of the ALU causing the ALU to be set to perform a particular arithmetic or logical operation. Another control signal is connected to the WriteEnable input of the memory so determining whether the memory will read or write.

These signals will be asserted one after the other, so producing the sequence of control signals that cause the instruction to be fetched into the IR and then to be executed. For example, if the pattern of bits in the IR represents an instruction to copy data from one register to another, the sequence of control signals will be similar to that described in section 5.3.

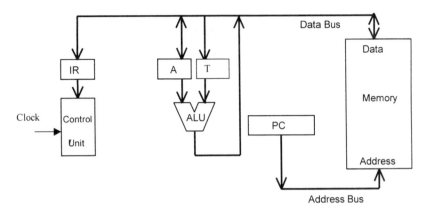

Figure 5.8 *Components and data paths within Simple Machine*

The Control Unit is the most complex of the major components of the computing machine. We shall consider its design in Chapter 13.

5.5 More general view of the design of Simple Machine*

Here we step back from the existing design of Simple Machine to consider how we arrived at its design. Consider a machine that performs only simple arithmetical and logical operations such as add, subtract, AND, and OR. We will encode each operation into a unique pattern of bits, called the **operation code**. For example, the operation 'add' might be encoded as 1000 0000, and the operation 'subtract' as 0110 0110.

The 8-bit operation code allows for up to 256 (2^8) different operations in the machine, more than enough for our machine.

In general, an arithmetical or logical operation requires two operands. For example, in $z = x \ add \ y$, the operation *add* has the operands x, y. Furthermore, the machine needs to be informed where to put the result, z. Remembering that in our machine we have decided to use 16 bits to specify the address of a storage location, the question arises: how are we to represent operations such as $z = x \ add \ y$ in one or more program instructions?

5.5.1 Four-address format

Taking $z = x \ add \ y$ as an example, assume that the number x is stored in the memory location having address, X. Also, number y is stored in memory location Y and location Z is reserved to store number z. A programmer would find it convenient to write an instruction such as 'add the contents of memory location X to the contents of memory Y, store the result in location Z, and fetch the next instruction from location P'. More concisely, this instruction might be written:

```
add (X), (Y), (Z), P
```

This instruction contains all the information for a machine to execute it. Specifically, this information is the five items:

- The required operation, here add.
- The address of the storage location holding the first operand, here X.
- The address of the storage location holding the second operand, here Y.
- The address of the storage location where the result is to be stored, here Z.
- The address of the storage location holding the next instruction, here P.

These four-address instructions require 72 bits: 8 bits for the operation code, plus 16 bits for each of the four addresses. Since each memory location stores a byte, these 72-bit instructions will be stored in nine consecutive memory locations. But, our machine can read only one byte at a time from the memory, so that it will have to read nine memory locations in order to get the instruction. This will make a slow machine. Fortunately, not all the items in the instruction need to be explicitly stated within the instruction itself.

5.5.2 Three-address format

We have noted before that the simple stratagem of storing program instructions in consecutive memory locations allows us to remove the need to specify P. Instead, we incorporated a Program Counter, PC, into the design of the machine. The PC will be incremented automatically after reading an instruction. Since we no longer need to specify P in the instruction, the instruction will now contain only three memory addresses:

```
add (X),(Y),(Z)
```

These three-address instructions can be encoded into $8 + 3 \times 16 = 56$ bits, requiring only seven locations in the memory.

Because we have removed the address of the next instruction from the current instruction we will have to provide an instruction that loads the PC with a new value, *nn*. This instruction *could* be written load PC, nn; however, the programmer will see this instruction as a **branch** or **jump** to a new location in memory, so we will write it as   jp nn.

5.5.3 Two-address format

Now let the output of the ALU always be stored in a special register within the machine, register A. The instruction will now specify two addresses:

```
add (X),(Y)
```

It is implicit that:

- the address of the next instruction is in the PC,
- the result of this operation is stored in register A.

In order to store the contents of register A in memory, we must provide for an instruction to do this, say `load(X),A`. Now, when the programmer wishes to program *z = x add y* he must write the sequence:

```
add (X),(Y)   ;add contents of memory location X to
              contents of memory location Y, and store
              result in register A
load (Z),A    ;store, in memory location Z, the
              contents of register A
```

These two-address instructions can be encoded into $8 + 2 \times 16 = 40$ bits, that is, five consecutive memory locations.

5.5.4 One-address format

We now let the first operand be obtained from register A. The instruction now specifies only one address, that of the second operand:

```
add (X)
```

It is implicit that:

- the address of the next instruction is in the PC,
- the first operand is in register A,
- the result of this operation is stored in register A.

In order to allow register A to be loaded from memory, we must provide the instruction `load A,(X)`.

Now, when the programmer wishes to program *z = x add y* she must write the sequence:

```
load A,(X)    ;load register A from memory location X
add (Y)       ;add contents of memory location Y to
              contents of register A, store result in
              register A
load (Z),A    ;store, in memory location Z, the
              contents of register A
```

These one-address instructions can be encoded into $8 + 1 \times 16 = 24$ bits, that is, three consecutive memory locations.

We have chosen to use this one address format as the basis of our machine design.

5.5.5 Zero-address format

Finally, we replace register A with an operand **stack**. This behaves like a stack of plates stored on top of a sprung base as may be found in a restaurant. When a new plate is placed on the top of the stack (a **push** operation), all the plates move down and when a plate is removed from the top (a **pop** operation), all the remaining plates move up.

Arithmetic and logic instructions do not specify an address:

```
add
```

It is implicit that:

- the address of the next instruction is in the PC,
- the first operand is on the top of the stack,
- the second operand is second on the stack,
- operands are popped off the stack and the result of the operation is then pushed onto the top of the stack.

Now, when the programmer wishes to program $z = x$ *add* y she must write the sequence:

```
push (X)      ;push contents of memory location X onto
              the stack
push (Y)      ;push contents of memory location Y onto
              the stack
add           ;add the top two elements of the stack,
              store result in the top of the stack
pop (Z)       ;store, in memory location Z, the
              contents of the top of the stack
```

The contents of the stack during these instructions are shown in Figure 5.9.

This form of processor is very simple and has been widely used for calculators and specialized arithmetic devices such as those that perform floating-point arithmetic.

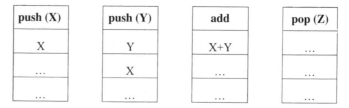

Figure 5.9 *Contents of stack during* $z = x$ *add* y

5.6 Improvements to Simple Machine

We now consider some improvements to Simple Machine. These are intended to make it easier to program or to make it operate faster. We shall call this improved design, the G80.

5.6.1 Data storage within the microprocessor

In order to read data stored within the memory, the G80 must first put the address of the required location onto the address bus, assert the signal to the memory that tells it to read, and then wait for the memory to place the data onto the data bus. This takes considerably more time than to move data from one G80 register to another, so it will be beneficial to provide a small amount of storage within the G80 itself. It will be left to the ingenuity of the programmer to decide which data is best stored within the G80 rather than in the main memory.

As an example, consider a calculation that uses a particular value many times. Clearly the programmer should store this data in a register within the G80, rather than in memory, since that will greatly speed up access to the data. Again, during many calculations, there occurs a need to store values temporarily so that they can be used at a later stage in the calculation. Suppose we wish to calculate an expression such as $5 \times x - 8 \times y$ where x, and y are numbers. We will do this by first calculating $8 \times y$, saving this temporary result, then calculating $5 \times x$ and finally subtracting the temporary result. While such temporary values could be stored in the memory, it will allow faster operation if the programmer uses a G80 register.

So, we add six 8-bit data registers to Simple Machine and call these registers B, C, D, E, H, and L. Because we often need 16-bit data, we shall arrange that registers B and C can both be accessed as though they formed one 16-bit **register pair**, BC. Similarly, we shall provide for DE and HL to be treated as 16-bit registers.

5.6.2 Status flags

We will often want our machine to perform different instructions depending on the value of some data[8]. For example, we may wish to compute:

```
if(x - 8 == 0)
      do_this …
else
      do_that …
```

Here, we want *either* do_this *or* do_that to be executed, depending on the value of x. The first requirement is to provide a circuit to detect that the result of a calculation is zero. We will store the output of this circuit in a flip-flop called the **Zero flag** or Z flag.

---

[8] This is the difference between a *calculation* and a *computation*.

Zero flag

The logic circuit to detect a zero output from the ALU is straightforward, Figure 5.10. The eight outputs of the ALU are inverted and then ANDed so that the Zero flag will be set only if all the ALU output bits are zero. We incorporate this hardware into the G80. To make use of this flag we need at least one machine instruction that takes account of the state of the flag. Our requirement is that, if the Zero flag is set, we want the machine to perform a different sequence of instructions to what it would do if the Zero flag were not set. Thus, we want an instruction such as:

jp z,nn   *fetch the next instruction from memory location nn if the Zero flag is set, otherwise do nothing.*

This type of instruction is called a **conditional branch** or **conditional jump**. When this instruction is executed, the Control Unit will load the Program Counter with nn if the zero flag is set, otherwise the Program Counter remains pointing to the next location in memory. Thus, if the Zero flag is set, the next instruction will be fetched from memory location nn, otherwise, the next instruction will be fetched from the next memory location. Our machine can now perform a different sequence of instructions depending on the value of an item of data. It has changed from being an automatic calculating machine to become an automatic computing machine or computer.

We give the programmer more freedom by having the complementary instruction:

jp nz,nn   *fetch the next instruction from memory location nn if the Zero flag is not set, otherwise do nothing.*

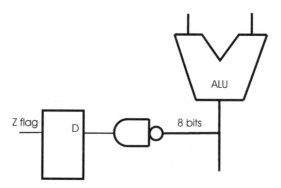

Figure 5.10 *Logic for the zero flag*

Sign flag

In many computations involving signed integers, we want to be able to detect if the ALU output is positive or negative. We can easily save the sign of the output from the ALU by storing bit 7 from the ALU in a flip-flop called the

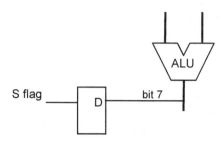

Figure 5.11 *Logic for Sign flag*

Sign flag or S flag, as shown in Figure 5.11. We incorporate this hardware into the G80 and provide the instructions:

jp m,nn   *fetch the next instruction from memory location nn if the Sign flag is set (ALU output is <u>m</u>inus), otherwise do nothing.*

jp p,nn   *fetch the next instruction from memory location nn if the Sign flag is not set (ALU output is <u>p</u>ositive), otherwise do nothing.*

Carry flag

Suppose we need to detect if the addition of two unsigned integers gives a sum that is too big to be stored within the Accumulator register. If this occurs, the ALU will generate a carry bit having the value of 1 instead of the normal value of 0. Clearly, it is important to save the carry from the ALU so that we can use it in some way to do something about the overflow. We provide a flip-flop that stores the carry bit; this flip-flop is referred to as the **Carry flag**, or C flag. We incorporate this hardware, Figure 5.12, into the G80 and provide the instructions:

jp c,nn   *fetch the next instruction from memory location nn if the Carry flag is set, otherwise do nothing.*

jp nc,nn   *fetch the next instruction from memory location nn if the Carry flag is <u>not</u> set, otherwise do nothing.*

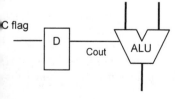

Figure 5.12 *Logic for Carry flag*

The Control Unit is required to load the Program Counter with nn if the Carry flag is set, otherwise the Program Counter remains pointing to the next location in memory. Thus, if the Carry flag is set, the next instruction will be fetched from memory location nn, otherwise, the next instruction will be fetched from the next memory location.

The individual flip-flops that store the flags are conveniently collected into a register, called variously the **Flag Register**, the **Status Register**, or the **Condition Code Register**.

5.7 Architecture of the G80 microprocessor

The architecture of the microprocessor with these improvements is shown in Figure 5.13. Data may travel from a source along the Data Bus to a destination along a path allowed by the arrowheads. The **register file** comprising registers B, C, D, E, H, L and PC is shown in diagrammatic form: all these registers have connections to and from the Data Bus and to the Address Bus. The architecture of this improved machine is similar to that of the Z80 manufactured by Zilog Inc. and the 8085 manufactured by Intel Inc. The Intel 80x86 family of processors is also based on a similar architecture.

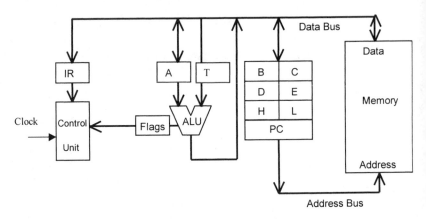

Figure 5.13 *Architecture of the improved computer*

We shall add more hardware and software facilities as their need arises. Let us summarize the design so far.

1 Programs comprise a list of instructions.
2 An instruction is stored in 1 or more bytes in the memory. The first byte of every instruction is the op-code, which indicates what the instruction is to do. The other bytes are an operand for the instruction.
3 Instructions are stored in sequential memory locations. Instructions are processed in the order that they are stored in memory. The programmer can change the sequence by using jump instructions. A jump instruction may be conditional on the state of one of the status flags, C, S, and Z.
4 The Program Counter, PC, stores the address of the next location in memory to be read. The op-code of the next instruction is read from the memory location whose address is in the PC. The op-code is transferred into the Instruction Register, IR. This is the fetch phase.
5 The content of the IR determines the sequence of control signals generated by the Control Unit, CU. These signals control the hardware so that it executes the operation indicated by the instruction. This is called the execute phase.
6 The Arithmetic and Logic Unit, ALU, performs arithmetic and logical operations on the data stored in registers A and T.
7 Some registers are included within the microprocessor in order to speed the operation of the computer. These are the general purpose registers, B, C, D, E, H, and L.

5.8 Problems

1   In the design of his Analytical Engine, Charles Babbage provided for two separate memories, one for the instructions and the other for the data. Suggest why such a computer might be faster than the single memory design used in the G80.

2   In our improvements to Simple Machine, we added six data registers to the machine. Why not add 60, 600, or even, 6000?

3   The Carry flag can be used to indicate that a result from the ALU has overflowed. This is true only if the data are unsigned integers. Devise logic that will detect overflow of signed integers. (We shall incorporate this **P flag** into the G80.)

4   Devise a program for a one-address machine that computes $v = w*x + y*z$ where w is stored in memory location W, etc. Assume that the machine has a multiply instruction.

5   Devise a program for a zero-address machine that computes $v = w*x + y*z$ where w is stored in memory location W, etc. Assume that the machine has a multiply instruction.

6 Instruction set and code assembly

In designing the hardware of the G80 we have noted a few instructions that it must be able to perform. In this chapter we introduce other useful instructions together with different **addressing modes**. We also see how these instructions, written in assembly language, can be converted to the 0s and 1s that will be stored in the computer memory. We do this initially by hand and then use a software tool called an **assembler**. By using the simulator software, we watch the activity of the G80 as it executes a program.

6.1 Programmer's model

The G80 microprocessor contains several registers that are accessible to the programmer. In order to write programs for it we must be aware of these registers; we have to keep in mind the 'programmer's model' of the computer, Figure 6.1. Later, we shall find that the addition of more registers to this model will assist the programmer in writing programs.

A	Flags
B	C
D	E
H	L
PC	

Figure 6.1 *Programmer's model of the computer at this stage of development*

6.2 Instruction format and addressing modes

We will define **mnemonics** for each instruction in such a way as to make them easy for the programmer to remember. We choose that the mnemonics for the G80 instructions will have the format[1]:

operation destination, source

A common requirement when we write a program will be to load a register with a number. These instructions have the form:

ld destination register, number

Here the **operation** is ld, the mnemonic for load[2].

e.g.   ld a, 0x42   Load number 0x42 into register A.

We will also want to copy data from one register to another register:

ld c, b   Load register C from register B.
           That is, copy the data in register B into register C.

Since our machine always puts the output of the ALU in register A, we must have an instruction to load the data from register A into a location in external memory. Similarly, since our machine always uses the data in register A as one of the inputs to the ALU, we must have an instruction to load register A with the data in a memory location:

ld a,(0x49C3)   Load register A from memory location
                 0x49C3.
ld (0x49C3),a   Load memory location 0x49C3 from
                 register A.

Note that in the mnemonics we use here, the parentheses around the address, distinguishes the load from memory instruction from the load with a number instruction[3].

The examples above show that the location of the data may be specified in various ways, or **addressing modes**. Thus the data referred to may be:

1 specified within the instruction itself, e.g. ld a,N. This is called **immediate** addressing;
2 in another G80 register which is specified within the instruction, e.g. ld a,e.
   This is called **register direct** addressing;

---

[1] We could equally as well have chosen the format operation source, destination. For example, Motorola Inc. chose this format for their 68000 microprocessors. Intel Corporation chose, for their 80 × 86 microprocessors, the same format as we have chosen for the G80.

[2] In the Motorola 68000 instruction set, move is used instead of ld. In the Intel 80 × 86 instruction set, mov is used instead of ld.

[3] Other manufacturers choose different ways of making this distinction; the programmer must read the manufacturers' documentation carefully.

3 in a memory location which is specified within the instruction, e.g. ld a, (0x49C3). This is called **memory direct** addressing.

Similar addressing modes are found on other computers. Larger computers tend to have many more addressing modes; indeed later, we shall find it helps the programmer if we add other addressing modes to the G80. An understanding of the addressing modes of a particular computer is one of the major challenges to a programmer using its assembly code.

These addressing modes are used in instructions other than the ld instructions. However, not all G80 instructions require both a destination and a source to be specified. For example:

```
inc a    Increment the contents of register A by 1.
dec b    Decrement the contents of register B by 1.
inc hl   Increment the contents of register pair HL.
```

Note that we do not provide the facility to use *all* combinations of addressing modes to specify the source and destination of the data. Although this would be convenient for the programmer, it would add to the complexity, and cost, of our microprocessor design. Thus, we have made no provision for instructions such as:

ld (0x49C3), 42 load the memory location 49C3 with 42

To achieve this transfer of data we would use the two instructions:

```
ld a,42
ld (0x49C3),a
```

The above example illustrates that, when programming any computer, we will have to use our ingenuity to work around the limitations of its instruction set.

Program Addrs1.asm, Figure 6.2, lets us see these addressing modes in operation. The source code begins with a semicolon followed by the name of the program. The semicolon is used to indicate that what follows on the remainder of the line is a **comment**; this is purely for the convenience of the person reading the program.

However, before we can run this program on the G80 we must first convert the mnemonics to machine code. That is, we must convert the mnemonics into the 0s and 1s that must be loaded into memory in order to control what the G80 does.

```
;Addrs1.asm

                          ;Addressing mode
    ld   c, 0x66          ;immediate
    ld   a, c             ;register direct
    ld   (0x0007), a      ;memory direct
    halt
```

Figure 6.2 *Source code of program Addrs1.asm*

6.3 Converting the source code to machine code – manual assembly

Our program has been written using mnemonics for the computer instructions because these are understandable by human programmers. However, the mnemonics must be converted to machine code before being transferred into the G80 computer memory. This translation from **source code** to **machine code** is called code **assembly**. Here we do this by looking up the machine code in the list of G80 instructions in Appendix A. Thus, for the first instruction of the source code, we find `ld c,N` in the list of G80 instructions; the corresponding machine code is 0E 20. Since the codes in the instruction list are given for N equal to 0x20, we replace the 20 with 66. The second instruction `ld a, c`, simply has the code 79. The code for instruction `ld (NN), a` is given as 32 84 05 for NN equal to 0584; noting that the order of the bytes NN is reversed, we write 32 0B 00. The machine code for `Addrs1.asm` is given in Figure 6.3.

Addrs1.asm		
Machine code	**Line number**	**Instruction mnemonic**
0E 66	1	`ld c,0x66`
79	2	`ld a, c`
32 07 00	3	`ld (0x0007), a`
76	4	`Halt`

Figure 6.3 *Translation of Addrs1.asm to machine code*

Address	Content
0000	0E
0001	66
0002	79
0003	32
0004	07
0005	00
0006	76

Figure 6.4 *Machine code for Addrs1.asm as it appears in memory*

Next we have to decide where to put the machine code in the G80 memory. This is easy since the G80 has been designed such that when it is powered up it sets its Program Counter to 0000[4]. So, we must place the machine code in memory location 0000 onwards. Thus, we want the contents of the G80 memory to be as shown in Figure 6.4.

Finally we will load this code into the G80 memory and see it in operation. To do this, run the `GDS.exe` program and select Simulator from the main menu. When the G80 simulator appears, point the cursor onto memory location 0000 and double click. When the dialog box appears, enter the code shown in Figure 6.4. After entering the code, the simulator should appear as shown in Figure 6.5. (You may notice that the G80 simulator automatically loads all unused memory locations with 0x76, which is the code for the `halt` instruction. This is so that, should your program erroneously attempt to access a memory location that you have not programmed, the simulator will execute the `halt` instruction. In practice, memory locations that have not been programmed are likely to contain 0xFF.)

Click on the yellow Single Instruction, SI, button in the GDS menu to execute the code one instruction at a time and observe what happens. When the program reaches the `halt` instruction in location 0006, click on the red Reset button, [0], and step through it again until you are happy that you

---

[4] Some microprocessors load their Program Counter with an address that is near the top of the memory space when they are powered up.

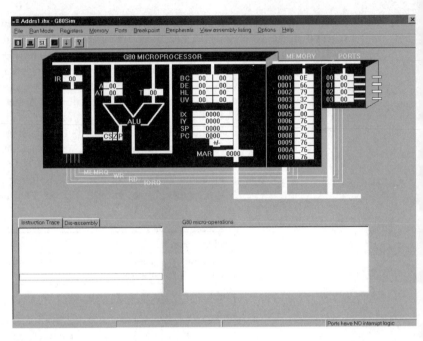

Figure 6.5 *Appearance of G80Sim after loading the machine code for Addrs1.asm*

understand what each instruction does. (If you accidentally click the green Run button, you will have to click the SI button before you can exit from the simulator.)

6.4 Using the assembler

When we manually converted the mnemonic code of `Addrs1.asm` into machine code, we looked up each instruction in the list of G80 instructions to get the corresponding machine code. This simple, but tedious, task is best carried out using a computer program that runs on your PC. This program, the **assembler** tool, forms part of GDS. This tool, together with the **linker** tool, does the translation from mnemonics to machine code for us. To use these tools you must first create a directory on a disk into which you will save all your work. GDS will do this for you if you wish.

Run GDS and in the upper part of the opening screen type the source code shown in Figure 6.2. Use the tab key to indent each line of code; this makes your code easier to read. Save this file as "`Addrs1.asm`" using main menu | File | Save As. Now click on Assembler in the main menu and observe that the lower part of the screen now reports what the assembler tool has done. Correct any typing errors that may be indicated by the assembler. Repeat this 'edit – assemble' cycle until the assembler reports no errors then click on main menu | View Assembly to see how the assembler has converted your source code to machine code. The display will appear as shown in Figure 6.6. The lower part of the screen displays a file produced by the assembler and stored in a disk file named `Addrs1.lst`. Observe that the assembler has

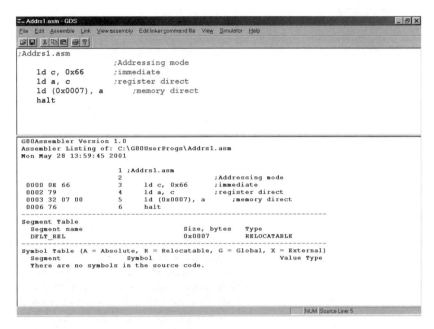

Figure 6.6 *Appearance of GDS after entering and assembling the source code for Addrs1.asm*

done the task of translating the instructions given in mnemonic code into their G80 machine codes.

Now click on Link, and observe that the linker program indicates a successful linking. We shall return to the purpose of the linker in Chapter 12. Now click on Simulator and observe that the G80 memory contains the same code as we produced by hand, Figure 6.4.

6.5 Assembly language

In program Addrs1.asm we made explicit reference to memory location 0007 but when we write source code in mnemonics, it is inconvenient to keep track of the actual memory locations used. Instead of writing actual, or physical, addresses it is more convenient to give the locations names, or **labels** or **symbols**. The programmer uses these **symbolic addresses** when writing the code; they are converted to real addresses when the program is assembled and linked. Thus, Addrs1.asm is more conveniently written as shown in Figure 6.7. The source code of the program now contains not only mnemonics for the computer instructions but also a **pseudo-operation**, or pseudo-op or **assembler directive**; this is a command to the assembler tool. Together, the mnemonics for the G80 instructions and the assembler directives comprise the G80 **assembly language**.

The memory location at the end of the program code has been given the symbolic name fred. The symbol is defined by writing it at the start of the line and following it with a colon. Now, instead of writing ld (0x0007), a we can more readily write ld (fred), a. Indeed, wherever fred appears in the program, it will be interpreted as 0x0007. In this example, location

```
;Addrs2.asm
;Program Addrs1.asm using assembly language
;
      ld c, 0x66
      ld a, c
      ld (fred), a     ;'fred' is a symbolic address
      halt
fred:
      .ds 1            ;Reserve 1 byte for storage
```

Figure 6.7 *Source code of Addrs2.asm*

fred is to store a byte so we reserve one byte of memory using the .ds 1 (define storage) directive.

Edit the source code for Addrs1.asm to that of Figure 6.7 and save it as Addrs2.asm. Then assemble and link it. View the assembly listing (main menu | View Assembly) and note that the assembler has produced the same machine code as it did for Addrs1.asm. Of course, if you now run the simulator, the program will behave exactly the same as Addrs1.asm did.

6.6 Types of instruction

Although the list of all the instructions in the instruction set of the G80 looks forbiddingly large, the instructions may be conveniently classified according to the type of operation they carry out. Thus, some instructions merely copy data from one register or memory location to another; these are **data transfer** instructions. A second type is the **arithmetical and logical** instructions. A third type of instruction controls which instruction will be executed next; these are **program control** instructions. Any other type of instruction we simply regard as belonging to a catch-all fourth classification. These instructions are illustrated in the following sections. To become familiar with the G80 instructions[5] you should type each of these examples into GDS, assemble, link, and step through them one instruction at a time. When running the simulator, you can put the assembly listing onto the screen by clicking on main menu | View Assembly listing.

6.6.1 Data transfer instructions

These instructions simply copy data from one place in the computer to another place. The data may be 1 or 2 bytes long. We have used some of these data transfer instructions in Addrs2.asm; Figure 6.8 illustrates more examples. Note that the instruction ld bc, 0x1234 loads register B with 0x12 and also loads register C with 0x34. We say that **register pair** BC has been loaded with 0x1234. The instruction ld hl, fred loads register pair HL with 0012, which is the value of fred.

---

[5] All microprocessors are capable of executing similar instructions to those described here.

```
;Move.asm
;Some single byte data transfers:-
;
        ld c, 66        ;Load reg C with decimal 66
        ld a, 10        ;Load reg A with decimal 10
        ld (fred), a    ;Load memory location 'fred'
                        ; from A
        ld a, c         ;Load reg A from C
        ld a, (fred)    ;Load reg A from 'fred'
        ;
;Some two byte transfers:-
        ld bc, 0x1234   ;Load register pair BC
                        ; with 0x1234
        ld hl, fred     ;Load register pair HL
                        ; with address of 'fred'
        halt
fred:
        .ds 1           ;Reserve 1 byte for storage
```

Figure 6.8 *Source code of Move.asm*

Our computer is of no practical use unless it can move data from the computer to the world outside the computer and move data from the outside world into the computer. Connections between our computer and the outside world are done through **ports**; the hardware of input and output ports is explored in Chapter 9. For the present, we see how data ports are used to transfer data between our computer and the outside world. In the following program, we input data from a bank of eight switches and output the state of the switches to a bank of light-emitting diodes, LEDs.

Run GDS, and type the source code for Sws_Leds.asm, Figure 6.9. Click Assemble in the main menu to assemble it. When you have corrected any errors the assembler objects to, click on the main menu item Link. Now click on the main menu Simulator to simulate your program. When the simulator appears, 'connect' the switches and the LEDs to the G80 computer by clicking on Peripherals | Switches and on Peripherals | LEDs. You may drag these devices to any position on the screen. The appearance of the simulator is shown in Figure 6.10.

```
;Sws_Leds.asm
;
;Define port addresses:
SWS = 0x90      ;Address of the switches port.
LEDS = 0x20     ;Address of the LEDS port.
;
loop:
        in a, (SWS)     ;Move data from switches to register A.
        out (LEDS), a   ;Move data from register A to LEDs.
        jp loop         ;Do the above forever.
```

Figure 6.9 *Source code of Sws_Leds.asm*

Now click on the green Run button. While the Sws_Leds program is running, toggle a switch by clicking on it and observe that the LEDs change to the state of the switches. You can see more detail of what is happening by repeatedly clicking on the yellow SI (Single Instruction) button. Observe that the instruction in a, (SWS) copies the data from the switches to register A. The out (LEDS), a instruction copies the data in register A to the LEDs. The program uses the jp loop instruction to repeat the sequence.

To exit from the simulator, you must first stop your program from running by pressing either the yellow SI button or the red Reset button.

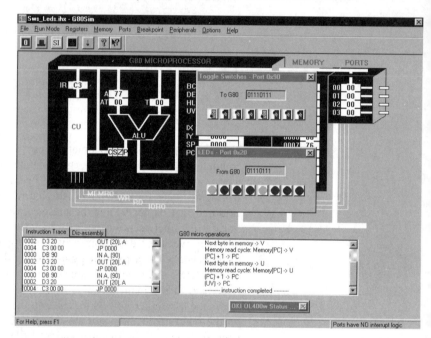

Figure 6.10 *Simulator running Sws_Leds.asm*

6.6.2 Arithmetical and logical instructions

These instructions process the data by performing arithmetical operations, such as addition and subtraction, or logical operations such as AND and OR. When logical operations are performed on multi-bit data, the data are processed bit by bit. Thus the logical AND of 10001100 with 11110110 is obtained by AND-ing corresponding bits in both patterns:

```
      1 0 0 0 1 1 0 0
AND   1 1 1 1 0 1 1 0
      - - - - - - - -
      1 0 0 0 0 1 0 0
```

Similarly, the logical OR gives:

```
          1 0 0 0 1 1 0 0
     OR   1 1 1 1 0 1 1 0
          _ _ _ _ _ _ _ _
          1 1 1 1 1 1 1 0
```

Some illustrative examples are given in `ALUops.asm`, Figure 6.11. Enter this source code, assemble and link it. Then use the simulator to single step through the program and observe the effect of each of the instructions. You will find it convenient to have the assembly listing on the screen; to show this, click on View assembly listing.

```
;ALUops.asm
;Some single byte arithmetical instructions.
      ld   a, 42
      ld   b,6
      add a,b          ;Add contents of reg B to contents of reg A.
                       ; Result is 48 = 0x30 in reg A.
      sub b            ;Subtract contents of reg B from contents of
                       ; reg A.  Result is 42 = 0x2A in reg A.
      inc b            ;Add 1 to reg B.  Result is 7 = 0x07 in reg B.
      dec a            ;Subtract 1 from reg A.  Result is 41 = 0x29 in
                       ; reg A.
;
;Some two byte arithmetical instructions.
      ld hl, 0x5566
      ld de, 0x3344
      add hl, de    ;Add contents of reg pair DE to contents of
                    ; reg pair HL.  Result is 0x88AA in reg HL.
      inc hl        ;Increment HL.  Result is 0x88AB in reg HL.
      dec de        ;Decrement DE.  Result is 0x3343 in reg DE.
;
;Some logical operations.
      ld a, 0x0F   ;00001111, 0x0F
      and 0x63     ;01100011, 0x63
                   ;00000011, 0x03 = 0x0F AND 0x63
      or 0x2C      ;00101100, 0x2C
                   ;00101111  0x2F = 0x03 OR 0x2C
      xor 6        ;00000110, 0x06
                   ;00101001  0x29 = 0x2F XOR 0x06
      cpl          ;11010110  0xd6 = bit complement of 0x29
      halt
```

Figure 6.11 *Source code of ALUops.asm*

6.6.3 Skew instructions

These instructions shift the data one place to the left or right. When data is shifted, one bit drops out one end of the data and a new bit enters the other end. In the G80, the bit that drops out the end is always stored in the Carry flag. However, the bit that enters the opposite end of the data depends on the particular skew instruction. The G80 skew instructions are summarized in Figure 6.12. Program `Skew.asm`, Figure 6.13, illustrates the use of some of the skew operations.

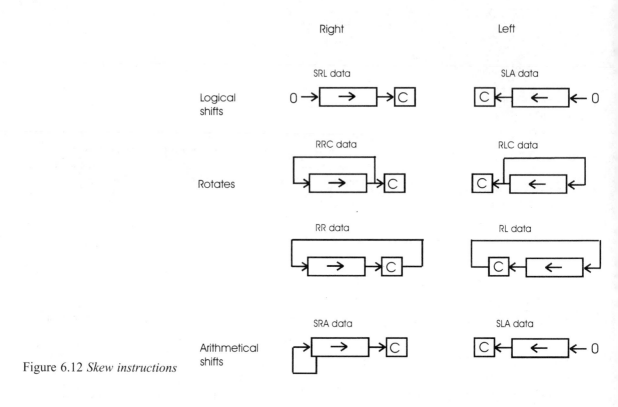

Figure 6.12 *Skew instructions*

```
;Skew.asm
;Some skew operations - shifts and rotates:-
        ld   d, 0xC2     ;D = 0xC2 = 1100 0010
        srl d            ;D = 0x61 = 0110 0001
                         ;Previous content of D shifted right
                         ;Previous lsb into Carry flag.
        srl d            ;D = 0x30 = 0011 0000    And again.
        ;
        rlc d            ;D = 0x60 = 0110 0000
                         ;Now shifted left, bit 7 shifts
                         ;   into bit 0 and to Carry.
        rlc d            ;D = 0xC0 = 1100 0000
        rlc d            ;D = 0x81 = 1000 0001, Carry flag set.
        rlc d            ;D = 0x03 = 0000 0011, Carry flag set.
        rlc d            ;D = 0x06 = 0000 0110, Carry flag reset.
        ;
;Arithmetical shift to the left doubles the value:-
        ld  a,-3         ;A = 1111 1101 = -3
        sla a            ;A = 1111 1010 = -6
;Arithmetical shift to the right halves the value:-
        sra a            ;A = 1111 1101 = -3
        sra a            ;A = 1111 1110 = -2, not -1½ !
```

Figure 6.13 *Source code of Skew.asm*

```
;Jump.asm
;Some instructions which change the sequence of operations.
     ld  a,1
again:
     dec a
②  jp z, is0   ;If the Zero flag is set,
                ; take next instruction from
                ; memory location is0,
                ;else, carry on as usual.
     ld b,42
①  jp again
;
is0:
     inc a
     inc a
①  jp  again
```

Figure 6.14 *Source code of Jump.asm*

6.6.4 Program control instructions

Some instructions, called jump or branch instructions, cause the Program Counter to be loaded with a new value so that the next instruction is fetched from a memory location other than the one following the jump instruction. They are illustrated in program Jump.asm, Figure 6.14. The jump will always happen in an unconditional jump instruction, ①. The jump may or may not occur in a conditional jump instruction, depending on the state of a particular flag, ②.

6.7 Problems

Manipulate bits of the data.

1   The temperature at three positions in a furnace is stored as 8-bit integers in the 3 bytes beginning in the memory location having address furnace. How can the temperature at the second position be transferred to register A?

2   The upper nibble (bits 7, 6, 5, and 4) of register A are required to be made zero while not changing the lower 4 bits (bits 3, 2, 1, and 0). How this can be achieved in one instruction?

3   The upper nibble of register A contains 0000. How can these bits be replaced with 0011 without affecting the lower nibble using one instruction?

4   How can the upper nibble of register A be replaced with 0011 whatever the existing contents of the upper nibble? The lower nibble is to be unchanged.

5   How can bits 1 and 2 of register A be inverted using one instruction?

Use data shifts.

6   Show that the instruction add hl, hl is effectively the same as shifting HL left one place. Do this by writing a short program that loads register pair HL with 0x4004 and then repeatedly performs add hl, hl. What information does the Carry flag contain when the add hl, hl instruction is executed?

7   The G80 does not have an instruction for shifting register pair DE to the right. How can this be achieved using two G80 instructions?

8   How can register pair BC be shifted to the left one place?

9   Modify Sws_Leds1.asm so that the LEDs display the contents of register A rotated two places to the left.

Use arithmetical instructions.

10   Assuming register A contains a number between 0 and 50, multiply the number by five. Hint: Shifting a number left one place doubles its value.

11   Multiply the unsigned number in register A by five, placing the result in register pair DE.

Overflow detection.

12   Observe how the C and P flags indicate overflow of unsigned and signed integers respectively by stepping through the following lines of code.

(a)
```
ld  a,  0x7F
add a,  1
```

If the programmer regards the numbers as unsigned integers, is the result correct? If the programmer regards the numbers as signed integers, is the result correct?

(b)
```
ld  a,  0xFF
add a,  1
```

If the programmer regards the numbers as unsigned integers, is the result correct? If the programmer regards the numbers as signed integers, is the result correct?

(c)
```
ld  a,  0x80
sub 1
```

If the programmer regards the numbers as unsigned integers, is the result correct? If the programmer regards the numbers as signed integers, is the result correct?

(d) ```
     ld a, 0
     sub 1
     ```

If the programmer regards the numbers as unsigned integers, is the result correct? If the programmer regards the numbers as signed integers, is the result correct?

(e)  Explain how the C flag may be used to detect unsigned overflow, and how the P flag may be used to detect signed overflow.

Use the status flags.

13  How can the G80 be programmed to detect that the contents of registers B and C are the same?

14  How can the G80 be programmed to detect that the contents of register B are greater than the contents of register C?

15  How can the G80 be programmed to detect that the contents of register B are less than the contents of register C?

16  How can the G80 be programmed to detect that the contents of register B are greater than or equal to the contents of register C?

17  How can the G80 be programmed to detect that the contents of register B are less than or equal to the contents of register C?
     ```

7 Program structures

In Chapter 6 we saw the variety of instructions that are available to a programmer of the G80. In this chapter we see how these instructions, and the data on which they operate, are best organized into various structures. Programs are written in order to process data; indeed, what is commonly referred to as a 'program' is an algorithm that processes data. Thus we have that 'Program = Data + Algorithm for processing the Data'. We use **program control structures** to define the algorithm; we use **data structures** to store data in a way that helps us devise simple algorithms.

In this chapter, we look first at how instructions may be organized into the three basic program control structures **sequence**, **while**, and **if/else**, and then we look at the often used data structures **tables**, **arrays**, and **stack**. Along the way, we shall add two **index registers** to the design of the G80.

7.1 Program control structures

```
DoThis;
NowThis;
AndThis;
```

Figure 7.1 *A sequence of instructions*

To create robust programs, we use a small number of program control structures. Any algorithm for a computer may be expressed using only the three control structures[1] called **sequence**, **while**, and **if/else**. Each structure has exactly one entry point and exactly one exit point. This discipline helps to keep programs comprehensible to the programmer and to another person having to understand it in order to make improvements. The discipline also leads to more reliable programs, that is, programs that behave exactly as the program designer intended. Another way of saying this is that the program has fewer 'bugs'.

Flowcharts illustrating these control structures are shown in Figures 7.1, 7.2, and 7.3 together with their equivalents in a high-level language based on the C language. In this chapter, we will see the use of these control structures.

7.1.1 Sequence

This structure is so simple that it is difficult to see it as a structure. It is simply a sequence of instructions, each one executed after the previous one. Thus, the following program segment is a sequence:

---

[1] Bohm and Jacopini in 1966 proved that these structures were *all* that were essential to specify an algorithm.

```
while(condition is met)
    DoThisOver;
```

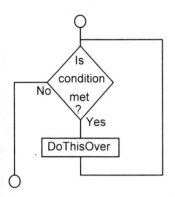

Figure 7.2 *A while loop of instructions*

```
getfred:
        ld a, (fred)
        add a, 42
        jp there

        ;
```

Although this structure is very simple, it is important to note that once the sequence is begun at `getfred`, all the instructions in the sequence will be executed. It has the property that all structures have: it has a single entry point, `getfred`, and a single exit point, the `jp there` instruction. Because there are no labels that could be used as another entry point, `getfred` is the only entry point. The `jp there` instruction determines the single exit point.

```
if(condition is met)
        MetCode
else
        ElseCode
```

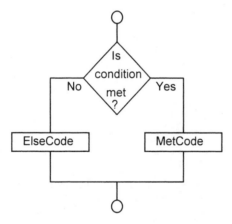

Figure 7.3 *An if/else structure of alternative sequences of instructions*

7.1.2 While loop

This structure allows the programmer to specify that a certain block of code will be executed all the while that a particular condition is met. Program `while1.asm`, Figure 7.4, illustrates this: it sets register A to zero, then enters a 'while' so that while the content of register A is not equal to 50, register A is incremented. When register A holds 50, the while ends and another 'while' is entered. This second 'while' repeats all the while that register A does not hold zero. When register A does hold zero, this 'while' terminates and the program stops. Just for fun, we make the program display the contents of register A on the chart recorder.

It is convenient to have a template for the code of a while loop. A programmer can use the template to help in writing the assembly code. Both while loops have been coded using the following template:

```
            WhileEntry:
                    Instruction(s) to affect a flag that indicates
                            whether or not the condition for the while
                            is met.
                    Conditional jump to WhileExit if the flag
                            indicates that the condition for the while
                            is not met.
                    ;
                    Code to execute while the condition is met.
                            'Body' of the loop.
                    ;
                    jp WhileEntry
            WhileExit:


;While1.asm
;
;Algorithm:
;reg A = 0
;while reg A != 50
;    increment reg A
;
;while reg A != 0
;    decrement reg A
;
CHART = 0x30
;
start:
    ld a, 0
while2:      while(A != 50)
    ;if( A == 50 ) exit this while loop
    cp 50           ;Affect Z flag
    jp z, while2end
    ;
    inc a           ;    A = A + 1
    out (CHART), a
    jp while2
    ;
while2end:
    ;
while3:      while(A != 0)
    ;if( A == 0 ) exit this while loop
    cp 0            ;Affect Z flag
    jp z, while3end
    ;
    dec a           ;    A = A - 1
    out (CHART), a
    jp while3
    ;
while3end:
    halt            ;OR jp start
```

Figure 7.4 *Source code of while1.asm*

If we replace the `halt` the end of `while1.asm` with `jp start`, the program code will repeat forever. We have effectively enclosed the two original 'whiles' within another 'while'. The condition for this outer 'while' to execute is always true so the code within it, the body of the 'while', will repeat forever. The program structure is then:

```
A = 0
while(TRUE)
      {
      while(A! = 50}   /! = is read as 'not the same as'
            {
            increment A
            write A to chart recorder
            }
      while( A ! = 0)
            {
            decrement A
            write A to chart recorder
            }
      }
```

7.1.3 If/Else

In a computation, the programmer will require that one or other blocks of program code will be executed depending on the data being processed. For example, in program `If_else1.asm`, Figure 7.5, it is required that if the toggle switch at bit 7 is set to 1, then registers B and C will be incremented, else registers B and C will be decremented. Just for fun, we output the contents of register B to a chart recorder, which is at port CHART. The `jp start` instruction at the end of the code effectively encloses the main body of the program code within a `while(TRUE)` loop so that it will repeat forever.

While this program is running, click on switch 7 and observe that registers B and C change as required by the program.

The following template has been used to write the assembly code for the if/else control structure:

```
IfEntry:
        Instruction(s) to affect a flag that indicates
             whether or not the condition for the
             if/else is met or not met.
        Conditional jump to IfElse if the flag indicates
             that the condition for the if/else is not
             met.
        ;
        Code to execute if the condition is met.
        jp IfExit
        ;
IfElse:
```

```
            Code to execute if the condition is not met.
    IfExit:
```

Quite often, the 'else' code is to do nothing. In this case the template becomes:

```
    IfEntry:
            Instruction(s) to affect a flag that indicates
                    whether or not the condition for the
                    if/else is met or not met.
            Conditional jump to IfExit if the flag indicates
                    that the condition for the if/else is not
                    met.
            ;
            Code to execute if the condition is met.
    IfExit:
```

```
;If_else1.asm
;
;while( TRUE )
;    if Switch7 is 1
;        increment reg B and C
;    else
;        decrement reg B and C
;
SWS     = 0x90
CHART   = 0x30
;
start:
    in a, (SWS)        ;if( SWS bit 7 == 0 )
    bit 7, a
    jp z, els
    ;
    inc b              ;    B = B + 1
    inc c              ;    C = C + 1
    jp ifend
    ;
els:                   ;else
    dec b              ;    B = B - 1
    dec c              ;    C = C - 1
ifend:
    ;output register B to chart recorder
    ld a, b
    out (CHART), a
    jp start           ;do forever
```

Figure 7.5 *Source code of If_else1.asm*

7.2 Data structures

A single number rarely gives a complete description of the state of a particular object. Thus the position of a ship at sea is defined by two numbers – its latitude and longitude – while the position of an aircraft requires three numbers – its latitude, longitude, and height above sea-level. More complex states such as that of a chemical reaction in a reaction vessel are likely to require many numbers such as the height of the liquid level, its temperature, its pressure, its pH value, and its oxygen content. Whatever the object to be described, the collection of numbers that describe it are best stored in the computer memory in a logical data structure. This allows the programmer to readily comprehend the data and to write efficient algorithms that access the numbers, or **elements**, within the data structure. Thus, the design of a 'good' program requires that the programmer store the data in a logical way. Here we look at some basic forms of data structures. We shall also see that, in order to access elements within a data structure, we shall have to add another method by which the G80 accesses data in memory locations.

7.2.1 Look-up table

This very simple data structure is widely used for, as its name suggests, looking up the answer to a particular question in a table that contains all the possible answers. As an example, suppose the question is 'Given a decimal digit, which segments of a seven-segment display must be illuminated in order to display the digit?'[2] The specification of the seven-segment display is given in Appendix C; from it we can readily obtain the table, Figure 7.6,

Decimal digit	Display segment								Hex
	dp	g	f	e	d	c	b	a	
0	0	0	1	1	1	1	1	1	3F
1	0	0	0	0	0	1	1	0	06
2	0	1	0	1	1	0	1	1	5B
3	0	1	0	0	1	1	1	1	4F
4	0	1	1	0	0	1	1	0	66
5	0	1	1	0	1	1	0	1	6D
6	0	1	1	1	1	1	0	1	7D
7	0	0	0	0	0	1	1	1	07
8	0	1	1	1	1	1	1	1	7F
9	0	1	1	0	1	1	1	1	6F
Error	0	1	1	1	1	0	0	1	79

Figure 7.6 *Table showing state of the seven segments to be illuminated*

[2] You might wish to try to devise an algorithm that **computes** which segments are to be illuminated. Your algorithm will be more complicated than the solution using a look-up table.

which indicates the segments to be illuminated. In answer to the question, a human would look up the answer in the table; we will copy this method by storing the table in the computer memory and devising an algorithm for looking up the required answer.

Assume that the start of the table is in memory location 0400: then, if the digit to display is *s*, the required answer is to be found in memory location 0400+*s*. Since *s* is a variable, the address, 0400+*s*, has to be calculated by our program. Let the result of this address calculation be stored in register-pair HL. We now wish to read the contents of the memory location whose address is in HL. However, our current design of the G80 does not facilitate this form of data access. We will make good this deficiency by adding hardware to the G80 that provides a data path from register-pair HL to the address bus. We also add instructions of the form:

```
ld a,(hl)   ;Load register A from the memory location
            ; whose address is in register pair HL.
ld (hl),a   ;Load the memory location whose address is
            ; in register pair HL from register A.
```

We say that the content of HL **points** to the required data. To give the programmer more than one pointer, and to add some regularity in the design of the G80, we shall also modify the G80 hardware so that the contents of register pairs BC and DE can be used as pointers to memory locations.

Program SegLut.asm, Figure 7.7, illustrates the use of these new instructions to access the seven-segment display table. The bit patterns in the table, which begins at memory location SegTab, are defined by writing the assembler directive .db followed by the value of a number in the list. The and 0x0F instruction forces the upper 4 bits of the data from the keyboard to zero. The remaining 4 bits of data are copied into register pair HL. We now want to add the value of SegTab to the number in HL – this is done by first loading the value of SegTab into register pair DE and then adding DE to HL. The address of the data we want is now in HL so we load that data into register A using ld a, (hl).

Normally, if a look-up table has *x* entries, in order to make our program code robust, we would have to check that the input data was not greater than *x*; otherwise the program would erroneously read a byte from a location not in the table. The SegLut.asm program code avoids having to check that the input data is a decimal digit by simply extending the segment table to make it contain 16 entries, one for each possible input data. All the table entries 10 to 15 are the bit pattern that displays 'E'.

Note that the look-up table is a powerful technique; in general, programs should be written so that they avoid wasting time computing a result that can be looked up in a 'reasonably sized' look-up table.

7.2.2 Lists of data

Suppose, for example, that five temperature sensors monitor the temperature of a furnace. A logical way of storing these temperatures is to put them into consecutive memory locations, so forming a **list** of temperatures.

```
;SegLut.asm
;
;while( TRUE )
;   Get a decimal digit from keypad
;   Display on right-hand seven-segment display.
;
;
;
KEYPAD = 0x80
SSEGR = 0xA0
;
start:
    in a, (KEYPAD)    ;get a key
    and 0x0F          ;strip off upper nibble
    ld l, a           ;Copy A to HL
    ld h, 0
    ld de, SegTab     ;DE holds SegTab
    add hl, de        ;add keypad number
    ld a, (hl)        ;get data from table
    out (SSEGR), a    ;display
    jp start          ;do forever
;
SegTab:
    .db 0x3F          ;0
    .db 0x06          ;1
    .db 0x5B          ;2
    .db 0x4F          ;3
    .db 0x66          ;4
    .db 0x6D          ;5
    .db 0x7D          ;6
    .db 0x07          ;7
    .db 0x7F          ;8
    .db 0x6F          ;9
    .db 0x79          ;E
    .db 0x79          ;E
    .db 0x79          ;E
    .db 0x79          ;E
    .db 0x79          ;E
    .db 0x79          ;E
```

Figure 7.7 *Source code of SegLut.asm*

Now suppose we wish to determine the sum of the five temperatures, each being an 8-bit unsigned integer. The program will have to count the number of temperatures that have been read from the list. One way to keep count is to set a register to 0, increment it each time a temperature is added, and checking for a count of 5. Alternatively, we can set a register to 5, decrement it each time a temperature is added, and check for a count of 0. Since the G80 and other microprocessors have special hardware to detect zero, this latter method is the more common. We choose to keep the length of the list in register B, which we decrement every time a number in the list has been added. The algorithm to form the sum is then:

```
B = 5
while( B ! = 0)
        {
        get next number from the list
        add the number obtained from the list
        decrement B
        }
```

The source code for this example, List1.asm, is shown in Figure 7.8. It begins by initializing the contents of the registers we shall use, then the while loop is entered at wh2. The condition for the while is evaluated by loading register A from register B then comparing it with zero. The next four instructions add the temperature and save it register E. The inc hl instruction adds one to the contents of HL so that HL points to the next temperature in the

```
;List1.asm
;Find sum of list of five unsigned integers.
;The list of numbers is stored at list.
;Algorithm:
;count = 5
;while( count != 0 )
;    {
;    get next number from list.
;    add it to sum_so_far
;    count = count - 1
;    }
;
;Register usage:
;           HL  pointer to data in list
;            E  sum_so_far
;            B  loop counter
;
start:
      ld   hl, list      ;Point to list
      ld   b,5           ;5 numbers in list
      ld   e,0           ;Initialise sum_so_far
      ;
;While( count != 0 )
wh2:
      ld   a, b          ;If( count == 0 ) done
      cp 0               ;Affect Z flag
      jp z, wh2end
      ;
      ld   a, (hl)       ;Get a number
      inc hl             ;Bump the pointer
      add a, e           ;Add sum_so_far
      ld   e,a           ;Save sum_so_far
      dec b              ;Count down
      jp   wh2
      ;
wh2end:
      halt
;
①list:                  ;Here is the list of five unsigned integers
      .db 2
      .db 29
      .db 130
      .db 79
      .db 7
```

Figure 7.8 *Source code of program List1.asm*

list. Finally, register B is decremented by one and the while loop is performed again because of the `jp wh2` instruction.

Note that if there were, say, 20 numbers in the list the only code change needed would be to load register C with 20 instead of 5.

7.2.3 Character strings

Often strings of characters are used in a program for messages that might be written to a display. Such strings are most easily stored in a simple list.

Alphanumeric characters are represented by an internationally agreed code, the International Standards Organization (ISO) Code which was derived from the **American Standard Code for Information Interchange** (ASCII). The seven-bit ASCII code represents all the letters of the alphabet, both upper and lower case, as well as the numerals 0 to 9 and various punctuation marks and control codes. The codes are given in Appendix B. The ISO codes extend this standard to cope with the additional characters required for international use, such as the character for the British pound, £, and various accented characters of European languages. However, it is still common to refer to the codes for characters as 'ASCII' codes.

Character strings are usually stored as a list of ASCII codes terminated by the NUL character (0x00). Thus, the string 'Hello!' is stored as shown in Figure 7.9 where `Msg1` is the address of the start of the string. Our algorithm for reading the string does not count the number of characters in the string; instead, it keeps reading until the NUL character is read. The technique of ending a list of values with a value that is not in the set of possible values is useful wherever the list does not have a fixed length; the ending value is called a **sentinel**.

In program `String1.asm`, it is required to count the number of occurrences of the character 'e' in a character string. The algorithm is:

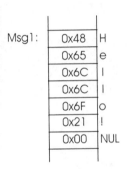

Msg1:

0x48	H
0x65	e
0x6C	l
0x6C	l
0x6F	o
0x21	!
0x00	NUL

Figure 7.9 *Storage of the character string Hello!*

```
e_count = 0;
get first character from list
while( character ! = 0)
        {
        if( character = = 'e')
                increment e_count
        get next character in list
        }
```

The corresponding assembly code is shown in Figure 7.10.

At ① we have used `and a` rather than `cp 0`; in this context the effect is the same but the `and a` instruction is encoded into only one byte while the `cp 0` instruction is encoded into two bytes. The instruction `and a` does not alter the contents of register A but, since the data is passed through the ALU, the flags are affected.

At ② a comparison between the contents of register A and the ASCII code for character 'e'. Note that we do not have to write this ASCII code explicitly since the assembler tool will convert `'e` to its ASCII code, 0x65. If the

```
;String1.asm
;Count "e" in a null-terminated string.
;Register usage:  HL  pointer to string
;                 E  count of "e"
;
;Initialise registers
    ld hl, msg1    ;Point to string
    ld e, 0        ;Counter
    ;
;While( character != 00 )
wh1:
    ld a, (hl)     ;Get a character
    inc hl         ;Bump pointer
    ;If( character == NUL ) wh1end
①  and a          ;Affect cpu flags
    jp z,   wh1end ;If end of string, jump
    ;
    ;If( letter == "e" ) E = E + 1
②  cp  'e         ;ASCII 'e' = 0x65
    jp nz, not_e   ;If not "e", jump
    ;
    inc e          ;Count "e" in register E
not_e:
    jp wh1
;
wh1end:
    halt
    ;

;Here is the message
msg1:
③  .db 'H, 'e, 'l     ;Hel
    .db 'l, 'o, '!     ;lo!
    .db 'e, 'e         ;ee
    .db 0              ;NUL, sentinel
;Could use the following line instead:
;    .asciz 'Hello!ee' ;Null terminated string.
```

Figure 7.10 *Program to count number of occurrences of 'e' in a string*

character is 'e', the compare instruction will set the Zero flag, otherwise the flag will be reset.

At ③ the string is defined using the .db directive. A more convenient way is to let the assembler look up the required ASCII codes; write .asciiz 'Hello!, where .asciiz is an assembler directive to insert the ASCII codes for the characters into the program and append a NUL character.

7.2.4 Jump table

Suppose we wish to get a command character from a keyboard and execute a particular code sequence according to the command character. In the following example, a single character command is read from the ASCII keyboard. The command is one of the characters a, c, e, p. After getting the

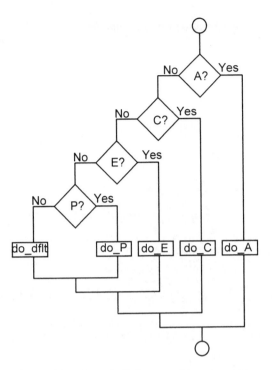

Figure 7.11 *Nested if/else to achieve a multi-way switch*

command character, the section of code that deals with the command is executed. This 'multi-way switch' is an extension of the two-way switch normally implemented by an if/else control structure. Indeed, one solution is to have a nest of if/else structures as shown in Figure 7.11. The code for this becomes difficult to read, particularly if the number of possible command characters is large, so we will use an alternative approach, the **jump table**.

In program Switch1.asm, Figure 7.12, we set up a jump table that contains the addresses of the start of each program section. We obtain the command character from the ASCII keyboard and look up the start address of the appropriate code in the table. The structure of the jump table is:

```
ASCII code for a command (1 byte)
Address of start of required program code (2 bytes)
ASCII code for a command (1 byte)
Address of start of required program code (2 bytes)
ASCII code for a command (1 byte)
Address of start of required program code (2 bytes)
...
...
00                      ;sentinel
Address of start of program code to deal with
                        ; unrecognised input
```

```
;Switch1.asm    - switch control structure
;while(TRUE)     ;do forever
;    {
;    Get a command <a,c,e,p> from KBD
;    Do code depending on command
;    }
;
KBD = 0xC0           ;ASCII keyboard
LCD = 0xD0           ;LCD
;
CRLF = 0x0A          ;newline character
;
start:
    in a, (KBD)
    ld c, a          ;save command
    ld hl, jtab      ;Pointer to jump table
lookup:
①   ld a, (hl)       ;Extract a command from table
    cp c             ;Does it match the command?
    jp z, getadr     ;If so, jump
                     ; else
②   and a            ;Is it the end of table?
    jp z, getadr     ;If so, jump
; else
③   inc hl           ;Bump pointer
    inc hl           ;   three
    inc hl           ;        times.
    jp lookup        ;Try again
    ;
    ;Found a match or end of table
getadr:
    inc hl           ;Bump pointer
    ld e, (hl)       ;Get address into...
    inc hl           ;      register pair
    ld d, (hl)       ;         DE.
    ex de, hl        ;DE into HL
    jp (hl)          ;Jump to required code
    ;
;
case_a: ;Code for command 'a'
    ld a, "a"
    out (LCD), a
    ld a, CRLF
    out (LCD), a
    jp start
    ;
case_c: ;Code for command 'c'
    ld a, "c"
    out (LCD), a
    ld a, CRLF
    out (LCD), a
    jp start
    ;
```

Figure 7.12 *Source code of Switch1.asm*

```
case_e: ;Code for command 'e'
    ld a, "e"
    out (LCD), a
    ld a, CRLF
    out (LCD), a
    jp start
    ;
case_p: ;Code for command 'p'
    ld a, "p"
    out (LCD), a
    ld a, CRLF
    out (LCD), a
    jp start
    ;
case_flt:    ;Code for unrecognised command
    ld a, "?"
    out (LCD), a
    ld a, CRLF
    out (LCD), a
    jp start
    ;
    ;Here is the jump table
jtab:
    .ascii  "a"      ;ASCII a
    .dw case_a       ;Address of case_a
    .ascii  "c"      ;ASCII c
    .dw case_c       ;Address of case_c
    .ascii  "e"      ;ASCII e
    .dw case_e       ;Address of case_e
    .ascii  "p"      ;ASCII p
    .dw case_p       ;Address of case_p
    .db 0            ;Sentinel
    .dw case_flt     ;Address of case_flt
```

Figure 7.12 *(cont.)*

Having input a command character, we search the jump table for a match. Now, from the structure of the jump table, we know that we should access every third byte of the table in this search. When we find a table entry that matches the input character, we read the following two bytes in the table as the start address of the instructions to be executed.

Run the program at full speed and a single instruction at a time until you have grasped the concept. Remember that the program looks up the memory address of the start of the instructions we want to execute in response to the command character. The response to the command is a very short message to the LCD; try changing these messages to something of your own devising.

A command code ①, is extracted, from the table and checked to see if it is zero ②. If an invalid command is held in register C, the command code extracted from the table will eventually be the sentinel and a jump will be made to the default code at **case_flt**. A valid command will match one of the character codes in the jump table. Then the address word, 2 bytes, in the table is copied into register pair DE and then HL, so that finally the **jp (hl)** transfers program control to the required code section.

In order to compare the letter of the required command with the command codes in the jump table, every third byte in the table must be read, hence the pointer is incremented by three each time through the loop ③.

7.2.5 Two-dimensional arrays

Sometimes data falls naturally into a two-dimensional array of values. Assume that we wish to determine the average temperature in four layers of a large storage vessel in a beer brewery. (The storage vessel is so tall that the beer tends to separate into layers.) The temperature of each layer of the vessel is obtained from the average value of two sensors in each layer. Thus, we have a total of eight temperature sensors.

An obvious way of regarding the temperatures is as a two-dimensional array having the format shown in Figure 7.13.

	Temp 0	**Temp 1**	**Average**
Layer 0	T00	T01	T02
Layer 1	T10	T11	T12
Layer 2	T20	T21	T22
Layer 3	T30	T31	T32

Figure 7.13 *Concept of two-dimensional array*

We can store this two-dimensional array in memory in two ways: store the elements of each row in turn or store the elements of each column in turn, as shown in Figure 7.14.

Figure 7.14 *Alternative ways of storing a two-dimensional array in memory:* (a) *by row, column;* (b) *by column, row*

Array

T00
T01
T02
T10
T11
T12
T20
T21
T22
T30
T31
T32

(a)

Array

T00
T10
T20
T30
T01
T11
T21
T31
T02
T12
T22
T32

(b)

Since we wish to process each row in turn, it is easier to use the storage scheme in Figure 7.14(a). The program code can then use register-pair HL to address each element in turn, incrementing HL after each access. Program RowSum.asm, Figure 7.15, uses this method.

```
;RowSum.asm
;Sum rows in an array.
;Register usage:   HL  pointer to array
;                  B   row counter
;
;Initialise registers
     ld hl, array   ;Point to array
     ld b,4         ;Number of rows
;
;Do until row count == 0
tloop:
     ld a, (hl)     ;Get number in col 0
     inc hl         ;Bump pointer to col 1
     add a, (hl)    ;Add number in col 1
     inc hl         ;Bump pointer to col 3
     ld (hl), a     ;Store sum in col 3
     inc hl         ;Bump pointer to start of next row
     djnz tloop     ;Decrement row count and test.
;
     halt
;
array:  ;temperature array.  Temperatures are 0 to 60.
     .db 50, 02,    0  ;Row 0
     .db 19, 21,    0  ;Row 1
     .db 60, 45,    0  ;Row 2
     .db 09, 01,    0  ;Row 3
```

Figure 7.15 *Program to sum row elements of an array*

7.2.6 Index registers IX and IY

If we wish to form the sum of the columns of the array stored as in Program ColSum.asm, Figure 7.16, we will find it useful to add another addressing method to the G80. (This is the last addition we shall make to the way in which the G80 can address memory locations.) We add **index registers** IX and IY to the G80 registers[3]. These may have a displacement added to their contents before being used as a pointer; the displacement is an 8-bit signed integer in the range $-128 \ldots +127$. This is illustrated by the instruction sequence:

---

[3] The G80 instruction set uses the term **indexed addressing** to refer to the addressing mode which uses the contents of an index register plus a displacement as a pointer. In other computers, this term is used to describe an addressing mode in which the displacement is held in a register or memory location and is therefore able to be modified when the program is run. In contrast, the displacement in the G80 index instructions is fixed when the program is assembled.

```
ld  ix, 0x5108
ld  a, (ix + 1)   ;Load reg A from memory location 0x5109
ld  a, (ix − 6)   ;Load reg A from memory location 0x5102
```

```
;ColSum.asm
;Sum columns in an array.
;Register usage:  IX  pointer to array
;                 B   col counter
;
;Initialise registers
        ld b,2              ;Number of cols
        ;
        ;Until col count == 0
        ld ix, array
tloop:
        ld a, (ix)          ;Get number in row 0
        add a, (ix+3)       ;Add number in row 1
        add a, (ix+6)       ;Add number in row 2
        add a, (ix+9)       ;Add number in row 3
        ld (ix+12), a       ;Store sum in row 4
        inc ix              ;Move pointer to start of next col
        djnz tloop          ;Decrement col count and test.
        ;
        halt
        ;
array:          ;temperature array.  Temperatures are 0 to 60.
        .db 50, 02, 0       ;Row 0
        .db 19, 21, 0       ;Row 1
        .db 60, 45, 0       ;Row 2
        .db 09, 01, 0       ;Row 3
        .db 0,  0,  0       ;Column sum
```

Figure 7.16 *Program to sum column elements of an array*

7.2.7 Stack

The stack is a special data structure that is maintained automatically by the G80. It behaves like a stack of plates in a restaurant, from which it is said it takes its name. The last plate put on the stack is the first plate available to be taken from the stack. In the stack structure, the last byte written, or **pushed**, onto the stack is the first byte available to be read from, or **popped**, from the stack. The stack is stored in a part of memory; the memory address of the current top-of-stack is held in a G80 register, the Stack Pointer, SP. We add logic to the G80 control unit so that whenever a byte is pushed onto the stack, the Stack Pointer is automatically decremented. Similarly, when a byte is popped from the stack, the Stack Pointer is automatically incremented.

We add to the G80 instruction set instructions of the form:

```
push rr    ;push the two registers rr onto the top of
           the stack
pop rr     ;pop the top two bytes off the stack into
           registers rr
```

where `rr` is AF, BC, DE, HL, IX, or IY.

```
;Stack.asm
;Illustration of stack operations
;The stack is stored in memory locations below 8000
;
      ld sp, 0x8000
      ld bc, 0xBBCC
      ld de, 0xDDEE
      push de
      push bc
      pop de
      pop bc
      halt
```

Figure 7.17 *Source code of Stack.asm*

The operation of the stack is shown in program `Stack.asm`, Figure 7.17. The instruction `ld sp,0x8000` initializes the Stack Pointer so that the stack is the region of memory below location 8000. Single-step through this program and observe both the behaviour of the Stack Pointer and the region of memory below 8000.

In most applications, the programmer need only have regard for the order of the stack operations and the depth of the stack itself. This last point is to prevent the stack encroaching onto an area of memory used for some other purpose.

7.3 Subroutines

Programs usually contain some functions that are performed several times. Typical of these are functions that multiply two numbers or generate a short delay. The code for the function can be written into the program each time it is required or, alternatively, it may be written just once as a **subroutine** and accessed each time it is required. This is achieved by a pair of instructions, `call nn`, which causes a jump to the subroutine at address nn, and `ret`, which causes a return from the subroutine back to the instruction immediately following the `call` instruction. These two instructions behave like 'smart' jump instructions.

The `call nn` appears to behave just like a `jp nn` instruction but it also causes the address of the next instruction, the **return address,** to be automatically saved. The `ret` instruction behaves like a jump to the return address, that is, the location following the call. How is this achieved? Modern microprocessors almost invariably save the return address on the stack. When the control unit has finished fetching the `call nn` instruction, its Program Counter is pointing to the following instruction, which is the required return address. The control unit then automatically pushes the PC on to the stack, so saving the return address, and then loads the PC with nn, the address of the start of the subroutine, so causing a jump to memory location nn. When the G80 executes the `ret` instruction, it performs what is effectively a 'pop pc' instruction, which puts the return address back into the PC so causing a jump back to the instruction immediately following the original call.

Where the subroutine contains more than just a few instructions, its use reduces the amount of memory required for the program. While this might be of crucial importance in some very small computers having a very small memory, an important benefit is for the programmer since programs using subroutines are easier to write and maintain. Because of the time required to save the return address and, perhaps other data, access to the code in the subroutine is always delayed slightly.

7.3.1 Example of subroutine

Program X5Sub.asm, Figure 7.18, includes a call to a subroutine named X5. When the subroutine is called, the number in register A is multiplied by five.

```
;X5Sub.asm
;Illustrates a call to subroutine X5.
;
     ld sp, 0x8000   ;Identify stack region
     ld a, (num)     ;Put number into reg A
     call X5         ;Multiply by 5
     ld (num), a     ;Store in num
     halt


;Subroutine to multiply integer in A by 5,
;   and return product in A.
X5:
     ld d, a         ;Save 1 x number
     sla a           ;Form 2 x number
     sla a           ;Form 4 x number
     add a, d        ;Form 5 x number
     ret             ;Return to caller

;Data
num:
     .db 3
```

Figure 7.18 *Source code of program X5Sub.asm*

When the call X5 instruction is executed, the next instruction is fetched from memory location X5, the start of the X5 subroutine. At the end of the subroutine, the ret instruction causes the microprocessor to fetch and execute the instruction following the call X5 instruction. This subroutine destroys the original contents of register D; it is good practice to code a subroutine so that registers that might contain current data are not modified by the subroutine. This is simply achieved by saving those registers at the beginning of the subroutine and restoring them just before returning; the stack is very convenient for this purpose. The subroutine is then written as shown in Figure 7.19.

```
;X5.asm
;Improved X5 subroutine.
;
;Subroutine to multiply integer in A by 5,
;  and return product in A.
X5:
     push de        ;Save regs D and E
     ld d, a        ;Save 1 x number
     sla a          ;Form 2 x number
     sla a          ;Form 4 x number
     add a, d       ;Form 5 x number
     pop de         ;Unsave regs D and E
     ret            ;Return to caller
```

Figure 7.19 *Improved subroutine X5*

```
;Mul16x16
;Tests the Mul16x16 subroutine
;0x7FFF x 0x7FFF = 0x3FFF 0001
     ld de, 0x7fff    ;Max possible integer
     ld bc, 0x7fff    ;Max possible integer
     call Mul16x16
     halt
```

```
;Subroutine to multiply
;  signed, but positive,
;  16-bit integers in DE and BC.
;  Product in DEHL.
;  DE x BC = DEHL
;  No overflow possible.
;
Mul16x16:
     xor a          ;Clear Cy flag and A
     ld h, a        ;Clear...
     ld l, a        ;...product
     ld a, 16       ;Iteration count
loop:
     ;Shift DE, and add Cy from previous HL shift
     ex de, hl
     adc hl, hl
     ex de, hl
     jp nc, mul     ;if D7 was 1,
     add hl, bc     ;  add BC
     jp nc, mul     ;    if Cy == 1,
     inc de         ;        put 1 into E0
mul:
     dec a          ;Decrement iteration counter
     ret z          ;If done, return
     add hl, hl     ;Shift HL left
     jp loop
```

Figure 7.20 *Source code of Mul16x16.asm*

7.3.2 Parameter passing

Usually, a subroutine is written to make use of some data that is **passed** to it. The data that is passed to a subroutine is called its **parameters**. Thus, X5Sub.asm has one parameter passed to it, the number to be multiplied by five. This parameter is passed to the subroutine via register A and the result is also passed back to the caller via register A. Program Mul16by16.asm, Figure 7.20, includes a subroutine that multiplies two 16-bit numbers. The two parameters, the multiplicand and the multiplier, are passed in register

```
;Div32by16.asm
;Test the Div_32by16 subroutine.
;0x3FFF 0001/0x7FFF = 0x7FFF
     ld hl, 0x3fff
     ld de, 0x0001
     ld bc, 0;x7fff
     call Div_32by16
     halt          ;stop



;Subroutine to divide the 32-bit signed,
; but positive,integer in HLDE by the
; 16-bit signed, but positive, integer
; in BC.
; Put the 16-bit quotient in DE,
;   remainder in HL
; HLDE/BC = DE, rem HL
; Quotient,DE, may overflow without warning!
;
Div_32by16:
     ld a, 16     ;iteration counter
loop:
     ;Shift HLDE left
     add hl, hl  ;shift HL left
     ex de, hl   ;shift..
     add hl,hl   ;..DE...
     ex de, hl   ;...left
     jr nc, jump1;if DE shift procuces a carry,
     inc hl      ;   pass it into HL
jump1:
     ;Subtract divisor,BC, from
     ; upper 16 bits of dividend, HL.
     or a           ;Carry=0, sbc follows
     sbc hl, bc    ;Subtract divisor
     inc de        ;1 into quotient, E0=1
     jr nc, jump2;if HL was > BC, jump
     add hl, bc  ;    else restore divisor
     res 0, e    ;          0 into quotient, E0=0
jump2:
     dec a          ;Examined all 16 bits?
     jr nz, loop ;  if not, next iteration
     ret         ;  else, done
```

Figure 7.21 *Source code of Div32by16.asm*

pairs DE and BC, and the 32-bit product is returned in registers DEHL. (The algorithm for this general-purpose multiplication is similar to the manual long multiplication method.) The two parameters for the 32-bit by 16-bit division, `Div32by16.asm`, Figure 7.21, are passed in registers HLDE and BC, while the quotient is returned in register pair DE and the remainder in HL. (The algorithm for this general-purpose division is similar to the manual long division method.)

The multiplication and division subroutines pass parameters via the microprocessor registers. This is simple but is limited by the number of registers in the microprocessor. Clearly, a data structure of many bytes cannot be passed directly using the microprocessor registers; instead, a pointer to the data structure is passed. An example of passing a pointer to the data is given in program `CntChar.asm`, Figure 7.22. This program is based on program `String1.asm`, which counts the occurrence of the character 'e' in a string. It has been made more general by providing that the character to be counted is a parameter, passed in register B, as well as the pointer to the string, passed in register pair HL. The result is returned in register C.

```
;CntChar.asm
;Subroutine to count the number of occurrences of a
; given character in a null-terminated string.
;Calling sequence: ld b, character    character to count
;                    ld hl, string      pointer to string
;                    call .ch_count
;Returns with the count in register C
;
ch_count:
        push    af          ;Save A and F.
        ld   c, 0           ;Counter
;
;While( letter != 00 )
cloop:
        ld   a, (hl)        ;Get a letter
        inc hl              ;Bump pointer
        ;If( letter == NUL ) return
        and a               ;For cpu flags
        ret z               ;If end of string, return
        ;
        ;If( letter == required character ) C = C + 1
        cp   b
        jp nz,notch         ;If not the character, jump
        ;
        inc c               ;Count in register C
notch:
        jp cloop
        pop af              ;Restore A and F.
        ret
```

Figure 7.22 *Source code of CntChar.asm*

7.4 Problems

1   Program `If_else1.asm` allows register B to be incremented from 255 to 0 and to be decremented from 0 to 255. This results in the chart recorder display swinging between maximum and minimum. Modify the program so that these swings do not occur. Do this by providing that when register B contains 255 it can only be decremented and when it contains 0 it can only be incremented.

2   Devise and test a program that generates a triangular waveform on the chart recorder. (The waveform starts at 0, ramps linearly up to 50, then ramps linearly down to 0, and repeats forever.)

3   Devise and test a program that generates a square waveform on the chart recorder. (The waveform switches between 0 and 50, staying at each level for ten steps. This is repeated forever.)

4   Devise and test a program that generates a sawtooth waveform on the chart recorder. (The waveform ramps linearly from 0 to 50, then jumps back to 0. This is repeated forever.)

5   Devise and test a program that generates a sine waveform on the chart recorder. (The middle of the waveform has a value of 100, and it swings 100 either side of this middle value. This is repeated forever. Use the data table in file `SineTab.asm`, which contains a list of values of the sinusoidal function.)

6   Do Problem 5 but use only the first half of the table of sine values. This will require the computation of the output values.

7   Do Problem 5 but use only the first quarter of the table of values.

8   Patterns of segments of a seven-segment display are shown in Figure P7.1. Assuming that register A contains an unsigned integer, devise and test a program that shows pattern (a) if register A contains an odd number, pattern (b) if an even number (not zero), and pattern (c) if zero.

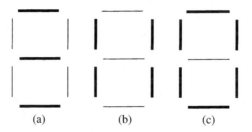

Figure P7.1   (a)   (b)   (c)

9   Patterns of segments of a seven-segment display are shown in Figure P7.1. Assuming that register A contains a signed integer, devise and test a program that shows pattern (a) if register A contains a negative number, pattern (b) if a positive number (not zero), and pattern (c) if zero.

10 Patterns of segments of a seven-segment display are shown in Figure P7.2. Assuming that register A contains a signed integer, devise and test a program that shows:

pattern (a) if the number is negative and even,
pattern (b) if the number is negative and odd,
pattern (c) if the number is positive and even,
pattern (d) if the number is positive and odd,
pattern (e) if the number is zero.

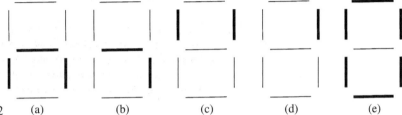

Figure P7.2   (a)   (b)   (c)   (d)   (e)

11 What useful function is performed by program `Stack.asm`?

12 Devise and test a subroutine that will display the contents of register A as two hexadecimal digits on the seven-segment displays.

13 Devise and test a subroutine that will display the contents of register A as two decimal digits on the two seven-segment displays. Register A normally contains a number from decimal 0 to 99. If register A erroneously contains a number outside this range, your routine should display '– –'.

14 Devise and test a subroutine that will display the contents of register A as three decimal digits on the LCD. Register A contains an unsigned integer.

15 Devise and test a subroutine that will display the contents of register A as a sign and three decimal digits on the LCD. Register A contains a signed integer.

16 Devise and test a program that steps the stepper motor continuously and displays the current position of the linear slider on the seven-segment displays as a decimal number in the range 0 to 79. You should use the subroutine from Problem 13.

17 Devise and test a subroutine that steps the stepper motor clockwise until the linear slider is at the position indicated by the value contained in register A when the subroutine is called.

18   Devise and test a subroutine that steps the stepper motor clockwise or counter-clockwise until the linear slider is at the position indicated by the value contained in register A when the subroutine is called. The direction of the stepper motor should be that which requires the smaller number of steps to reach the desired position.

19   Devise a subroutine that will concatenate two null-terminated strings.

20   Rewrite `Switch1.asm` using two simple tables, one of which contains the ASCII codes and the other contains the start addresses.

21   A program checks to see if the average of five temperatures is greater or less than 40. Programmer A sums the five temperatures, divides by 5 to get the average, and compares the average with 40. Programmer B sums the five temperatures, and compares the sum with 200. Comment on the two program designs.

8 Simple computer circuits

In this chapter we look at how a small computer may be constructed using the G80 microprocessor. We begin with the design of the simplest computer, COMP1, which comprises just a G80 microprocessor and a single read-only memory (ROM) chip that stores the program code. This computer is then developed into COMP2, which is the same as COMP1 but with the addition of a single RAM chip. Computer COMP3 has a single ROM chip and two RAM chips. The sequence of events for both memory read and memory write operations are discussed.

8.1 G80 external connections

Let us assume that the G80 is to be fabricated on a piece of silicon semi conductor. What signals should we bring into the outside world, that is, what is the **pin-out** to be? This is mostly straightforward: clearly the contents of the memory address register, MAR, and the G80 data bus, must be brought out to pins on the chip to allow communication with the external memory chips. Also, the control signals that indicate to the memory whether it is to read or write data must be made available. In our design these are called RD and WR[1]. Thus when RD is asserted, the memory will output data stored within it, while when WR is asserted, the memory will write the data on its data pins into the location indicated by the address on its address pins. Remember that by 'asserted' we mean 'set to the voltage level that makes the signal active'.

We also bring out a signal, MREQ, that indicates that the address bus is carrying a new memory address. We will be able to use this to alert the memory chips that a request for their use is being made. In addition, when the G80 is powered-up, or **reset**, it must go its reset state, which sets the Program Counter to 0000 in order to start executing program code from memory location 0000. The RESET input signal performs this function. We shall make use of these signals in the circuit diagrams of the computers that are designed in the following sections.

8.2 Read-only memory device – ROM

A typical read-only memory chip contains 16K locations, each of 1 byte; it is known as a 16 KB or 16K8 ROM. Such a device has the product number 27128, where the 128 indicates the number of bits (16 KByte * 8 = 128 Kbits) and the prefacing digits, 27, were used by the original manufacturer to iden tify this type of memory. These devices, or **chips**, use a special transistor on which to store a single bit. The individual bits in the ROM are set to 0 or 1 before it is used in a computer; the ROM retains this information even when

---

[1] Some microprocessors combine these signals into one control signal, which, when asserted, indicates Read, and otherwise indicates Write.

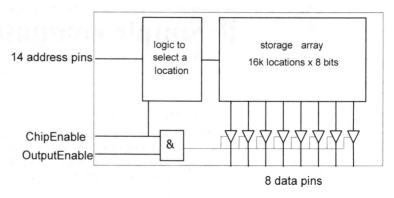

Figure 8.1 *Pins on a 16K8 ROM chip*

it has no power supplied to it; it is said to be a form of **non-volatile** storage. The data can be erased from the memory by exposing it to ultraviolet light; the devices are therefore known as ultraviolet erasable, programmable ROM, UV-EPROM, or simply EPROM. EPROMs are often used to store the code for the program that is executed when the computer is reset or powered up. (It is, of course, essential that a computer has some instructions in its memory space when it is first powered up, otherwise it has no instructions about what to do next.)

A 16K8 ROM has $16 \times 2^{10} = 2^{14}$ locations and thus has 14 address pins on the chip. In addition, there are eight data pins and other pins that carry control signals to the chip. The chip is shown in Figure 8.1.

Two pins for control signals are shown, OutputEnable and ChipEnable. The OutputEnable signal enables the three state buffers that connect the 8-bit output of the storage array to the data pins. These buffers allow the data pins to be connected directly to the computer data bus that may be shared by other chips in the computer. ChipEnable is a signal which effectively turns the chip on or off. Unless ChipEnable is asserted, the ROM chip does nothing and, because the three-state buffers are disabled, it is effectively disconnected from the computer circuit. In order to read a particular location, that is, connect a particular location to the data pins:

> the address pins must carry the address of the location, AND
> the chip must be enabled by asserting ChipEnable, AND
> the output buffers must be enabled by asserting OutputEnable.

Control signals, but not address and data signals, are usually asserted by a logic low level on the pin that carries the signal. Manufacturers use various conventions to indicate this: they are illustrated in Figure 8.2.

The signal names shown are often abbreviated to CE and OE, and ChipEnable is often called ChipSelect, CS. The circuit designer must become familiar with all the conventions, particularly so since it is not uncommon for the conventions to be mixed on the same diagram!

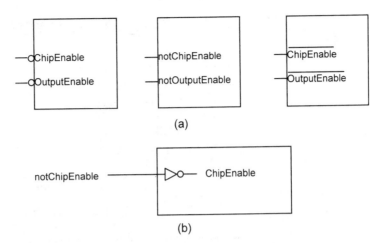

Figure 8.2 (a) *Equivalent conventions for indicating active low signals;* (b) *interpretation*

8.3 COMP1 computer – G80 with ROM only

The COMP1 computer comprises a G80 microprocessor and a 16K8 ROM chip; its circuit is shown in Figure 8.3. Since the RESET signal must be asserted when power is first applied to the circuit we generate this signal cheaply using a capacitor and resistor, as shown. To assert the RESET signal the pin must be driven to zero volts as indicated by the bubble on the RESET input of the G80. The capacitor initially has zero volts across it, so asserting RESET; it eventually charges to 5 V so de-asserting RESET. This cheap circuit will not work well if the power supply to COMP1 is turned off then on again before the capacitor has had time to fully discharge back to 0 V. Special chips, called microprocessor supervisors, are widely used to provide a more reliable way of generating the RESET signal. They also include a variety of other useful functions. We would normally use one of these unless the cost of manufacture is the dominant design criterion.

The box labelled 'clock' represents a circuit that generates a square wave at a fixed frequency. All the signals generated by the G80 are related to cycles of this clock waveform, as we see next in the sequence of signals that are generated when the G80 reads a memory location.

8.3.1 G80 read cycle

The timing of the G80 signals when it is reading a memory location, that is, performing a **memory read cycle**, is shown in Figure 8.4. When the G80 begins the memory read cycle, it connects the contents of its Memory Address Register, MAR, to the address bus at the beginning of the first clock cycle, ①. The system clock signal then causes it to assert MREQ, ②, to indicate that the address bus now carries a valid memory address. Signal MREQ is connected to the ChipEnable, CE, on the ROM chip, so that the ROM chip is enabled. The circuit within the ROM selects the location whose address is on its address pins. Almost at the same time, ③, as asserting MREQ, the G80

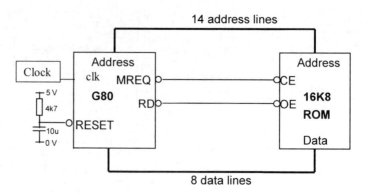

Figure 8.3 *Circuit of the COMP1 computer*

asserts RD. We connect this to the OutputEnable, OE, of the ROM, so that
the ROM output buffers are enabled. When the logic circuits within the ROM
have had time to work, the data stored in the addressed ROM location eventually appears on the data pins of the ROM, ④, and therefore on the data
pins of the G80. The G80 allows the time of about two clock cycles for the
ROM to output data. During the third clock cycle after starting to read the
memory, ⑤, the G80 reads this data into an internal register at the same time
as de-asserting both MREQ and RD. The memory read cycle ends at ⑥.

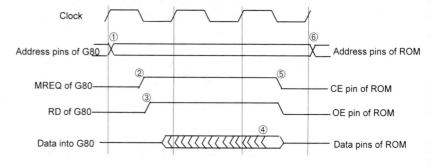

Figure 8.4 *Memory read cycle*

Summarizing the timing diagram:

At time 1:

G80 places the address of the location to be read onto the address bus
and so to the address pins of the ROM.

At time 2:

G80 asserts its MREQ signal and so enables the ROM.

At time 3:

G80 asserts its RD signal and so enables the outputs of the ROM. The circuit within the ROM responds to these signals and ...

At time 4:

ROM places the 8 bits of data stored at the location being read onto its eight data pins and the data bus.

At time 5:

G80 reads the data on the data bus into one of its registers and de-asserts both MREQ and RD.

At time 6:

G80 begins the next cycle.

In the COMP1 circuit, the ROM control signals are given by:

$$CE_{ROM} = MREQ$$
$$OE_{ROM} = RD$$

We must derive these logic equations in order to draw the circuit. The equations indicate that the ROM is enabled during the time that the G80 indicates that the address bus carries a valid memory address; this is when the G80 is asserting its MREQ output signal. The output buffers of the ROM connect

Address

	Hexadecimal	Binary
	0000	0000 0000 0000 0000
ROM 16K		
	3FFF	0011 1111 1111 1111
	4000	0100 0000 0000 0000
Not Used 48K		
	FFFF	1111 1111 1111 1111

Figure 8.5 *Memory map of the COMP1 computer*

the data from the ROM to its data pins. These are enabled by OE during the time that the G80 is performing a memory read operation, that is, when the G80 is asserting its RD signal.

The memory available to the programmer is conveniently given by a **memory map**, which shows the usage of the possible 64K addresses in the G80 memory space, Figure 8.5. When the G80 is reset, its Program Counter is reset to 0000. It is therefore a normal requirement that there be some program code stored at memory location 0000. The map shows the 16K ROM occupying memory space 0000 to 3FFF, with the remaining memory space unused.

8.4 RAM device

Few computations can be done without having memory locations that can be written to as well as read from. A memory device that can be read and written is called a read/write device. Semiconductor read/write devices are called, for historical reasons, **random access memory**, RAM. This name is a little misleading since the ROM is also a random access device! Strictly, the term 'random access' means that the time to access a location is the same whatever the address of the location in the memory device. Thus, a magnetic disk memory is not a random access device since the time taken to access a location on the disk depends on where the location is situated on the disk.

RAM chips are available in many different forms. In some, the number of bits stored at each location is 8 while in others it is just 1; some (static RAM or SRAM) store each bit in a flip-flop, while others (dynamic RAM or DRAM) store a bit as a charge on a capacitor. Small computers typically use 8-bit wide SRAM chips that have similar pins to the ROM but with the addition of a pin for a signal that indicates whether the RAM is to be written or read. This signal is usually called WriteEnable, WE, it being understood that if WE is not asserted then the chip is in its read mode. Thus, in order to write to a particular memory location in a RAM device:

> the address pins on the RAM must carry the address of the location, AND
> the data pins on the RAM must carry the data to be written, AND
> the RAM chip must be enabled by asserting its ChipEnable, CE, input signal, AND
> the RAM chip must be set to its write mode by asserting its WE input signal.

To read a location in the RAM device, similar conditions apply, except that WE is not asserted and the RAM data pins are not driven with data. At the end of the read operation, the RAM data pins will carry the data read from the RAM.

We will now extend COMP1 by adding some RAM.

8.5 COMP2 computer – G80 with ROM and RAM

The COMP2 computer is the same as COMP1 with the addition of a single 16 KB RAM chip. The first step in its design is to decide where in the memory space we wish the RAM to reside; we choose to have the memory map shown in Figure 8.6.

Address

	Hexadecimal	Binary
	0000	0000 0000 0000 0000
ROM 16K		
	3FFF	0011 1111 1111 1111
	4000	0100 0000 0000 0000
ROM 16K		
	7FFF	0111 1111 1111 1111
	8000	1000 0000 0000 0000
Not Used 32K		
	FFFF	1111 1111 1111 1111

Figure 8.6 *Memory map of the COMP2 computer*

When the G80 performs a memory read cycle with the address bus carrying an address in the range 4000 to 7FFF, the RAM chip must be enabled. If the address is in the range 0000 to 3FFF, the ROM chip must be enabled. (Note that since only half of the 64 KB in the G80 memory space is used, only 15 address bits are used, that is, address line A15 is not used.) From an examination of the memory map, Figure 8.6, we see that address bit A14 distinguishes between the two memory chips. That is, the address of all the locations within the ROM have address bit A14 $= = 0$, those within the RAM have A14 $= = 1$. That is:

$$\mathrm{CE_{ROM}} = (\text{Address Bus} = = 00xx\ xxxx\ xxxx\ xxxx).\mathrm{MREQ}$$
$$\mathrm{CE_{RAM}} = (\text{Address Bus} = = 01xx\ xxxx\ xxxx\ xxxx).\mathrm{MREQ}$$

Since A15 is not used, we can write:

$$CE_{ROM} = /A14.MREQ.$$
$$CE_{RAM} = A14.MREQ.$$

This is a convenient way of saying that the ROM chip is enabled when (A14 = = 0) AND (MREQ is asserted). Also, the RAM chip is enabled when (A14 = = 1) AND (MREQ is asserted).

We can check this by considering what happens when MREQ is asserted with the address bus carrying the 16-bit address 0000 0000 0000 0011. Since A14 = = 0, the ROM chip is enabled. Address bits A13 to A0, which are connected to the address pins of the ROM chip, select location 00 0000 0000 0011 within the ROM. Similarly, when the address bus carries 0100 0000 0000 0011, the RAM chip is enabled because A14 = = 1. Address

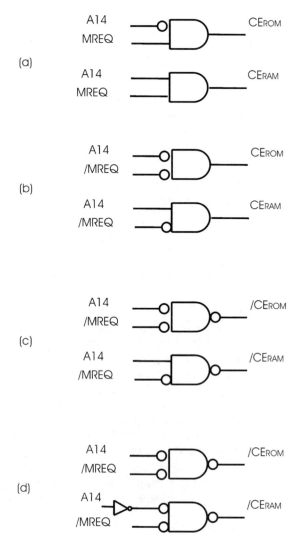

Figure 8.7 *Selecting one of the two memory chips in the COMP2 computer*

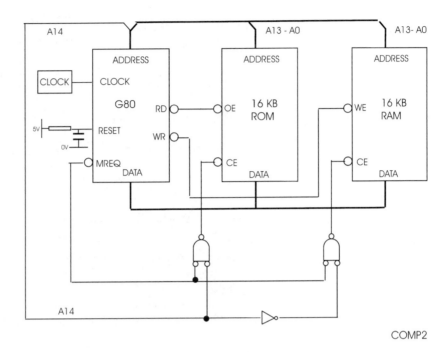

Figure 8.8 *Circuit diagram of the COMP2 computer*

bits A13 to A0, which are also connected to the address pins of the RAM chip, select location 00 0000 0000 0011 within the RAM chip.

The logic equations give the logic diagram shown in Figure 8.7a. But /MREQ is generated by the G80 so the diagram is written as in Figure 8.7b. Further, the chip enable signals are asserted when low, leading to the diagram Figure 8.7c. Finally, Figure 8.7d shows a diagram of the **chip-select logic** using standard OR gates. Note that the use of this symbol for the OR gates makes it easy to understand the logic function that the circuit performs.

The OE_{ROM} connection remains as on the COMP1 computer, that is, $OE_{ROM} = RD$. However, this signal will have no effect unless the ROM chip is selected. The WE input to the RAM must be asserted when the G80 is writing data; this is indicated by asserting WR. Thus, we write: WE = WR. The circuit of the COMP2 computer is shown in Figure 8.8.

8.5.1 G80 write cycle

The G80 timing for the write cycle is given in Figure 8.9. This diagram is drawn using a different convention to the timing diagram of the read cycle: the control signals are shown as they would be seen on an oscilloscope, that is, by voltage levels. This is the more usual way that timing diagrams are drawn in the technical literature. A signal that is **logically** asserted may actually be an **electrically** low, 0 V, signal or an **electrically** high, 5 V, signal. The reader must remember that MREQ, for example, is asserted when the waveform for /MREQ is at zero volts.

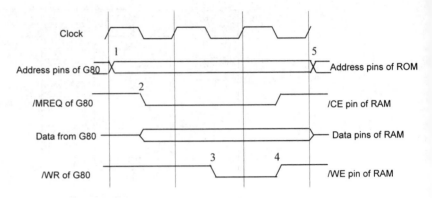

Figure 8.9 *Memory write cycle*

The timing diagram for the memory write cycle is interpreted as follows.

At time 1:
> G80 places the address of the location to be written (between 4000 and 7FFF) onto the address bus and so to the address pins of the RAM.

At time 2:
> G80 asserts its MREQ signal and so enables the RAM via the gate having inputs /A14 and /MREQ.
> G80 places the data to be written on the data bus and thus to the data pins of the RAM.

At time 3:
> G80 asserts its WR signal and so selects the write mode of the RAM. The circuit within the RAM responds to these signals.

Between times 3 and 4:

> RAM writes the 8 bits of data on the data bus into the addressed location.

At time 4:
> G80 de-asserts both MREQ and WR.

At time 5:
> G80 begins the next cycle.

8.6 COMP3 computer

This computer is to have 32 KB of ROM and 32 KB of RAM. The ROM is a single 32 KB chip while the RAM is two 16 KB chips. We want the memory map shown in Figure 8.10.

Three chip enable signals must be produced: CE_{ROM}, CE_{RAM0}, and CE_{RAM1}. From the memory map it is seen that the addresses of all locations within ROM are uniquely identified by address line A15 = = 0. That is,

Address

Hexadecimal   Binary

	0000	0000 0000 0000 0000
ROM		
32K		
	7FFF	0111 1111 1111 1111
	8000	1000 0000 0000 0000
RAM0		
16K		
	BFFF	1011 1111 1111 1111
	C000	1100 0000 0000 0000
RAM1		
16K		
	FFFF	1111 1111 1111 1111

Figure 8.10 *Memory map of the COMP3 computer*

$$CE_{ROM} = (\text{Address Bus} == 0xxx\ xxxx\ xxxx\ xxxx).\ MREQ$$

so that we can write

$$CE_{ROM} = /A15\ .\ MREQ$$

For locations within RAM0, $<A15\ A14> == <1\ 0>$, and for locations within RAM1, $<A15\ A14> = <1\ 1>$. That is:

$$CE_{RAM0} = (\text{Address Bus} == 10xx\ xxxx\ xxxx\ xxxx).\ MREQ$$
$$CE_{RAM1} = (\text{Address Bus} == 11xx\ xxxx\ xxxx\ xxxx).\ MREQ$$

so that we can write:

$$CE_{RAM0} = A15\ .\ /A14\ .\ MREQ$$
$$CE_{RAM1} = A15\ .\ A14\ .\ MREQ$$

The logic diagram and circuit diagram for this chip select logic is shown in Figure 8.11. As before, we write the circuit literally then add bubbles to

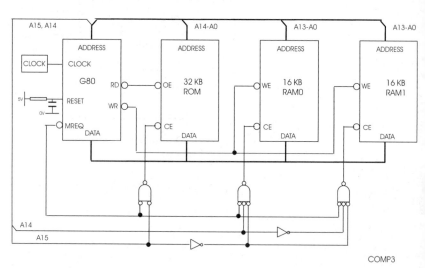

Figure 8.11 *Chip select logic for the COMP3 computer:* (a) *logic diagram;* (b) *logic using standard logic gates and producing active low outputs*

convert to standard gates with the required assertion levels. The complete circuit diagram of the COMP3 computer is shown in Figure 8.12.

The chip select logic circuits in our designs have been constructed from standard logic gates. In practice, it is more likely that we would put most of the small logic circuits in a computer into a programmable logic chip, a device that may be configured (or 'programmed') to generate the required logic function.

Figure 8.12 *Circuit of the COMP3 computer*

8.7 Microprocessor control signals

The G80 control signals used in the circuits of this chapter are found in one form or another on all microprocessors. The G80 signal, MREQ, which indicates that a memory address has been placed on the Address Bus, is sometimes called **valid memory address**, VMA. The G80 has 24 pins that carry the 16 address lines and the eight data lines, but this is not essential. Some microprocessors reduce the number of pins on the chip by having only 16 pins for both address and data signals. Eight pins carry both the data and the lower 8 bits of the address, though at different times; the particular use of the pins is indicated by a signal on an extra pin, having a name such as Address Latch Enable.

8.8 Problems   Design chip-select logic for the computers having the memory maps shown. All chip select signals are asserted by a low level signal and your logic should use the G80 control signals directly, for example your logic must use the G80 signal /MREQ rather than MREQ. The shaded areas in the memory maps are not used.

1   The computer has the memory map shown in Figure P8.1(a).

2   The computer has the memory map shown in Figure P8.1(b).

3   The computer has the memory map shown in Figure P8.1(c).

Figure P8.1

ROM0 8K	ROM 32K	ROM 8K	0000 1FFF
ROM1 8K		RAM0 16K	2000 3FFF
			4000 5FFF
Not used		RAM1 16K	6000 7FFF
	Not used		8000 9FFF
		Not used	A000 BFFF
		Not used	C000 DFFF
	RAM 8K		E000 FFFF
(a)	(b)	(c)	

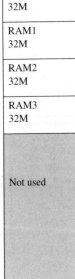

Figure P8.6

RAM0 32M

RAM1 32M

RAM2 32M

RAM3 32M

Not used

4   A memory chip is 4 bits wide, that is, each location stores 4 bits. Show how two of these devices can be connected so that they appear to the G80 as a single 8-bit wide memory device.

5   A memory chip is 1 bit wide, that is, each location stores 1 bit. Show how eight of these devices can be connected so that they appear to the G80 as a single 8-bit wide memory device.

6   A large computer has an address bus that is 32 bits wide.

How many bytes of memory can it address?

Devise chip-select logic for such a computer that has the following memory map. Shown in Figure p8.6.

9 Input and output ports

To be useful a computer must be able to read data from the outside world and write data to the outside world. In personal computers, input and output are usually from a keyboard and to a visual display unit or sound generator. Computers which are embedded into products such as photocopiers and industrial process controllers read data from devices such as pressure and temperature sensors and write data to devices such as flow control valves, heaters, and motors. Whatever the computer, data enters the computer via an **input port** and data leaves the computer via an **output port**. In this chapter we see how simple input and output ports are constructed and how they are accessed within a program. The design of a **programmable port** that may be either an input or an output is developed from the circuits of simple ports. The function and operation of a UART is discussed. Many different devices may be connected to the G80 via its ports; the specifications of these devices are given in Appendix C.

9.1 Simple output port

We make an 8-bit output port from eight flip-flops, the inputs of which are connected to the data bus and the outputs connect to the outside world, Figure 9.1. It is only necessary to generate a rising edge on *OutSelect* a short time after the microprocessor has placed the data to be output on the data bus. The data will then be latched into the flip-flops and remain there until new data is written to the port.

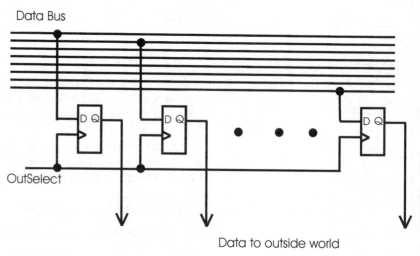

Figure 9.1 *Output port*

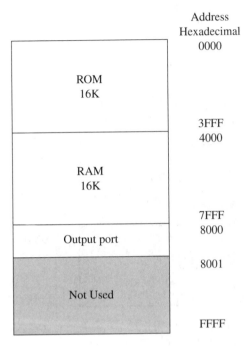

Address
Hexadecimal
0000

ROM
16K

3FFF
4000

RAM
16K

7FFF
8000

Output port

8001

Not Used

FFFF

Figure 9.2 *Memory map of COMP2 computer with an output port at 8000*

The port may be regarded as a single memory location chip so that OutSelect may be generated in the same way as the ChipEnables for the memory chips. The port thus occupies an address in the memory space; it is said to be **memory mapped**. If the port were to be added to the COMP2 computer of Chapter 8 a suitable address would be 8000 giving the memory map shown in Figure 9.2. Data will be written to the port using the same instructions as writing to memory, for example `ld (0x8000), a`.

The port is to be enabled when the Address Bus carries 8000 and the G80 is performing a memory write operation, that is:

OutSelect = (AddressBus = = 8000) . MREQ . WR

= (AddressBus = = 1000 0000 0000 0000). MREQ . WR

= A15. /A14 . /A13 . /A12 ... /A1 . /A0 . MREQ . WR

This address decoding, to select a single location, requires all 16 of the address lines. An alternative memory map that results in simpler selection logic is shown in Figure 9.3.

In this map, the single port is mapped not to one memory location but to 32K locations. This is quite acceptable since this memory space is otherwise unused. It means that a write to any memory location with address in the range 8000 to FFFF will write to the port. The port select logic is now greatly simplified to:

Address

Hexadecimal | Binary

ROM 16K	0000 0000 0000 0000 0000
	3FFF 0011 1111 1111 1111
RAM 16K	4000 0100 0000 0000 0000
	7FFF 0111 1111 1111 1111
Output Port	8000 1000 0000 0000 0000
	FFFF 1111 1111 1111 1111

Figure 9.3 *Memory map of the COMP2 computer with a single output port at 8000 to FFFF*

$$\text{OutSelect} = (\text{AddressBus} == 1xxx\ xxxx\ xxxx\ xxxx) \cdot \text{MREQ} \cdot \text{WR}$$
$$= \text{A15} \cdot \text{MREQ} \cdot \text{WR}$$

since all addresses in the range 8000 to FFFF have A15 == 1.

9.2 Port address space

Using the memory address space for the port limits the use of that space for memory. This is particularly inconvenient where all the available memory address space is likely to be used by memory devices. To overcome this inconvenience, we provide the G80 with an alternative method of addressing ports, a method used in many other microprocessors. Quite simply, we let the G80 assert a new signal, IORQ, when it has placed a port address on the address bus, and we add to the G80 instruction set an instruction out (port_address),a which transfers data from register A to the port having port address *port_address*.

Note that, just as the MREQ signal indicates that the address bus is carrying a memory address, the IORQ signal indicates that the address bus is carrying a port address. In concept, we now have two address spaces, one for memory and another for ports. This allows ports to be **I/O-mapped** rather than memory-mapped.

We let port addresses be just 8 bits since this allows 256 input ports and 256 output ports – more than enough. It also allows us to specify the address in the out (N),a instruction in just 1 byte, instead of the 2 bytes that would have to be provided if we used a 16-bit port address.

Assume there are three output ports in the computer, at port addresses 00, 01, and 02. The selection logic is:

$$OutSelect0 = (AddressBus == 00).\ IORQ\ .\ WR$$
$$= (AddressBus == 0000\ 0000).\ IORQ\ .\ WR$$
$$= /A7\ ./A6\ ./A5\ ./A4\ ./A3\ ./A2\ ./A1\ ./A0\ .\ IORQ\ .\ WR$$
$$OutSelect1 = (AddressBus == 01).\ IORQ\ .\ WR$$
$$= (AddressBus == 0000\ 0001)\ .\ IORQ\ .\ WR$$
$$= /A7\ ./A6\ ./A5\ ./A4\ ./A3\ ./A2\ ./A1\ .\ A0\ .\ IORQ\ .\ WR$$
$$OutSelect2 = (AddressBus == 02).\ IORQ\ .\ WR$$
$$= (AddressBus == 0000\ 0010)\ .\ IORQ\ .\ WR$$
$$= /A7\ ./A6\ ./A5\ ./A4\ ./A3\ ./A2\ .\ A1\ ./A0\ .\ IORQ\ .\ WR$$

If these ports are the only output ports in the computer, only two address lines, A1 and A0, are actually needed to distinguish between them, so giving the simpler selection logic:

$$OutSelect0 = /A1\ ./A0\ .\ IORQ\ .\ WR$$
$$OutSelect1 = /A1\ .\ A0\ .\ IORQ\ .\ WR$$
$$OutSelect2 = A1\ ./A0\ .\ IORQ\ .\ WR$$

Just as the memory map shows the usage of the memory space, the port address map shows the usage of the I/O space; the map for the current example is shown in Figure 9.4.

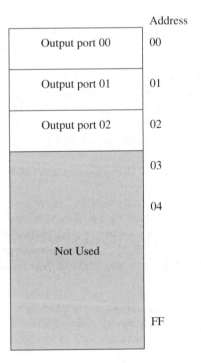

Figure 9.4 *Port map for computer having three output ports*

9.3 A simple input port

An 8-bit input port is simply eight three-state buffers, the outputs of which are connected to the data bus and the inputs connect to the outside world, Figure 9.5. It is only necessary to assert *InSelect*[1] during the time that the microprocessor indicates that it is about to read the Data Bus. The data will then be read into the microprocessor.

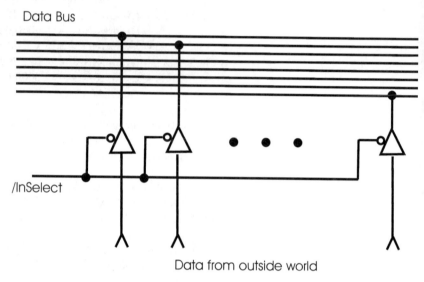

Figure 9.5 *Input port*

Like an output port, we may use the MREQ signal in the selection logic for an input port so that it will be selected as though it were a memory location. However, we choose to place all the G80 ports in the port address space. To accommodate this, we add an instruction to the G80 instruction set: `in a, (port_address)`. This transfers data from the port having address *port_address* to the G80 register A. During the execution of this instruction, the G80 asserts IORQ and RD while the Address Bus carries the port address.

Hence, the *InSelect* signal may be generated by:

$$\text{InSelect} = (\text{AddressBus} == \text{port address}) \cdot \text{IORQ} \cdot \text{RD}$$

The G80 actually reads the Data Bus when the RD signal is finally de-asserted. This allows the three state buffers to have time to place their data on the bus.

Note that it is possible, indeed, common practice, to have an output port and an input port share the same port address since an output port is selected using the WR signal and an input port is selected using the RD signal.

9.4 Programmable ports*

When a computer circuit is designed for a specific application, the dedicated ports described in the previous sections can be used. However, consider a small computer that is intended to be sold for use in a variety of applications.

---

[1] To assert InSelect, we must make InSelect high, that is, /InSelect must be low.

How many input and output ports should the designer provide? We can give the designers of these computers some flexibility by providing ports that may be configured by the programmer to be either input or output ports. That is, the port pins may be either input or output at the choice of the user. These devices are variously called PPI, parallel port interface, PIA, parallel interface adapter, or, more generally, **PIO**, programmable/parallel input output devices.

We make a programmable port by combining the logic of an input port with that of an output port. In addition, we use a second output port that is not connected to the outside world, but instead is used to configure the circuit to the direction required by the user. The logic for 1 bit of a programmable port is shown in Figure 9.6. This logic is repeated for all 8 bits of an 8-bit port. The I/O connection may be either an input or an output, as determined by the programmer. The three-state buffer, TB1, is the 1-bit input port that allows the microprocessor to read the signal on I/O. Flip-flop DataFF is the 1-bit output port that allows the microprocessor to write a signal to I/O. The output port is connected to I/O via three-state buffer TB2. The purpose of TB2 is to allow the output of DataFF to be disconnected from I/O when the port is to be an input. In this situation, an external signal will be driving I/O, so we cannot allow that signal and the output of DataFF to both drive the I/O wire. This would create a **data contention**.

If the programmer wishes the I/O connection to be an output, TB2 must be enabled. Alternatively, if the programmer wishes the I/O connection to be an output, TB2 must be disabled to avoid the possible data contention. The fact that I/O is also connected to the input port is not a problem.

The enable signal for the three-state buffer TB2 comes from the second output port, flip-flop ControlFF. This port, the control port, determines the data direction of connection I/O. The control port is used to configure the circuit rather than to send data to the outside world. The programmer must

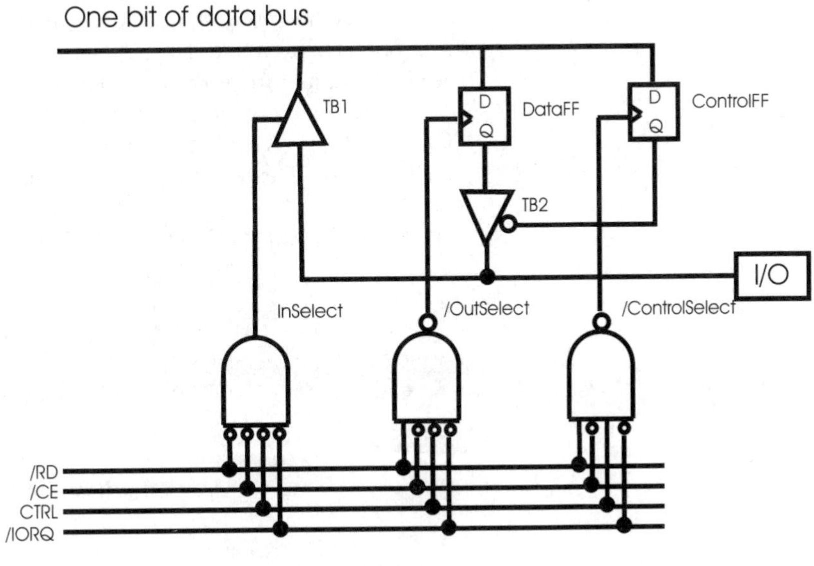

Figure 9.6 *One bit of a programmable port*

write to the control port in order to configure the port as an input or an output before attempting to use the port. This is called **initializing** the port.

Although the circuit contains three physical ports, it appears to the programmer as two ports. One port is the control port (an output port), and the other port is the data port (either input or output and having the same port address). The port selection logic is designed so that when CTRL is asserted, the control port is addressed, otherwise the data port is addressed. Also, the device does nothing unless the ChipEnable, CE, and the IORQ signals are asserted. We have chosen the RD signal from the microprocessor to indicate whether a read or write is to be performed. Thus, when RD is asserted, the data port will be read, otherwise, one of the two output ports will be written.

The select logic for a write to the control port is therefore:

ControlSelect = CTRL . /RD . IORQ . CE

The select logic for a write to the output data port is:

OutSelect = /CTRL . /RD . IORQ . CE

The select logic for a read from the input port is:

InSelect = /CTRL . RD . IORQ . CE

The OutSelect and the ControlSelect signals are inverted before being connected to the flip-flops. This is because we want the selected flip-flop to be triggered by the rising edge produced when the select signal changes from low to high at the end of the G80 write cycle.

To connect one of these programmable ports to the G80, we must assign two port addresses to the device, one for the control port and one for the data port. For example, let the control port be at 0x80 and the data port at 0x81. Assuming there are no other ports in the port address space 0x80 to 0xFF, the programmable port device may be selected by address line A7. That is, CE = A7. The control port is selected by A0 = = 0, giving CTRL = /A0. The select signals are thus:

ControlSelect = CTRL . /RD . IORQ . CE

= /A0 . /RD . IORQ . A7

= A7 . /A0 . /RD . IORQ   i.e. write to port 0x80

OutSelect   = /CTRL . /RD . IORQ . CE

= A0 . /RD . IORQ . A7

= A7 . A0 . /RD . IORQ   i.e. write to port 0x81

$$\text{InSelect} \quad = /CTRL \cdot RD \cdot IORQ \cdot CE$$
$$= A0 \cdot RD \cdot IORQ \cdot A7$$
$$= A7 \cdot A0 \cdot RD \cdot IORQ \qquad \text{i.e. read from port } 0x81$$

9.5 Serial data transmission – UART*

Although the G80 computer does not have provision for serial data transmission, this section discusses the technique because of its popularity for sending data between two computing devices.

Parallel transmission of data between two points requires a wire for each bit of data together with a reference signal or ground. Where the two points are more than a few metres apart, the cabling becomes costly. The solution is to send the data in serial, that is, one bit after another so that each bit of data is separated from another by a period of time rather than being on a different wire. The basic method of serial transmission, Figure 9.7, is to, first, load the data into the flip-flops of a shift register, then shift the data eight times. At each shift pulse, 1 bit of data is shifted into the receiver shift register and, after eight shift pulses, the data may be read in parallel from the receiver register. This form of transmission requires three wires between the transmitter and receiver – the data line, the shift (or clock) line, and a reference line. It is sometimes used to connect devices such as multi-digit displays and keyboards to a computer because it simplifies the connections. When data is sent between points connected by the public telephone system, the serial transmission must take place *without* sending the clock pulses along a separate wire.

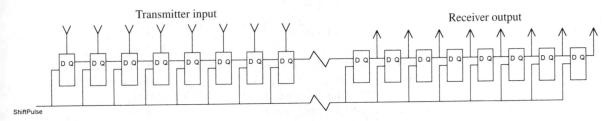

Figure 9.7 *Using shift registers as serial to parallel converters*

The **universal asynchronous receiver/transmitter**, UART, is a device that includes all the logic necessary to both transmit and receive data serially without a common clock, hence the term 'asynchronous' in its name. Using three wires between two UARTs allows data to be sent in both directions between two computers, Figure 9.8.

When the transmission is over the telephone network, the telephone line must carry data in both directions and the signals must be compatible with a system originally designed for audio frequencies. In this case a modem (*modulator/demodulator*) connects between the UART and the telephone network, Figure 9.9. The modem modulates binary signals to audio frequency signals and demodulates audio signals to binary signals. Modems of yesteryear simply converted a bit to one of two audio frequencies; modern day modems use more complex modulation schemes to achieve much higher data rates.

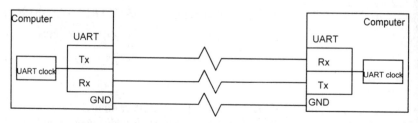

Figure 9.8 *Direct connection between two UARTs*

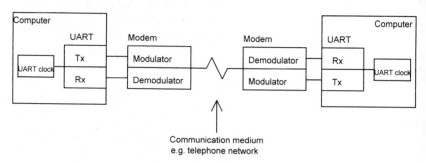

Communication medium
e.g. telephone network

Figure 9.9 *Two UARTs connected via modems*

The design of the UART is based on the method of Figure 9.7 but instead of both the receiver and transmitter using the same shift pulses, each uses shift pulses obtained from its own clock generator. Both these clock generators must have nominally the same frequency, although in practice they will not be exactly the same.

The format of each byte as transmitted is shown in Figure 9.10. When not transmitting data, the UART output carries a high logic level, that is, the serial line **idles** high. To indicate the start of a byte, the line is brought low so that the data bits are prefaced by a logic 0. After the data bits, the line returns to the idling level, ready for the start of another byte. The data bits are said to be **framed** between a **Start bit** and a **Stop bit**.

Once the receiver has detected the Start transition from the high to the low level, it can begin reading the data. The best time to read the incoming data is in the middle of each bit time; a slight difference between the speeds of the transmitter and receiver clocks will cause the time of reading the data to vary a little about this mid-bit time. This will allow up to a half-bit time difference before the wrong bit is read. To accommodate this sampling near the middle of the bit, the UART receiver clock frequency is such that, typically, 16 clock pulses occur within each bit time. Then, following the high to low transition at the start of a data frame, a counter begins to count the receiver clock cycles. When this counter reaches eight, the time is very nearly the middle of the Start bit and the Start bit is read. Subsequently, the receiver reads the incoming signal every 16 receiver clock cycles (that is, near the middle of each data bit) and shifts the data into the receiver data register.

The transmitter may append a **parity bit** to the data. This bit is used to check that the data has been correctly received. If the transmitter uses even

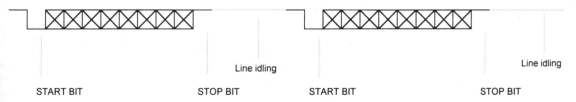

START BIT   STOP BIT   START BIT   STOP BIT

Line idling   Line idling

Figure 9.10 *Format of an asynchronous data frame*

parity, it will set the parity bit to whatever value makes the total number of ones in the data bits and the parity bit even. The receiver checks for an even number of bits and, should this be odd, it will set a **ParityError** flag to indicate that there has been a parity error. The UART allows the user to choose odd parity (number of 1s is odd) or no parity (parity bit not inserted).

For successful communication between transmitter and receiver, both must agree as to the nominal speed, the number of data bits (usually 8), the number of Stop bits (usually 1), and the type of parity (odd, even, none). When there are no errors in the data transmission, the circuit sets the DataReady flag to indicate that a byte has been assembled and is ready to be read by the computer. When the computer reads the data, this flag is automatically reset. If the data is not read before another byte is received, an **OverrunError** flag is set, indicating an error. Two other sources of error can also be detected. Thus, if the initial high to low transition was caused by a short duration noise spike on the line, the transition is ignored. In addition, if the bit following the data (the Stop bit) is not high, a **FramingError** flag is set.

9.6 Problems

1   A computer using a G80 microprocessor has three output ports at port addresses 0x80, 0x81, and 0x82. Devise logic to produce the required port select signals.

2   A computer using a G80 microprocessor has three input ports at port addresses 0x00, 0x01, and 0x02. Devise logic to produce the required port select signals.

3   A computer using a G80 microprocessor uses a PIO at port addresses 0x00 and 0x01. Sketch a circuit showing how the PIO will be connected to the microprocessor. Assume the PIO has the control signals shown in Figure 9.6.

10 Input and output methods

We have seen in Chapter 9 that input and output ports provide the hardware for transferring data into and out of the computer. Here we look at how we can use these ports in programs that transfer data to and from various types of peripheral devices such as a keypad and a stepper motor. A fundamental problem is the difference in the rate at which a peripheral device and the G80 can write and read data. We will see that data transfer cannot take place without taking into account the characteristics of the device that is connected to the port. In general, the programmer must cause the computer to adhere to a **protocol** that governs how the data transfer will take place. We begin by considering data transfers that occur at a particular point in the program, as determined by the programmer. This is known as **programmed input/ output**; the name indicates that the program initiates the data transfer. We then consider methods by which the input/output device itself initiates the data transfer, this is known as **interrupt-driven input/output**. We consider various mechanisms in which the G80 may respond to an interrupt request from a peripheral device. Finally, we see a third method of transferring data, **direct memory access**.

10.1 Simple input and output

If we wish to write data to a display comprising several light-emitting diodes, LEDs, the output data may be written at any time since the LEDs are always ready to receive new data. This simple data transfer protocol is variously called **direct transfer**, or **unconditional transfer**. The program Sws_Leds. asm uses this protocol both for writing to the LEDs and reading from the switches.

10.2 Handshaking

When we attempt to use the unconditional transfer method to read a 4-bit number from a keypad, the unconditional transfer protocol gives an unsatisfactory result. The source code for this unsatisfactory program is shown in Figure 10.1. In addition to the input and output instructions, the source code contains some instructions which convert the 4-bit number from the keypad to the ASCII code for the corresponding hexadecimal digit. The character is displayed on the LCD using an unconditional transfer. A list of ASCII codes is given in Appendix B.

When this program is run, the character corresponding to the last keypad button pressed is repeatedly displayed. However, we want a character to be displayed only once when a keypad button has been pressed.

A solution lies in the hardware of the keypad itself. When a keypad button is pressed the keypad logic circuit sets bit 7 of its data register to 1, and

```
;Pad_LCDX.asm
;Read output of keypad, convert to ASCII, display on LCD.
;No handshake - so reads keypad repeatedly !!
;
LCD = 0xD0
KEYPAD = 0x80
loop:
      in a, (KEYPAD)
      and 0x0F              ;force unused bits to zero
      ;Convert key_number to ASCII
      ; if key_number > 9, add 0x37, else add 0x30
      cp 0x0A
      jp c, asc1            ;if key_number > 9, jump to asc1
      ;
      add a, 0x37
      jp ifex
asc1:
      add a, 0x30           ;
ifex:
      out (LCD), a
      jp loop
```

Figure 10.1 *Listing of program Pad_LCDx.asm*

when the data register is read the keypad automatically resets bit 7 to zero. Bit 7 of the keypad data register thus holds a 1 if a button has been pressed but has not yet been read; otherwise, it holds a 0. The bit is used to signal whether or not the keypad has unread data; it is called the **DataReady** signal. In the improved program, `Pad_LCD.asm`, Figure 10.2, we repeatedly input from the keypad data register until the program detects that the DataReady signal is set to 1:

```
;while( DataReady = = 0 ) do nothing
wloop:
      in a, (KEYPAD)    ;read keypad data register
      bit 7,a           ;Z flag indicates whether or not
                             this
                        ; bit is 0
      jp z, wloop       ;if Z flag is set, jump to wloop
      ...               ; else continue
```

When this program is run it has the required behaviour; a character is displayed on the LCD only when a new keypad button has been pressed. The program code, together with the hardware of the keypad, uses a **handshake** mechanism.

10.2.1 More about handshaking

There are enough bits in the keypad data register to include the DataReady signal, but what if another keypad were to produce 8 bits of data? Clearly

```
;Pad_LCD.asm
;Read output of keypad, convert to ASCII, display on LCD.
;Keypad is handshaken - so reads keypad correctly.
;
LCD = 0xD0
KEYPAD = 0x80
;
;while( not DataReady ) do nothing
loop:
    in a, (KEYPAD)
    bit 7,a
    jp z, loop
    ;
    and 0x0F        ;force unused bits to zero
    ;Convert key_number to ASCII
    ; if key_number > 9, add 0x37, else add 0x30
    cp 10
    jp c, asc1          ;if key_number > 9, jump to asc1
    ;
    add a, 0x37
    jp ifex
asc1:
    add a, 0x30
ifex:
    out (LCD), a    ;reg A holds ASCII code
    jp loop
```

Figure 10.2 *Source code of program Pad_LCD.asm*

we will have to use an additional port; one port, the data port, will hold the data while another port, the control port, will hold the DataReady signal. Our program will then read the control port until it detects that DataReady is asserted, then it will read the data port.

Not all devices reset DataReady automatically when the port is read; such devices must have an additional input signal that can reset the DataReady flag. This signal is called **DataReadyReset** or **DataAcknowledge**; whatever its name, when it is asserted, it resets the DataReady signal. A keyboard with

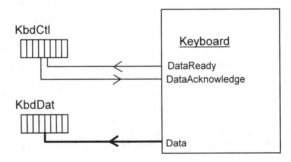

Figure 10.3 *Hardware interface for keyboard. KbdDat is the data port, KbdCtl is the control port*

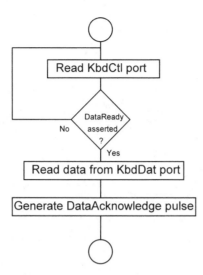

Figure 10.4 *Software interface for keyboard using a two-wire handshake*

this structure is shown in Figure 10.3. A program will then have to assert the DataAcknowledge signal at an appropriate time; a flowchart for this is shown in Figure 10.4.

In general, a handshaking protocol employs a signal from the device that indicates its status and another signal from the computer that acknowledges the data transfer. When these are the only two control signals, the protocol is called a **two-wire handshake***;* it is very common at all levels of a computer system.

10.3 Simple output to a slow device

Not all devices have a handshake facility, yet may not always be ready to accept data. The stepper motor is such a device, it has no signal to indicate when the step has been completed and is ready to receive another step signal. After being given a signal to step it must be allowed sufficient time to complete the step before giving it another step signal. We can do this by simply making the G80 use up time doing nothing after outputting a step signal; the nop instruction does just this. Program Pad_Step.asm, Figure 10.5, shows how we can use a few nop instructions to allow time for the motor to settle at its new position. (This source code also introduces assembler directives, .seg CODE (abs) and .org 0x100. These allow the programmer to specify the actual address where the code will be located in the G80 memory space. The effect of these directives in this source code is that the code following the .org 0x100 directive starts at memory location 0100. You can see this by viewing the output of the assembler.)

Assemble, link, and simulate Pad_Step.asm. To 'connect' the motor and the keypad to the G80 computer, click on Peripherals | Motor and Peripherals | Keypad. When running, the simulator will appear as in Figure 10.6.

Experiment by removing the nop instructions and observe that the motor behaves erratically when not given enough time to settle down after stepping.

```
;Pad_Step.asm

;Requires -
;      - keypad
;      - motor
;
;Steps the motor the number of steps from the keypad
;Uses Motor and Keypad
;
;Port address definitions
KEYPAD    = 0x80
KEYPAD_C  = 0x81
MOTOR     = 0xB0
;
      .seg CODE (abs)
      ;
      jp start
;
      .org 0x0100
start:

Lp1: ;Loop reads keypad, then steps the motor
      in a, (KEYPAD)
      bit 7,a
      jp z, Lp1        ;if DataReady bit is zero, jump
      ;
      ;Now have a key press
      and a, 0x0F      ;remove upper nibble
      jp z, Lp1        ;if zero number of steps, jump
      ;
      ld b, a          ;number of steps in reg B
      ld a, 1
step:
      xor 1            ;toggle bit 0
      out (MOTOR), a
      nop  ;;allow time for motor to step
      nop
      nop
      nop
      xor 1            ;toggle bit 0
      out (MOTOR), a
      nop
      nop
      nop
      nop
      djnz step
      ;
      jp Lp1
```

Figure 10.5 *Source code for program Pad_Step.asm*

10.4 Do-forever loop

Consider a program that controls an industrial process by reading from various sensing devices and writing to various actuators. Ideally, we would like the program to have the simple form:

```
while( TRUE )
     {
     Read all inputs
```

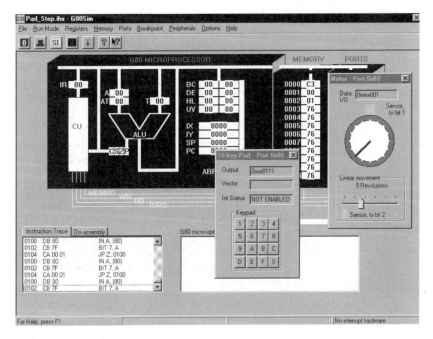

Figure 10.6 *Appearance of simulator when running program Pad_Step.asm*

```
Decide what the outputs should be
Write the outputs
}
```

This ideal program comprises a do-forever loop within which it reads the data from the sensors, decides what the outputs should be, then writes the outputs to the actuators. (In order to avoid having to wait for an input/output device that is not ready for a data transfer, we could simply use the previous value.)

Unfortunately, this simple model often results in an inadequate system. The reason lies in the time taken for the program to pass once through the do-forever loop. Let this be T seconds. Since the program does not wait for an input/output device that is not ready, T is virtually the time taken to decide what the outputs should be. Now consider what happens if a dangerous state of the industrial process is signalled, at an input port, just after the program has read the inputs. This emergency will not be read until T seconds later and the program will write the outputs to respond to the emergency only after 2.T seconds. If 2.T seconds is too long a time to respond to the emergency, the system will fail to respond in time. A solution to this problem is to use an interrupt-driven input.

10.5 Processor interrupt In the programmed input/output protocol discussed so far, the data transfer is initiated by the microprocessor when it executes input or output instructions in the program. This suggests an alternative approach – let the peripheral device itself initiate the data transfer. This technique is known as **interrupt-driven input/output**.

In this protocol, a peripheral device that has new data ready for input or is ready to receive new output data is allowed to initiate the data transfer. This implies that the microprocessor can somehow be made to stop its current activity, execute the instructions required for the data transfer, and then return to what it was doing. This is similar to someone working at a desk; when the telephone rings, she interrupts what she is doing in order to respond to a telephone call. After answering the call, the interrupted work is resumed at the point where it was interrupted by the telephone.

The principal benefit of this protocol is that the device can be dealt with, or **serviced**, speedily. Speed may be of crucial importance, such as where a potentially dangerous condition has been detected in the industrial plant being controlled by the computer or where a UART receives a character that must be read before the next character arrives. Another benefit accrues from the fact that the microprocessor will not have to waste time waiting for slow devices to become ready for the data transfer as is inherent in the handshake protocol. We now explore various ways of how this protocol can be implemented on a microprocessor.

10.6 Possible interrupt mechanisms

We want to interrupt the current activity of the microprocessor, execute the code (the **interrupt service routine**) which performs the required data transfer, and resume the original activity. There are many ways of achieving this in a microprocessor. The G80 is designed to respond in one of three ways, any of which can be chosen by the designer of a computer using the G80 microprocessor. The three ways are called interrupt mode 0, interrupt mode 1, and interrupt mode 2. These three ways have been chosen in response to the following design questions.

Design Question 1: How is the microprocessor to be signalled that an interrupt has been requested?
Clearly, there must be a signal from the device making the interrupt request and going into the microprocessor. Since we expect to have more than one input/output device capable of making an interrupt request, will we provide a separate interrupt request input for each input/output device? Alternatively, do we provide a single interrupt request signal that can be shared by all input/output devices capable of making interrupt requests?

A seemingly obvious solution is to have an interrupt request line for each device. However, this raises the question as to the number of interrupt request lines that should be provided, a question akin to asking how long is a piece of string. While some microprocessors have a handful of interrupt request lines, it is common to have a single interrupt request line, which is shared by all input/output devices. Any device that is capable of generating an interrupt request signal will be able to assert this shared interrupt request line. This allows an arbitrary number of input/output devices to be connected to the microprocessor. We choose this technique for the G80.

Design Question 2: When is the microprocessor to respond to an interrupt request?

Is this to be in the middle of the current instruction, at the end of the current instruction, or only at the end of certain instructions?

To respond to an interrupt request in mid-instruction would require that a considerable amount of information about the internal state of the microprocessor be saved in order to resume the instruction. It is simpler to provide that the microprocessor responds at the end of the current instruction to avoid this complication. Usually the response is at the end of any instruction although in a few microprocessors, the response follows only certain instructions. In common with most microprocessors, we choose to respond to an interrupt request signal at the end of the current instruction. Thus, the G80 will fetch an instruction, execute it, and then, if the interrupt request signal is asserted, it will respond to the interrupt request instead of proceeding to fetch the next instruction.

Design Question 3: Assuming there are several input/output devices capable of making an interrupt request, how will the microprocessor identify which device made the request?

If our answer to Design Question 1 was to have an interrupt request line for each input/output device, then the requesting device is implicitly identified by the interrupt request signal itself. Since we have chosen to have a shared request line, the immediate response of the microprocessor must be to identify the input/output device that made the interrupt request.

One possibility is that, in response to the interrupt request signal, we design our microprocessor to jump to a pre-determined address that is the start of an **interrupt polling routine**. This routine will read, in turn, a single bit from each input/output device. This bit, the **interrupt flag**, within every device indicates whether that device made an interrupt request. When this **interrupt polling routine** detects that a flag in a device is set, a jump is made to the code that services that device. We provide this facility in the G80 microprocessor as the **interrupt mode 1** response. However, the execution of the interrupt polling routine delays entry to the code that actually services the interrupting device. We will design into the G80 an additional method of responding to an interrupt request, which provides a quicker access to the required interrupt service routine.

A widely used technique is to provide that in response to the interrupt request signal, which is an input to the microprocessor, the microprocessor asserts an output signal, Interrupt Acknowledge. This is connected to all the input/output devices. When Interrupt Acknowledge is asserted, the logic within the input/output device that made the interrupt request is designed to place a unique pattern of bits onto the Data Bus. The microprocessor reads this pattern so identifying the requesting device. In the G80, this byte is used to access a table that contains the addresses of the start of all the interrupt service routines. This way of responding to an interrupt request signal is called **interrupt mode 2**.

Design Question 4: Once the device making the interrupt request has been identified, how is the microprocessor to make a jump to the beginning of the appropriate interrupt service routine? Further, how will it resume executing the code that was interrupted?

Where there are several interrupt request inputs to the microprocessor, the microprocessor hardware may be designed to jump automatically to a pre-assigned memory address at which the interrupt service routine begins.

Where there is a shared interrupt request line, the identifier read from the input/output device during the time when the microprocessor asserted its Interrupt Acknowledge, may be used to determine the start address of the interrupt service routine. In this case, the identifier is used as a pointer into a table of the start addresses of the interrupt service routines, Figure 10.7. The 2 bytes at table locations $2x$ and $2x+1$ hold the start address of the interrupt service routine for the device having identifier x. Thus, if the identifier has a value of 2, table locations 4 and 5 hold the start address of the interrupt service routine for the device that identifies itself as 2. The table effectively translates the identifier into the start address of the appropriate interrupt service routine; it performs a pointing or vectoring function. This form of interrupt response is called a **vectored interrupt**.

How to allow the microprocessor to return to where it was before it was interrupted? A common mechanism is to use the stack region of memory. Before jumping to the interrupt service routine (that is, loading the Program Counter with the start address of the interrupt service routine), the microprocessor automatically pushes the current contents of the Program Counter onto the top of the stack. Then it loads the address of the start of the service routine into the Program Counter, so executing a jump to the service routine. At the end of the service routine, a return to the interrupted code is achieved by a computer instruction, such as `reti`, or `return from interrupt`, which pops the top of the stack into the Program Counter.

This mechanism requires that, if the programmer uses the stack within the service routine, she must ensure that the top of the stack is the same as it was when the service routine began. The G80 maintains one stack region, but some microprocessors maintain two stacks, one for use by the computer

Table location	Contents
00	Start address
01	of Interrupt Service routine 0
02	Start address
03	of Interrupt Service routine 1
04	Start address
05	of Interrupt Service routine 2
06	...

Figure 10.7 *Table giving the start addresses of the interrupt service routines*

system itself, the other for use by the programmer, so separating the requirements of the computer system from the requirements of the programmer.

Design Question 5:   How is the microprocessor to cope with simultaneous interrupt requests from more than one device? Further, what is the microprocessor to do if, while it is executing the service routine for one device, it receives an interrupt request from another input/output device?
This requires that the designer of the computer system must be able to assign a 'pecking order', or **interrupt priority**, to each of the input/output devices. Then, a device regarded as having a higher priority will be serviced in preference to a device having a lower priority. The details of how this might be achieved are discussed in the following section.

10.7 Interrupt priority mechanisms

The design problem is to decide what the microprocessor will do if it receives an interrupt request while it is currently executing the service routine for another device that made an earlier interrupt request. A similar problem arises if more than one device make simultaneous interrupt requests.

A common solution is to provide a signal that enters and leaves every device in the manner of a **daisy chain**. One way of achieving this is shown in Figure 10.8 where the daisy chain signal at the start of the daisy chain is permanently asserted. It then enters a device as InterruptEnableIn, IEI, and leaves that device as InterruptEnableOut, IEO. Every device contains the logic:

    IEO = IEI . InterruptNotRequested

where InterruptNotRequested is asserted when the device does not request interrupt service. Thus, when IEI = = 1 and InterruptNotRequested is asserted, IEO is set to 1 and this signal enters the next device in the daisy chain. If that device is requesting interrupt service, it will set its IEO to 0 and hence all devices further down the daisy chain will set IEO to 0. Only if IEI is asserted will a device respond to the interrupt acknowledge signal from the microprocessor. In this way, a device near the start of the daisy chain will be serviced in preference to a device further from the start, that is it will have higher interrupt priority.

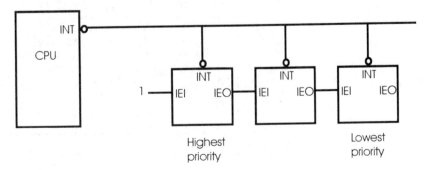

Figure 10.8 *Daisy chain interrupt priority logic*

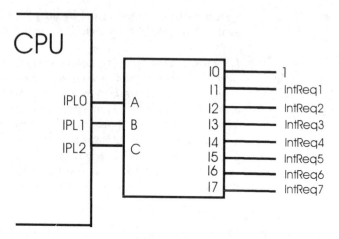

Figure 10.9 *Priority inputs*

An alternative solution is illustrated in Figure 10.9. Here, the microprocessor has not one interrupt request input but three Interrupt Priority Level inputs, IPL0, IPL1, and IPL2. These signals indicate a 3-bit number that gives the priority of the interrupt request. The microprocessor contains a 3-bit register that holds the priority level of the code it is currently executing. The Input Priority Level and this number are connected to a comparator within the microprocessor and the interrupt request is acknowledged only if its priority is greater than the priority of the code that the microprocessor is currently executing.

It can be seen from the truth table of the Interrupt Priority Encoder, Figure 10.10, that its output is a 3-bit number: this number is that of the highest active input. For example, if I4, I2 and I1 are all active, the output number is 4. If there are no interrupt requests, the Interrupt Priority Encoder generates a zero priority number. There are therefore seven levels of priority, the highest of which is level 7. In large computers, it may be that each of the seven inputs to the Interrupt Priority Encoder is itself generated from a daisy chain of devices.

I7	I6	I5	I4	I3	I2	I1	I0	CBA
1	X	X	X	X	X	X	X	111
0	1	X	X	X	X	X	X	110
0	0	1	X	X	X	X	X	101
0	0	0	1	X	X	X	X	100
0	0	0	0	1	X	X	X	011
0	0	0	0	0	1	X	X	010
0	0	0	0	0	0	1	X	001
0	0	0	0	0	0	0	1	000

Figure 10.10 *Priority encoder truth table*

10.8 Non-maskable interrupt

The normal interrupt mechanism of a microprocessor may be enabled and disabled by the programmer; it is said to be **maskable**. Usually a microprocessor has an interrupt mechanism that is not maskable, that is, it cannot be disabled by the programmer. This **non-maskable interrupt**, NMI, has a higher priority than any of the maskable interrupt requests and is typically used to handle potentially catastrophic events such as the impending loss of power. (The loss of the electricity supply can be detected electronically in sufficient time for the computer to use the stored energy in the power supply unit to execute many instructions. These would normally perform an orderly end to the program.) In some microprocessors, an NMI is simply the general interrupt request having highest priority, while in others such as the G80, a special NMI pin is used. The G80 always responds to an asserted NMI input by automatically calling the code at memory location 0066.

In the following examples, the NMI response is programmed to activate the beeper:

```
;On NMI, beep
.org 0x66 ;NMI routine always begins at 0x0066
out (BEEP), a
retn       ;return from NMI
```

10.9 G80 interrupt mechanisms

Any interrupt mechanism must incorporate a consistent set of answers to the design questions asked earlier in this chapter. The G80 is designed to deal with interrupt requests in not one but three ways. The programmer must select one of these ways using an interrupt mode instruction, im 0, im 1, or im 2. Since interrupt mode 2 is most commonly used, you may skip the sections on the other interrupt modes on a first reading.

10.9.1 Interrupt mode 0 – RSTn*

In this mode, the interrupting device is designed to place the code for an instruction on the Data Bus when the G80 asserts its INTAK signal. This instruction is transferred to the Instruction Register; thus, the interrupting device provides the next instruction to be executed. These instructions are usually one of several **restart** instructions, which are effectively single byte calls to fixed memory locations. Program Int0.asm, Figure 10.11, illustrates this interrupt mode.

Note that the logic in the port making the interrupt request must be designed to place one of the rst n instructions on the Data Bus when the G80 asserts its INTAK signal. This is the response expected by the G80 when programmed to respond in interrupt mode 0. The ports at addresses 00, 01, 02, and 03 incorporate this logic when Peripherals | Interrupt hardware | RSTn is selected. The simulator then appears as shown in Figure 10.12.

The interrupt logic within the ports is designed such that when any of IR1, IR2, or IR3 is asserted, a code is automatically loaded into port 03. For IR1 this code is 0xD7 which is the op code for the instruction rst 0x10. This instruction is effectively a call 0x0010 instruction. Similarly, when IR2 is

```
;int0.asm - Test IM0 response
;Uses RSTn interrupt mode
;
;Main loop outputs a count on port 0
;On IR1 increment register B
;On IR2 increment register C
;On IR3 increment register D
;On NMI beep
;
     .seg CODE (abs);This segment uses absolute addresses
;
     ld sp, 0xFFFF  ;Initialise Stack Pointer
     jp start
     ;
     .org 0x0100    ;Locate this code at 0100
     ;
start:
     ;Clear registers used for counting
     ld a, 0
     ld b, 0
     ld c, 0
     ld d, 0
     ;Now set up and ready to go...
     im 0 ;... select G80 interrupt, Mode 0
     ei   ;... and  enable G80 interrupt logic
;Main loop, outputs binary count to port 0
lp1:
     inc a
     out (0), a
     jr lp1

;Service IR1 - increment reg B
     .org 0x0010
     inc b
     ei
     reti
;
;Service IR2 - increment reg C
     .org 0x0020
     inc c
     ei
     reti
;
;Service IR3 - increment reg D
     .org 0x0030
     inc d
     ei
     reti
;
;Service NMI - beep

 BEEP = 0x60
     .org 0x0066
     out (BEEP), a
     ei
     retn
```

Figure 10.11 *Listing of program Int0.asm*

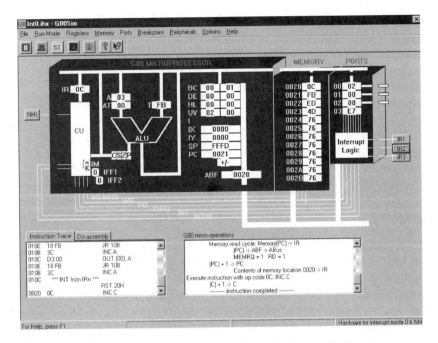

Figure 10.12 *Appearance of simulator with mode 0 or mode 1 ports*

asserted, 0xE7, the code for rst 0x20 (call 0x0020) is loaded into port 03, and when IR3 is asserted, 0xF7, the code for rst 0x30 (call 0x0030) is loaded into port 03. The G80 acknowledges an interrupt request from these ports, by asserting INTAK. This causes the logic in the ports to connect port 03 to the Data Bus so that the contents of port 03 can be transferred into the G80 Instruction Register.

After observing the behaviour of this program when running at full speed (by clicking the yellow button), press the Single Instruction button, SI. Now click on one or more of the IRn buttons and continue to step through the program code one instruction at a time.

Since each input/output device requires its own interrupt service routine, the number of devices is limited to the number of restart instructions. It is therefore restrictive and is no longer popular.

10.9.2 Interrupt mode 1 – poll*

When interrupt mode 1 is selected by the programmer by means of the im 1 instruction, the G80 responds to an interrupt request by calling the code at memory location 0x0038. The code beginning at this location is normally a routine that reads the interrupt flag from each device in turn; this is called **polling**. This is illustrated by program Int1.asm, shown in Figure 10.13. Note that the logic in the port making the interrupt request must be designed to set a flag in the control port, port 03. The polling routine then reads this port in order to identify which interrupt request signal, or signals, occurred. The ports at

```
;Int1.asm - Test IM1 response
;Requires ports in poll mode (1) and KeyPad
;
;Main loop            output count to port 0x00
;On interrupt IR1     inc B
;On interrupt IR2     inc C
;On interrupt IR3     inc D
;On interrupt KeyPad  key number in reg H
;On NMI               beep
;
;Port address definitions
BEEP     = 0x60
KEYPAD   = 0x80
KEYPAD_C = 0x81

Control  = 3
;
     .seg CODE (abs)
     .org 0
     ;
     ld sp, 0xFFFF
     jp start
     ;
     .org 0x38
     ;This routine is entered on every interrupt request.
     ;Poll the interrupt bits to determine the source of
the INT
     ;;;;;;;;;;;;;;;
     ;Destroys reg E
     ;;;;;;;;;;;;;;;
     ;First poll the ports in the GPP
     push af
     in a, (Control)
     ld e, a           ;Int id in reg E
     ;Clear GPP flags
     xor a
     out (Control), a
     ;Test each GPP  flag in turn
     bit 0, e
     call nz, servIR1
     ;
     bit 1, e
     call nz, servIR2
     ;
     bit 2, e
     call nz, servIR3
     ;
     ;Now poll the HexPad
     in a, (KEYPAD_C)
     bit 7, a
     call nz, servPad
```

Figure 10.13 *Listing of program Int1.asm*

```
        ;
        ;End of polling routine so tidy up and return
        pop af
        ei
        reti

;On NMI, beep
        .org 0x66
        out (BEEP), a
        ei
        retn

;Here is the main program
        .org 0x0100
start:
        ;Clear control port
        xor a
        out (Control), a
        ;
        ;Enable KeyPad int
        ld a, 0x83
        out (KEYPAD_C), a
        ;
        ;Clear registers used for counting
        ld a, 0
        ld b, 0
        ld c, 0
        ld d, 0
        ld h, 0
        ;Select interrupt mode 1 and enable G80 interrupt
logic
        im 1
        ei
;
;       Main loop outputs binary count to port 0x00
lp1:
        inc a
        out (0), a
        jr lp1

servIR1:        ;Increments register B
        inc b
        ret

servIR2:        ;Increments register C
        inc c
        ret

servIR3:        ;Increments register D
        inc d
        ret

servPad:        ;Puts keypad number into re H
        in a, (KEYPAD)
        and 0x0F
        ld h, a
        ret
```

Figure 10.13 *(cont.)*

addresses 00, 01, 02, and 03 incorporate this logic when Peripherals | Interrupt hardware | Poll is selected. The simulator then appears the same as for mode 0 port logic, Figure 10.12; however, port 03 now holds bits which indicate the source, or sources, of the interrupt request(s).

After observing the behaviour of this program when running at full speed, click the Single Instruction button, SI. Now click on one or more of the IRn buttons and continue to step through the program code one instruction at a time.

The order in which the polling routine examines the interrupt request flags from the devices implicitly assigns a priority to the devices since the first interrupting device polled will be serviced first. Unfortunately, the polling routine creates a delay before the required service routine is entered so slowing the response of the microprocessor to an interrupt request.

10.9.3 Interrupt mode 2 – vectored

Interrupt mode 2 is the most flexible of the three interrupt modes; it allows the interrupt service routines to be placed in any memory location. The G80 is put into this mode by an `im 2` instruction. The interrupting device is designed to place a vector on the Data Bus when the G80 asserts its INTAK signal. This vector is read by the G80, which then automatically uses it to obtain the address of the start of the interrupt service routine. The G80 does this by using a look-up table to convert the vector to the start address of the appropriate interrupt service routine. The overall concept is depicted in Figure 10.14.

The required program structure is a little more complicated than for the other interrupt modes but, fortunately, the structure is the same for all programs using mode 2 interrupt devices. Indeed, the following example may be used as the basis of all programs using this interrupt mode.

In the program `Int2.asm`, shown in Figure 10.15, the start of the look-up table that contains the start addresses of all the interrupt service routines

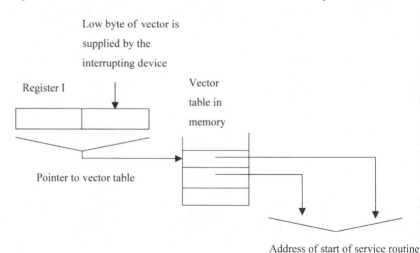

Figure 10.14 *Concept of mode 2 interrupt response*

is at memory location 0x8020. This location has been named VTab; that is, vTab = 0x8020. The assembly listing shows how this table contains the 2-byte address of the start of routine servA (0x001D) followed by the start address of routine servB (0x0021):

```
              56 ; Vector table
              57      .org 0x8020 ;NB Must be even address
8020          58 VTab:
8020 1D.00    59      .dw servA   ;Address of start of
                                  ; servA routine
8022.21.00    60      .dw servB   ;Address of start of
                                  ; servB routine
```

The high byte of the table address is stored in register I; in lines 14–18, this register is loaded with 0x80, the high byte of vtab. When an interrupt request from a device occurs, the device will supply the low byte of an address in the table. This is concatenated[1] with the contents of register I to form the address of a memory location within the table. Obviously, the byte from the device must have been stored within the device before this can happen. How is this done? Actually, each data port has an associated vector port. Thus, when Peripherals | Interrupt hardware | Vectored is selected, port 00 is a data port and port 01 is its associated vector port. Similarly, ports 02 and 03 are respectively a data port and its associated vector port. In lines 19–23, the program loads port 01 with 0x20, the low byte of VTab + 0. Similarly, in lines 24–28, the program loads port 03 with 0x22, the low byte of VTab + 2.

Run the program at full speed and observe that it has the behaviour given at the beginning of the program listing. After observing the behaviour of this program when running at full speed, click the Single Instruction button, SI. Now click on one or both of the StA, StB buttons and observe the operation of the program by stepping through the code one instruction at a time.

10.9.4 Vectored interrupt sequence of events

Let us follow the sequence of activity that occurs when a device makes an interrupt request. A conceptual view of the logic for the interrupt mechanism is shown in Figure 10.16. An I/O device, such as a printer or a keyboard, is attached to port 02/03. Register I within the G80 has been loaded with 0x80 and the Program Counter indicates that the next instruction is to be fetched from memory location 0x0019. During the execution of the current instruction, the device connected to port 02/03 asserts its Int Req signal, ①, indicating that it requires attention. This signal sets the flip-flop so that the Interrupt Request signal to the G80, INT, is asserted, ②. At the end of the current instruction, the G80 does not fetch the next instruction from the memory location indicated by the Program Counter. Instead, because INT is asserted,

---

[1] That is, the 16-bit address is formed by taking the contents of register I and appending the byte from the device. For example, if register I contains 0x80 and the byte from the device is 0x22, the resulting address is 0x8022.

```
                                      1 ;int2.asm - Test IM2 response
                                      2 ;Requires vectored ports.
                                      3 ;
                                      4 ;Main loop            count to port 2
                                      5 ;On interrupt StA     increment reg B
                                      6 ;On interrupt StB     increment reg C
                                      7 ;On NMI               beep
                                      8 ;
        0060                          9 BEEP = 0x60          ;address of beeper port
                                     10     .seg CODE (abs)
                                     11     ;
        0000 31 FF FF                12     ld sp, 0xFFFF  ;Initialise SP
        0003 ED 5E                   13     im 2           ;Interrupt mode 2
                                     14     ;Initialise register I
        0005 01`20`80                15     ld bc,  VTab
        0008 78                      16     ld a, b          ;Send the high byte of the
                                     17                      ; two-byte address VTab
        0009 ED 47                   18     ld i, a          ; to I register
                                     19     ;Initialise PPP device
        000B 79                      20     ld a, c          ;Send the low byte of the
                                     21                      ; two-byte address VTab
        000C D3 01                   22     out (1), a       ; to PIO device vector
                                     23                      ; port for port 0
        000E 01`22`80                24     ld bc, VTab+2
        0011 79                      25     ld a, c          ;Send the low byte of the
                                     26                      ; two-byte address VTab+2
        0012 D3 03                   27     out (3), a       ; to PIO device vector
                                     28                      ; port for port 1
        0014 FB                      29     ei               ;Interrupt data now set up,
                                     30                      ; so enable it
        0015 01 00 00                31     ld bc, 0
                                     32     ;
                                     33
        0018                         34 lp1:    ;Main program outputs binary
                                     35     ; count to port 2
        0018 3C                      36     inc a
        0019 D3 02                   37     out (2), a
        001B 18 FB                   38     jr lp1
                                     39
                                     40
                                     41 ;Service routine servA - increment register B
        001D 04                      42 servA:  inc b
        001E FB                      43     ei
        001F ED 4D                   44     reti
                                     45
                                     46 ;Service routine servB - increment register C
        0021 0C                      47 servB:  inc c
        0022 FB                      48     ei
        0023 ED 4D                   49     reti
                                     50
                                     51 ;NMI service - beep
                                     52     .org 0x0066
        0066 D3 60                   53     out (BEEP), a
        0068 ED 45                   54     retn
                                     55
                                     56 ; Vector table
                                     57     .org 0x8020      ;NB Must be even address
        8020                         58 VTab:
        8020`1D`00                   59     .dw servA        ;Address of start of servA
routine
        8022`21`00                   60     .dw servB        ;Address of start of servB
routine
                                     61
-----------------------------------------------------------------------
Segment Table
   Segment name                          Size, bytes    Type
   CODE                                  0x8024         ABSOLUTE
-----------------------------------------------------------------------
Symbol Table (A = Absolute, R = Relocatable, G = Global, X = External)
   Segment                  Symbol                         Value Type
   =                        BEEP                         = 0060
   CODE                     VTab                           8020  A
   CODE                     lp1                            0018  A
   CODE                     servA                          001D  A
   CODE                     servB                          0021  A
```

Figure 10.15 *Listing of program Int2.asm*

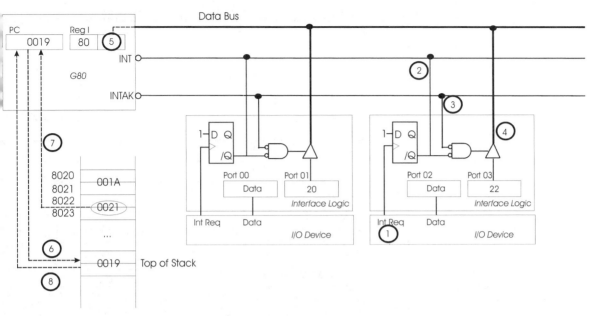

Figure 10.16 *Vectored interrupt response of G80*

the G80 asserts its Interrupt Acknowledge output signal, INTAK, ③. The three-state buffer that connects the vector port to the Data Bus is now enabled. Thus, the content of the vector register, 0x22, is placed on the Data Bus, ④. This byte is read and stored within the G80, ⑤. The G80 now pushes the contents of the Program Counter (0019) onto the stack, ⑥. The contents of register I and the number read from the vector register at step ⑤, are concatenated to form 0x8022. This address is used to transfer the 2 bytes at locations 0x8022 and 0x8023 into the Program Counter, ⑦, so that the Program Counter now holds 0x0021. This address is where the code for the interrupt service routine for port 02 begins.

The G80 now proceeds with its normal activity of fetching and executing instructions from the memory location pointed to by its Program Counter; that is, it executes the interrupt service routine, servB, which begins at memory location 0x0021. The programmer must end an interrupt service routine with a Return from Interrupt instruction, reti. When executing this instruction, the G80 pops the stack into the Program Counter, ⑧, and fetches the next instruction from memory location 0x0019 so returning to the code that was interrupted.

During the interrupt acknowledge cycle, the G80 automatically disables its interrupt mechanism. Thus, at some point in the interrupt service routine, the programmer must include an Enable Interrupt instruction, ei, to re-enable the interrupt facility. This is often done just before the reti instruction.

10.10 Direct memory access

Some I/O devices require a block of data to be transferred to or from the RAM. For example, a magnetic disk store will transfer a block of data between the RAM and the disk. Similarly, a data acquisition device might produce the temperature at 100 points in a furnace and the whole list of temperatures is to be transferred into consecutive RAM locations. We *could* transfer a

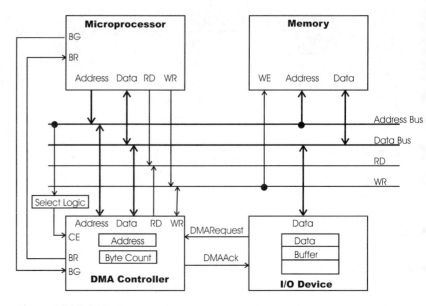

Figure 10.17 *Direct memory access*

block of data by letting the device generate an interrupt request and providing a service routine that transfers the block of data byte by byte. Thus, to input a block of data, the service routine will input a byte from the device, hold it in a microprocessor register, and then write it to a RAM location. Clearly, we can speed the data transfer by providing that the data be transferred directly between the RAM and the I/O device, so bypassing the microprocessor. This technique is known as **direct memory access** or **DMA**.

This technique will require a device, a **DMA controller**, that, during the data transfer, replaces the microprocessor as the device that controls the system bus[2]. In turn, this will require a signal to the microprocessor telling it that another device wishes to take control of the system bus. This is the BusRequest signal, BR, shown in Figure 10.17. The microprocessor will not be able to relinquish control of the bus immediately when BusRequest is asserted because it will be executing a program instruction. So, when it is able to respond, we arrange for it to assert a BusGrant, BG, signal[3]. Thus, when the DMA controller asserts BusRequest, the microprocessor finishes its current instruction and then effectively disconnects most of its pins from the bus. It can do this by disabling the three-state buffers that connect the pins to the bus. The microprocessor then asserts its BusGrant signal. The microprocessor cannot now perform any program instruction that requires use of the bus. The DMA controller causes the microprocessor to wait while the DMA controller has access to the bus and RAM.

The asserted BusGrant signal informs the DMA controller that it can now control the bus. That is, this signal enables the three-state buffers that connect

---

[2] Here, we use the term system bus, or simply bus, to refer to the wires that make up the Address Bus, the Data Bus, and control signals such as RD, WR, INT, and INTAK.
[3] BusRequest and BusGrant are often called Hold and HoldAcknowledge respectively.

the DMA controller pins to the bus. The DMA controller now behaves like a special purpose microprocessor and transfers a block of data between the RAM and the I/O device. In order to be able to do this, the DMA controller must have been loaded with the start address of the block in the RAM, the number of bytes in the block, and the direction of the data transfer. This initialization sequence must occur early in the computer program and before the DMA controller is loaded with a bit that enables it to respond to a DMA request signal from the I/O device.

In summary, when the I/O device wishes to transfer data, it asserts the DMARequest signal to the DMA controller. The controller then responds by asserting its BusRequest to the microprocessor. The microprocessor responds by asserting its BusGrant signal to the DMA controller. The DMA controller then puts the current content of its Address register onto the Address Bus, asserts RD or WR depending on the direction of the data transfer, and pulses the DMAAck to the I/O device. In response, the I/O device puts a byte onto the Data Bus (if an input) or receives a byte (if an output). Subsequently, the DMA controller increments its Address register, decrements its Byte Count register, puts the content of its Address register onto the Address Bus, asserts RD or WR, and pulses the DMAAck again. It repeats this sequence until the content of the Byte Count register reaches zero. Then, the DMA controller de-asserts its BusRequest signal, so allowing the microprocessor to regain control of the bus and continue with its programmed instructions.

10.11 Problems

Devise and test programs to perform the following actions.

No use of processor interrupt.

1   When bit 0 of the toggle switches is changed from 0 to 1, the stepper motor moves one step. When bit 0 of the toggle switches is changed from 1 to 0, the motor does not move. The direction of rotation is clockwise if bit 7 of the switches is 0 else it moves counterclockwise.

2   When bit 0 of the toggle switches is toggled, the stepper motor moves one step. The direction of rotation is clockwise if bit 7 of the switches is 0 else it moves counterclockwise.

3   Move the stepper motor clockwise from its 12 o'clock position until it reaches this position again, then reverse the motor. This action repeats indefinitely so that the motor oscillates one revolution clockwise followed by one rotation anticlockwise.

4   Move the stepper motor two revolutions clockwise from its 12 o'clock position. The motor then reverses and completes one revolution. This action repeats indefinitely so that the motor rotates two revolutions clockwise followed by one revolution anticlockwise.

5   Move the linear device attached to the stepper motor to its extreme left position.

6   Move the linear device attached to the stepper motor to the position indicated by the slider on the digital potentiometer. Let three slider units correspond to one linear device unit.

7   Input a multi-digit number from the keypad and display it on the LCD. Use the F key on the keypad to indicate the end of the number, that is, use the F key as the 'Enter' key.

8   Input two numbers, in the range 0 to 99, from the keypad and display their sum on the LCD. Use the F key on the keypad to indicate the end of the number.

9   While any toggle switch is set to 1, display the date and time on the LCD in the format:

       dd:mm:yy hh:mm:ss.

10   While any toggle switch is set to 1, display the date and time on the LCD in the format:

       Sat 25 Dec 01 12:30:05.

11   Read characters from the ASCII keyboard and display them on the LCD. The Enter key terminates the input string.

Use vectored processor interrupt, mode 2.

12   The main loop of the program outputs a count continuously to port 0x00. When a keypad key is pressed, it generates an interrupt request signal; in response, the stepper motor steps clockwise the number of steps, 1 to 15, as indicated by the keypad key. The 0 key does nothing. The StrobeA, StrobeB and NMI inputs do nothing.

13   The main loop of the program outputs a count continuously to port 0x02. When a keypad key is pressed, it generates an interrupt request signal; in response, the stepper motor steps the number of steps, 1 to 15, as indicated by the keypad key. The 0 key reverses the direction of subsequent steps. The StrobeA, StrobeB and NMI inputs do nothing.

14   The main loop of the program outputs a count continuously to port 0x00. After every five inputs from StrobeA, the LCD displays '5 done'. The StrobeB and NMI inputs do nothing.

Use polled processor interrupt, mode 1.

15   The main loop of the program outputs a count continuously to port 0x00. When a keypad key is pressed, it generates an interrupt request signal; in response, the stepper motor steps clockwise the number of steps, 1 to 15, as indicated by the keypad key. The 0 key does nothing. The IR1, IR2, IR3 and NMI inputs do nothing.

16   The main loop of the program outputs a count continuously to port 0x00. When a keypad key is pressed, it generates an interrupt request signal; in response, the stepper motor steps clockwise the number of steps, 1 to 15, as indicated by the keypad key. The 0 key does nothing. The IR1 input steps the motor clockwise from its current position to its 12 o'clock position. Inputs IR2, IR3 and NMI do nothing.

Processor design.

17   An interrupt priority scheme using a daisy chain is described in this chapter. Suggest another way of daisy chaining input/output devices that achieves the same result.

DMA.

18   Why are the DMA controller Address, Data, and WR signals in Figure 10.17 shown as bidirectional?

11 More devices

We describe here some of the more complex devices that may be included in an embedded system. Many embedded systems use **counter** devices, **timer** devices, and **calendar** devices; these are introduced here. The counter device is incorporated into a model of a **conveyor belt** in a factory where the counter counts the number of objects that pass along the conveyor. A model of a **kiln** is described as an example of hardware that is controlled by an embedded computer control system. The specification of these devices is given in Appendix C. Finally, we see how a timer may be used to make it appear that a computer is performing a number of programs simultaneously, a technique called **multitasking**.

11.1 Counter device and its use in a conveyor belt

Consider an embedded system that is controlling a conveyor belt in a factory. One of its many tasks is to count objects as they pass under an object-detecting sensor on the conveyor belt. When a certain number of objects has been counted, the system does another task, perhaps controlling a machine that places the batch of objects into a box. How are we to implement the counting? We *could* arrange that every signal from the sensor generates an interrupt request to the G80; the interrupt service routine decrements a counter and, if the count is zero, calls the routine to place the objects in a box. However, if the time between successive objects is short and the computer has many tasks to do, it may not be able to keep up with the flow of objects. Alternatively, we can delegate the job of counting to a separate piece of hardware, a counter device. The most common use of this device is to generate an interrupt request to the G80 when a certain number of objects has been counted. The interrupt service routine does whatever is required when the required count has been reached.

The counter device, Figure 11.1, is essentially a down counter; each pulse on the Decrement input decrements the counter. (In the conveyor belt each object on the conveyor belt generates a Decrement signal as it passes under a sensor.) A count of zero is detected by the gate and, when the content of the counter is zero, the down counter is reloaded with the value stored in the Time Constant register, so making the counter ready to count the next batch. If the interrupt facility of the device has been enabled, a zero count causes the Interrupt Control Logic to assert the InterruptRequest signal, INT, to the G80.

The interrupt facility is enabled or disabled by writing a particular pattern of bits to the Control Register. The Interrupt Control Logic circuit detects the bit patterns 0x83 and 0x03 as the interrupt enable and interrupt disable signals respectively. Finally, note that the current count may be read at any time by the instruction in a, (CTR).

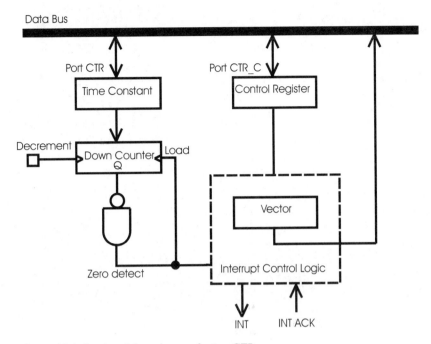

Figure 11.1 *Logic of the counter device CTR*

Program `Belt1.asm`, Figure 11.2, shows how the counter device may be used to step a motor at the end of a batch of four objects on the conveyor belt while the main program outputs a binary count to port 0.

11.2 Timer device

A common requirement of a computer is to perform a particular sequence of instructions at regular intervals of time. We can detect the end of an interval of time by using a variant of the counter device; in the timer device, the system clock is used to generate the Decrement input to the counter. However, since the system clock has a high frequency it is divided down so that the counter is actually decremented after a fixed number of system clock cycles. Thus the G80 timer device effectively counts system clock pulses and can be programmed to generate an interrupt request when a time interval, determined by the programmer, has expired.

Program `Timer1.asm`, Figure 11.3, shows how the timer device may be used to display a message on the LCD at intervals while the main program outputs a binary count to port 0.

```
;Belt1.asm
;Main loop - count to LEDs
;Interrupt on CTR==0 - msg to LCD
;Port addresses
CTR        = 0xE0
CTR_C      = 0xE1
LEDS       = 0x20
MOTOR      = 0xB0
BEEP       = 0x60
;
BATCH      = 4                      ;size of a batch
;
      ld sp, 0xFFFF
      jp start
;
;Service routine for NMI - beep
      .org 0x0066
      out (BEEP), a
      retn
;
      .org 0x0070
VTab:
      .dw ctrserv
      .dw StAserv
      .dw StBserv
;
start:
      ld a, BATCH
      out (CTR), a
      ;
      ld a, 0x00
      ld i, a          ;G80 high byte of VTab
      ;
      ld a, 0x70           ;CTR int vector
      out (CTR_C), a
      ;
      ld a, 0x72           ;StA vector
      out (1), a
      ld a, 0x74           ;StB vector
      out (3), a
;
      ld a, 0x83       ;enable CTR int
      out (CTR_C), a
      ;
      im 2             ;G80 int mode
      ei               ;enable G80 int
;
;Main
      xor a                ;clear A

mloop:
      out (0), a
      inc a
      jr mloop
;
;Service routine for interrupt from CTR
ctrserv:
      push af
      ld a, 1
      out (MOTOR), a
      nop
      nop
      xor a
      out (MOTOR), a
```

Figure 11.2 *Source code of program Belt1.asm*

```
            pop af
            ei
            reti
      ;
      ;Service routine for interrupt from StA and StB
      ;These simply beep.
      StAserv:
      StBserv:
            out (BEEP), a
            ei
            reti
```

Figure 11.2 *(cont.)*

```
;Timer1.asm
;Displays message on LCD when timer times out.
;Needs TIM, LCD
;
TIM        = 0x70
TIM_C      = 0x71
LCD        = 0xD0
;
      .seg CODE (abs)
      .org 0x0000
      jp start
      ;
      .org 0x0010
VTab:       ;Vector table
      .dw timserv
;
      .org 0x0100     ;Entry point
start:
      ld a, 0x06            ;Initialise TIM
      out (TIM), a  ;CTC TC
      ld a, VTab           ;Low byte of TIM vector...
      out (TIM_C), a ;... to TIM
      ld a, 0x83           ;TIM enb int
      out (TIM_C), a
      ;Init G80 int
      ld a, 0x00           ;All vectors at 00XX
      ld i, a
      ;clear LCD
      ld a , 0xFF
      out (LCD), a
      im 2
      ei
;
mloop:    ;main loop
      inc a
      out (0), a
      jp mloop
;
timserv:                      ;service routine - msg to LCD
      push af
      ;write msg to LCD
      ld hl, msg               ;pointer to start of msg
      ld b, msgend - msg  ;length of msg
      ld c, LCD
      otir
      pop af
      ei
      reti
msg:
      .db 0xA
      .ascii  /Timer interrupt!/
msgend:
```

Figure 11.3 *Source code of program Timer1.asm*

```
;Clock1.asm
;Display current time on LCD
;Repeats forever
;
;Port addresses
CLNDR = 0x10
LCD   = 0xD0
CRLF  = 0x0A
;
Loop:
    ld a, CRLF   ;newline to begin
    out (LCD), a
    in a,(CLNDR + 4)      ;hour, 0...23
    call byt2LCD
    ld a, ':
    out (LCD), a
    in a,(CLNDR + 5)      ;minute. 0...59
    call byt2LCD
    ld a, ':
    out (LCD), a
    in a,(CLNDR + 6)      ;second, 0...59
    call byt2LCD
    jp Loop


;Subroutine to display unsigned byte, 0...99, in reg A
;   on LCD as two decimal digits
;!!!No check that argument is 0...99.
CRLF = 0x0A
byt2LCD:
    push de      ;save current DE
    ;count tens in the number in reg A
    ;   by subtracting 10 until negative.
    ld d, 0      ;count of number of tens
tens:
    sub 10
    jp c, tensdun    ;if too many subtractions, jump
    ;
    inc d
    jr tens      ;subtract another 10
    ;
tensdun:    ;
    add 10       ;replace the 10
    ld e, a      ;save reg A
    ld a, d      ;the number of tens
                     ;!!! Could be > 9
    or 0x30      ;convert to ASCII character
    out (LCD), a     ;display the character
;
    ;whats left is units, so display it
    ld a, e      ;unsave reg A
    or 0x30      ;convert to ASCII character
    out (LCD), a     ;display the character
    pop de       ;restore original DE
    ret
```

Figure 11.4 *Source code of program Clock1.asm*

11.3 Calendar device

Many embedded controllers make use of the calendar date and time in order to determine a course of action. A typical calendar device will keep track of the current time from the year down to the second by using a series of counters. The calendar device in GDS appears to the user as a set of input ports at port addresses CLNDR to CLNDR + 6. Each of these ports contains data about the current time, including the day of the week. Program Clock1.asm, Figure 11.4, shows how the current time may be displayed on the LCD.

11.4 Pottery kiln

The pottery kiln is a typical plant that is controlled by an embedded computer. In general, a potter will wish to heat the clay at a given temperature and for a given time. To accommodate the needs of the potter, the kiln is equipped with a temperature sensor and an analogue to digital converter that produces a binary number output that is proportional to the current temperature. This data is placed into input port KTEMP. When the analogue to digital converter has generated a new temperature value, it automatically sets bit 7 of port KCTRL. This bit allows the embedded controlling computer to detect when the contents of port KTEMP have been updated. (This bit performs the same purpose as the DataReady bit in the keypad.) The kiln heater is switched on and off by writing to bit 0 of port KCTRL.

Program Kiln1.asm, Figure 11.5, shows how the kiln may be switched on and off using a toggle switch; the current temperature is plotted on a chart plotter.

```
;Kiln1.asm
;Hand control of kiln
;Switch 0 switches kiln heater on/off
;
KILNTEMP  = 0xF0
KILNCTRL  = 0xF1
CHART     = 0x30
SWS       = 0x90
;
;
        ld sp, 0xFFFF
loop:
        in a, (SWS)
        and 1                       ;strip off unused bits
        out (KILNCTRL), a
        call kilntemp       ;wait for new temp, then get it
        out (CHART), a      ;plot kiln temperature
        jr loop

;Subroutine to wait for a new temperature,
;     then get it into reg A
;Kiln hardware automatically converts temperature to
; a number at regular intervals.
kilntemp:                   ;Wait for new temperature
        in a, (KILNCTRL)
        bit 7, a            ;is there new data?
        jr Z, kilntemp      ;if no, jump
        ;
        in a, (KILNTEMP)            ;get new temperature
        ret
```

Figure 11.5 *Source code of program Kiln1.asm*

11.5 Multitasking*

When program `Timer1.asm` is running, we can regard it as appearing to be performing two tasks at the same time; one task outputs a binary count to port 0 while the second writes to the LCD. In practice we often want an embedded system to perform many tasks at the same time. For example, in a chemical plant, it might be required to control the temperature of some chemicals in a tank, regulate the flow of several fluids into the tank, measure the acidity of the chemicals, and display a mimic diagram of the state of the chemical process. All of these tasks need to be performed concurrently, that is, at the same time.

We *could* have a computer for each of the process control tasks, with each of them sending data about the process to another computer that displays the mimic diagram. Alternatively, we can arrange for one computer to perform all the tasks. Then, the basic idea is that the computer will run one task for a few milliseconds and then switch to run another task. Because the computer switches rapidly between the tasks, it will appear to be running all the tasks concurrently. Of course, with only one computer only one task can be running at any instant and this will be very obvious when we simulate multitasking because the simulator slows things down.

How do we program a single computer to run several tasks concurrently? The short answer is 'Not easily!' We must recognize that, in addition to the program code for each of the separate tasks, we also require code for a task that is capable of running the code for each of the tasks in turn. This additional task is known as a **scheduler** or **dispatcher**.

The problem now is how to construct the scheduler task. The scheduler task will run at regular intervals of time so we will use a timer device that generates interrupt requests at regular intervals of time. The interrupt service routine will be the scheduler task that stops the task currently being run and starts a new task. We have chosen a **round robin scheduling policy**; that is, each task will run in turn. Program `Sched.asm`, Figure 11.6, demonstrates how this can be done. This program runs three tasks in turn; each task is very simple. Task1, lines 200 to 205, simply writes '1' repeatedly to the LCD, Task2, lines 209 to 215, displays a binary count on the LEDs, and Task3, lines 219 to 221, generates a beep repeatedly.

If we are to switch from one task to another with the ability to resume the task at a later time, when a task switch occurs we must save the contents of the PC and all the CPU data registers for the current task. We save all this data in a region of memory called the Task Control Block, TCB. Each task has its own TCB. To resume a task, we must copy all the saved registers from the TCB back into the CPU registers and put the saved PC contents back into the PC. Thus, each time the scheduler runs, which is when the timer device generates an interrupt request, it must do two things. First, it must save the contents of the PC and the CPU data registers in the TCB for the task that has just been interrupted. Second, it must load the CPU data registers with the data stored in the TCB for the new task and load the PC with the saved resume address. Since the PC is loaded with the address at which the new task is to resume, the new task will run from where it was before it was interrupted.

To facilitate saving all the data registers, we shall add some registers, the Alternate Registers, to the design of the G80. These Alternate Registers are

```
                              1 ;Sched.asm - A simple scheduler
                              2 ;Runs a number of tasks in turn at
                              3 ;    fixed intervals of time.
                              4 ; - needs TIM
                              5 ;
                              6 ;Port addresses
0070                          7 TIM       = 0x70
0071                          8 TIM_C     = 0x71
0060                          9 BEEP      = 0x60
                             10 ;
000E                         11 TCBSIZE   = 14
                             12 ;
                             13     .seg CODE (abs)
0000 31 FF FF                14     ld sp, 0xFFFF
0003 C3`00`08                15     jp Start
                             16 ;
                             17 ;**********************************************
                             18 ;NMI service routine - beep
                             19     .org 0x0066
0066 D3 60                   20     out (BEEP), a
0068 ED 45                   21     retn
                             22 ;**********************************************
                             23 ;StrobeA and StrobeB interupts clear the LCD
006A                         24 StAserv:
006A                         25 StBserv:
006A F5                      26     push af
006B 3E FF                   27     ld a, 0xFF
006D D3 D0                   28     out (LCD), a
006F F1                      29     pop af
0070 FB                      30     ei
0071 ED 4D                   31     reti
                             32 ;**********************************************
                             33     .org 0x0100
0100                         34 VTab:              ;vector table
0100`1C`08                   35     .dw dispatch
0102`6A`00                   36     .dw StAserv    ;trivial dummy
0104`6A`00                   37     .dw StBserv    ;trivial dummy
                             38 ;**********************************************
                             39 ;Storage of data about the tasks.
0106                         40 NumTasks:
0106 04                      41     .db    4          ;Number of tasks plus 1
0107                         42 IDCurTask:
0107 01                      43     .db    1          ;Current task number,
                             44                  ; base 1
0108                         45 SPsave:            ;Here store the stack
0108                         46     .ds 2          ; pointer, SP
010A                         47 ResumeAddress:
010A                         48     .ds 2
                             49 ;**********************************************
                             50 ;Task control blocks.  Each is TCBSIZE bytes.
                             51 ;Each TCB is:
                             52 ; Task.Registers 12 bytes for registers,
                             53 ; Task.Address   2 bytes for resume address.
010C                         54 TCBs:
                             55 ;Task1
010C 00 00 00 00             56     .db    0,0,0,0,0,0,0,0,0,0,0,0
     00 00 00 00
     00 00 00 00
0118`00`10                   57     .dw    task1
```

Figure 11.6 *Source code of program Sched.asm (continued overleaf)*

```
                              58    ;
                              59  ;Task2
011A 00 00 00 00              60      .db     0,0,0,0,0,0,0,0,0,0,0,0
     00 00 00 00
     00 00 00 00
0126`00`20                    61      .dw     task2
                              62    ;
                              63  ;Task3
0128 00 00 00 00              64      .db     0,0,0,0,0,0,0,0,0,0,0,0
     00 00 00 00
     00 00 00 00
0134`00`30                    65      .dw     task3
                              66  ;Control blocks for additional tasks go here.
                              67  ;***********************************************
                              68      .org 0x0800
                              69  ;Initialise everything and start task1.
0800                          70  Start:
                              71  ;    Initialise port 0 & 3 interrupt vectors
                              72  ;      for StA and StB interrupts.
0800 3E`02                    73      ld a, VTab+2      ;NB low byte only
0802 D3 01                    74      out (1), a
0804 D3 03                    75      out (3),a
                              76  ;
                              77      ;Initialise TIM
0806 3E 08                    78      ld a, 8           ;Time Constant
0808 D3 70                    79      out (TIM), a
080A 3E`00                    80      ld a, VTab        ;Lo byte of TIM vector 0100
080C D3 71                    81      out (TIM_C), a
080E 3E 83                    82      ld a, 0x83        ;Enable TIM interrupt
0810 D3 71                    83      out (TIM_C), a
                              84  ;
                              85      ;Initialise G80 interrupt
0812 3E 01                    86      ld a, 0x01        ;Hi byte of Vector table
                              87                        ; at 0x0100
0814 ED 47                    88      ld i, a
0816 ED 5E                    89      im 2              ;Vectored interrupt mode
0818 FB                       90      ei                ;Enable G80 interrupt
0819 C3`00`10                 91      jp task1          ;Start off with task1
                              92  ;
                              93  ;***********************************************
                              94  ;On interrupt from TIM, run the dispatcher.
081C                          95  dispatch:
081C D3 60                    96      out (BEEP), a       ;So we can hear
                              97                          ; a task switch!
                              98  ;+++++++++++++++++++++++++++++++++++++++++++++++
                              99  ;Save all regs, including PC, in Task.Regs
                             100  ;+++++++++++++++++++++++++++++++++++++++++++++++
                             101      ;Save current regs on stack
                             102      ;NB. Address at which to resume the
                             103      ; current task is on top of stack, TOS.
                             104      ;
                             105      ;Save all data registers in alt regs.
081E 08                      106      ex af, af'
081F D9                      107      exx
0820 E1                      108      pop hl              ;Get Resume Address
0821 22`0A`01                109      ld (ResumeAddress), hl   ; and save it
0824 ED 73`08`01             110      ld (SPsave), sp     ;save current SP
0828 3A`07`01                111      ld a, (IDCurTask)   ;get task ID
                             112      ;Calculate address of TCB for the
                             113      ; task just stopped.
082B 47                      114      ld b, a
```

Figure 11.6 *(cont)*

```
082C 21`0C`01      115      ld hl, TCBs
082F 11 0E 00      116      ld de, TCBSIZE
0832               117  pp1:
0832 19            118      add hl, de
0833 10 FD         119      djnz pp1
                   120  ;Here HL holds address of the top end
                   121  ; of the TCB for the task just stopped.
0835 F9            122      ld sp, hl        ;Stack region now the TCB
0836 2A`0A`01      123      ld hl, (ResumeAddress)    ;Save...
0839 E5            124      push hl                   ; ... in TCB.
083A 08            125      ex af, af'       ;Save af,...
083B D9            126      exx              ; ...bc, de, hl
083C E5            127      push hl          ;  in alt regs.
083D F5            128      push af
083E C5            129      push bc
083F D5            130      push de
0840 DD E5         131      push ix
0842 FD E5         132      push iy
                   133  ;++++++++++++++++++++++++++++++++++++++++++++
                   134  ;Round-robin
                   135  ;Increment current task number cyclically,
                   136  ;    (1,2,3.1,2..)
                   137  ;++++++++++++++++++++++++++++++++++++++++++++
                   138  ;if( IDCurTask + 1 == NumTasks )
                   139  ;    IDCurTask = 1;
0844 3A`06`01      140      ld a, (NumTasks)     ;Number of tasks+1...
0847 47            141      ld b, a              ;...into reg B
0848 3A`07`01      142      ld a, (IDCurTask)    ;Get current task ID
084B 3C            143      inc a
084C B8            144      cp b
084D C2`52`08      145      jp nz, nomod
                   146      ;
0850 3E 01         147      ld a, 1
0852               148  nomod:
0852 32`07`01      149      ld (IDCurTask), a
                   150  ;++++++++++++++++++++++++++++++++++++++++++++
                   151  ;Load new Task.Registers to cpu
                   152  ;++++++++++++++++++++++++++++++++++++++++++++
                   153      ;Calculate address of top end of new TCB.
0855 47            154      ld b, a
0856 21`0C`01      155      ld hl, TCBs
0859 11 0E 00      156      ld de, TCBSIZE
085C               157  pp2:
085C 19            158      add hl, de
085D 10 FD         159      djnz pp2
                   160      ;Here HL holds address of top end of the
                   161      ; TCB of the new task.
085F 2B            162      dec hl
0860 56            163      ld d, (hl)   ;Get resume address
0861 2B            164      dec hl           ;... into de.
0862 5E            165      ld e, (hl)
0863 23            166      inc hl
0864 23            167      inc hl
0865 ED 7B`08`01   168      ld sp, (SPsave)  ;Restore original SP.
0869 D5            169      push de          ;Resume addrs to stack
086A ED 73`08`01   170      ld (SPsave), sp
                   171      ;
086E 11 F2 FF      172      ld de, -TCBSIZE
0871 19            173      add hl, de
0872 F9            174      ld sp, hl        ;Stack now the TCB
                   175      ;Now pop TCB into CPU registers.
```

Figure 11.6 *(cont)*

```
0873 FD E1        176        pop iy
0875 DD E1        177        pop ix
0877 D1           178        pop de
0878 C1           179        pop bc
0879 F1           180        pop af
087A E1           181        pop hl
                  182 ;++++++++++++++++++++++++++++++++++++++++++++
                  183 ;Invoke new Task
                  184 ;++++++++++++++++++++++++++++++++++++++++++++
087B ED 7B`08`01  185        ld sp, (SPsave)    ;Restore original SP
087F FB           186        ei                 ;Enable G80 int
0880 C9           187        ret                ;PC of new task
                  188                           ; from TOS to PC
                  189 ;********************************************
                  190 ;********************************************
                  191 ;Here are the tasks.
                  192 ;Note that the task dispatcher takes care of
                  193 ;  saving the cpu registers.
                  194 ;The tasks are located at specific addresses
                  195 ;  only so that we can see which task is
                  196 ;  running on the simulator by watching the PC.
                  197 ;********************************************
                  198
                  199        .org 0x1000
00D0              200 LCD    = 0xD0
1000              201 task1:     ;Display 1 on LCD
1000 3E 31        202        ld a, '1
1002              203 t1:
1002 D3 D0        204        out (LCD), a
1004 C3`02`10     205        jp t1
                  206 ;********************************************
                  207
                  208        .org 0x2000
0020              209 LEDS = 0x20
2000              210 task2:     ;Display count on LEDS
2000 3E FF        211        ld a, 255
2002              212 t2:
2002 D3 20        213        out (LEDS), a
2004 3C           214        inc a
2005 C3`02`20     215        jp t2
                  216 ;********************************************
                  217
                  218        .org 0x3000
3000              219 task3:     ;Beep continuously
3000 D3 60        220        out (BEEP),a
3002 C3`00`30     221        jp task3
                  222 ;********************************************
```

Figure 11.6 *(cont)*

effectively a duplicate set of the regular registers AF, BC, DE, and HL. The instruction `ex af,af'` exchanges the contents of the regular registers AF with the Alternate Registers AF′ and `exx` exchanges the contents of the regular registers BC, DE, and HL with their corresponding Alternate Registers.

In `Sched.asm`, the TCBs are stored at memory location TCBs , line 54. Each TCB has a size of 14 (line 11: `TCBSIZE = 14`) bytes. Thus the TCB for Task1 begins at memory location TCBs, that for Task2 begins at `TCBs + TCBSIZE`, and that for Task3 begins at `TCBs + 2*TCBSIZE`. The dispatcher actually calculates the *end* of the TCB for task number N from `TCBs + N*TCBSIZE`. This calculation occurs at lines 112 to 120 and lines 153 to 160.

In order to save the contents of the CPU registers in the TCB, the scheduler first saves the CPU data registers in the Alternate Registers in the G80, lines 106 and 107. The CPU data registers can now be used to calculate the high address end of the TCB for the current task, lines 112 to 120. The Stack Pointer is then set to this address, line 122, and the resume address of the current task pushed into the TCB, lines 123 and 124. The data registers that were earlier saved in the Alternate Registers are then pushed into the TCB, lines 125 to 132.

The task number is then incremented, lines 138 to 149, and the high address end of the TCB for the new task is calculated, lines 153 to 160. The resume address is in the 2 bytes just before the calculated address, it is extracted and pushed onto the stack, lines 162 to 170. The low address end of the TCB is calculated and loaded into the stack pointer, lines 172 to 174. The CPU registers are then loaded by popping the TCB, lines 176 to 181.

Finally, the new task is invoked by resetting the stack pointer to what it was just before the timer generated its interrupt request. The top of the stack contains the resume address for the new task (placed there at line 169), so that the `ret` instruction in line 187 pops the resume address into the PC and the new task runs.

11.6 Problems

Use the counter device.

1 Modify program `Belt1.asm` so that, at the end of each batch, it displays the batch number on the LCD in the format '(new line)Batch xx', where xx is the number of the batch.

2 As for Problem 1, but display the total number of objects in addition to the batch number.

Use the timer device.

3 Use the timer device in a program that writes a binary count to port 0x00 and, when the timer interrupt occurs, moves the stepper motor one step.

4 Use the timer device in a program that writes a binary count to port 0x03 and at regular intervals of time, displays the current state of port 0x03 on the two seven-segment displays as two decimal digits.

5 Devise a program that continually steps the stepper motor and, at regular intervals of time, shows the current linear traverse position as two decimal digits, 00 to 79, on the two seven-segment displays.

Use the calendar device.

6 In program `Clock1.asm`, the calendar hours, minutes, and seconds are read at times separated by the time that the G80 takes to display each number. Explain why this is not a good practice. Devise a program that reads all three numbers sequentially and then displays them.

7   Devise a program that continually reads the calendar device and beeps continuously after a time that has been entered by the user.

8   Devise a program that continually reads the calendar device and beeps continuously if the current time is between two times that have been entered by the user.

9   Devise a program that continually reads the calendar device and beeps for 10 seconds if the current time is one of a list of times that have been entered by the user.

Use the kiln plant.

10   Devise a program that switches the kiln heater off when its temperature is greater than 205°C and switches it on when its temperature is less than 195°C.

11   Devise a program that switches the kiln heater off when the temperature is less than a value Lower that is stored in a memory location, and off when its temperature is greater than Upper that is stored in a memory location.

12   To Problem 11, add an LCD that displays the following information:

> Upper temperature: XXXX
> Lower temperature: XXXX
> Current temperature: XXXX
> Heater ON/OFF

The display is to be updated every time the kiln updates its temperature port.

13   To Problem 11, add a keypad to allow the user to enter the required upper and lower temperatures.

14   Combine Problems 11, 12, and 13.

15   Devise a kiln control program that allows the user to:

> enter the required temperature,
> enter a time of day when the kiln will automatically switch on,
> enter a time of day when the kiln will automatically switch off,
> display useful information to the user.

The kiln controller will maintain a temperature 5°C either side of the required temperature. The temperature is also to be displayed on a chart recorder.

Use multitasking.

16   Change the tasks in program `Sched.asm` so that task1 steps a stepper motor, task2 displays the current position of the motor, and task3 displays the current time of day on the LCD.

12 Assembler and linker tools

The purpose of the assembler and linker tools is to automatically convert the statements, written in assembly language, into code that can be executed by the microprocessor. Without these tools, the programmer would find the task of building reliable programs a forbiddingly difficult task. There is an old saying that a good workman understands his tools; in this chapter we take a brief look at how the assembler and linker tools work.

A major factor in the process of creating reliable programs is that the programmer is able to identify each of the various functions of the program and write the code for each of the functions independently of the other functions. Thus the tools available to the programmer should accommodate the need to be able to write the code for a particular function as though it existed alone, and then to bring together, or **link**, all the functions of the program into the code for the complete program.

Figure 12.1 shows how the GDS program **development environment** accommodates the needs of a programmer who wishes to bring together three source code files in order to make an application program, BigProg. The programmer writes three source code files *.asm. She then converts each of the three source code files into three **relocatable files**, *.rel, by running the assembler tool three times, once for each source code file. She then uses the linker tool to link the three *.rel files into a single file, BigProg.ihx, which contains the executable code.

The process of generating executable code thus requires two steps: first, the assembly of all source files containing the various functions, second, the linking of the relocatable files to form executable code. (Even if the whole of the program is contained within just one source code file, the linking process is still required.)

12.1 How an assembler works

Assume that we are the designers of an assembler tool. We know, from Chapter 6, how to assemble source code manually so we shall base our simple design of the assembler tool along similar lines. When assembling a program manually, we made use of the table of all possible G80 instructions given in Appendix A. Thus, our assembler tool will contain a table containing the mnemonic for every G80 instruction together with the bytes of the machine code for the instruction. The basic design is that our assembler tool will read each line of the source code in turn, look up the mnemonic in the table, and write the required machine code to a file. Consider how our assembler will process the source code shown in Figure 12.2. The assembler directives in

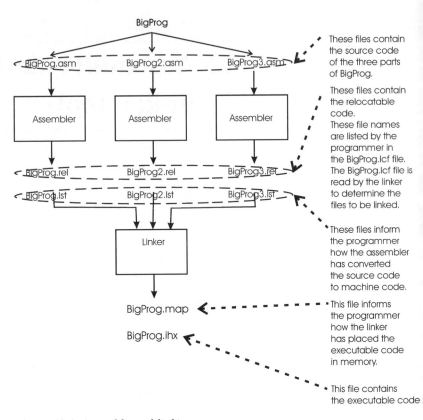

These files contain the source code of the three parts of BigProg.

These files contain the relocatable code.
These file names are listed by the programmer in the BigProg.lcf file. The BigProg.lcf file is read by the linker to determine the files to be linked.

These files inform the programmer how the assembler has converted the source code to machine code.

This file informs the programmer how the linker has placed the executable code in memory.

This file contains the executable code

Figure 12.1 *Assembly and linking processes*

```
1          .seg CODE (abs)
2          .org 0x2000
3          ld a, (fred)
4          ld b, a
5          ld a, (jane)
6          halt
7   fred:
8          .db 7
9   jane:
10         .db 4
```

Figure 12.2 *Sample source code*

lines 1 and 2 indicate that the code is to be assembled to begin in memory location 0x2000.

We immediately encounter a problem: when the instruction in line 3 is read, the assembler cannot form the binary code for the instruction. This is because it contains a reference to the memory location named `fred`, but the actual address value of `fred` is not known. Thus, in our design of the assembler tool, we adopt the strategy of first reading through all the lines in the source file to form the actual value of each of the symbols. We shall then read the source file a second time and use the actual values of the symbols to form the required code. Thus, we shall have a **two-pass** assembler.

12.1.1 First pass

To calculate the actual values of the symbolic addresses, we let the assembler program contain a variable called **LocationCounter**. When line 2 is read, the assembler will set LocationCounter to 0x2000. When line 3 is read, the assembler simply determines how many bytes there are in the instruction `ld a, (NN)`; it can do this by looking up the instruction in the instruction table stored within the assembler tool. Having determined that the instruction is 3 bytes long, the assembler adds 3 to the current value of

LocationCounter, making its value 0x2003. After reading and processing line 4, the assembler LocationCounter has the value 0x2004 since the ld b, a instruction is 1 byte long. Similarly, after line 5, LocationCounter has the value 0x2007, and after line 6, LocationCounter has the value 0x2008.

When the assembler reads line 7, it detects the symbol fred and saves fred and the current value of the LocationCounter (0x2008) in a table, the **Symbol Table**. After line 8, LocationCounter has the value 0x2009. When line 9 is read, the assembler detects the symbol jane and stores it together with its actual value, 0x2009, in the Symbol Table. After reading all the source code lines, the Symbol Table in the assembler has stored the information:

```
fred = 0x2008
jane = 0x2009
```

12.1.2 Second pass

During the second pass through the source code, the assembler again reads each line of the source code. This time it looks up the binary code for each of the instructions and, if the instruction contains a reference to a symbol, it looks up the actual value in the Symbol Table. For example, when line 3 is processed, the operation code for ld a, (NN) is looked up to get 0x3A. The symbol fred is then looked up in the Symbol Table to find 0x2008. So the machine code for this instruction is the 3 bytes 0x3A 0x08 0x20. Thus, after the second pass, the source code has been converted to machine code.

12.1.3 Practical assemblers

To make a more useful assembler tool, our basic design must be developed to accommodate the errors that programmers make when writing their source code. These mistakes may be simple typing errors or more serious errors such as defining a symbol more than once. When an error is detected, the assembler tool should produce messages to the programmer that help her to make the required corrections. The flowcharts, Figure 12.3, show the two passes of a simple assembler that informs the user of the most obvious programming errors.

The G80 assembler is actually somewhat more sophisticated than our simple design. One difference is that it does not contain a look-up table for every possible instruction; instead it makes use of the way the operation codes have been constructed by the microprocessor designers. For example, all the ld register, register operation codes take the form, in binary, 01 ddd sss where both ddd and sss are 3 bits that identify one of the eight registers, A, B,..L. Thus, once the assembler has detected an instruction of this type, it is able to **compute** the corresponding operation code rather than look it up in a table.

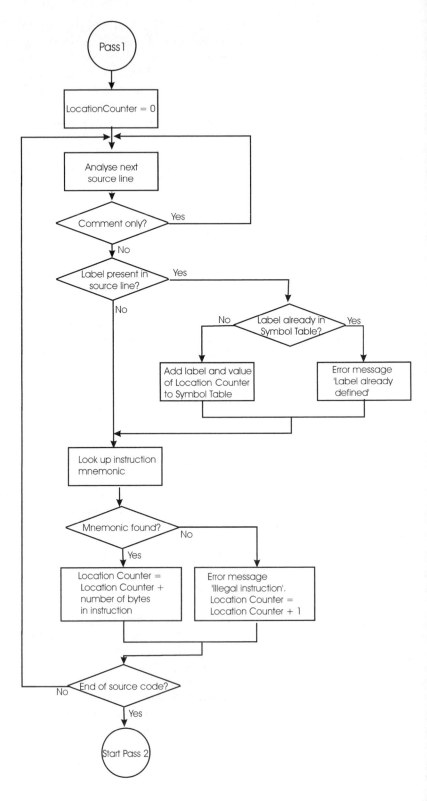

Figure 12.3(a) *First pass of a simple assembler*

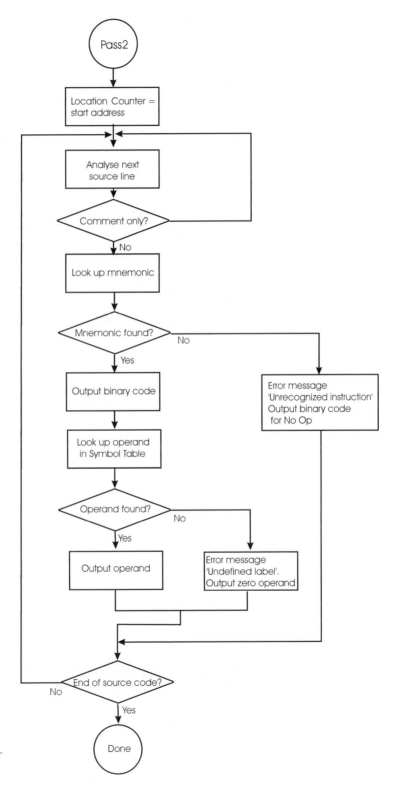

Figure 12.3(b) *Second pass of a simple assembler*

12.1.4 Relocatable segments

In an embedded system, the program code is stored in ROM and data is stored in RAM. It will assist the programmer if she can separate these different uses of the computer memory space within different program **segments** or **areas** within her program. Thus, the programmer may specify that all program instructions are placed in a segment called, say, CODE while all data storage is placed in a segment called, say, DATA. Each individual source code file may then contain one or both segments. (If the programmer does not specify a segment, the G80 assembler assumes that the code is in a relocatable segment.)

For example, Figure 12.4(a) shows three source code files. Source file `BigProg.asm` contains program instructions in segment CODE and the data to which these instructions refer are contained within segment DATA. File `BigProg.asm` contains only program instructions in segment CODE and `BigProg.asm` contains the two segments, CODE and DATA. The intention is to produce one file, which, when loaded into memory, appears as shown in Figure 12.4(b). Here it is assumed that the computer memory contains ROM at 0000 to 7FFF and RAM at 8000 to FFFF. Note that all the CODE segments, A, C, and D, are placed in ROM, while DATA segments B and E are placed in RAM. The assembler must therefore generate files that can be combined in this way. The combining is effected by the linker tool. We discuss the use of the G80 linker next.

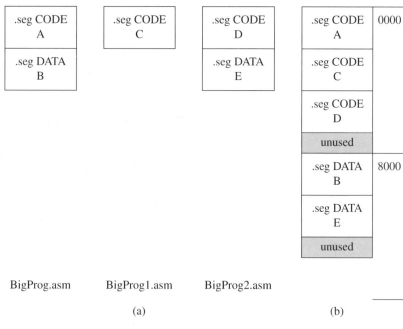

BigProg.asm   BigProg1.asm   BigProg2.asm

(a)   (b)

Figure 12.4 (a) *Three source files with segments;* (b) *use of memory*

12.2 Linker

The programmer's project is to produce the 0s and 1s that, when loaded into the memory of the microprocessor, will perform the required functions. In making the project the programmer will usually write the source code of the functions in separate source code files, `*.asm`. The assembler tool converts each of the source code files into a relocatable file, `*.rel`. The purpose of the linker tool is to join, or link, these relocatable files into a single file that can be loaded into the memory of the computer.

In the programs we have considered until now, all the code has been in one source file. Unless instructed otherwise, the linker tool locates the code at memory address 0000. But, given two or more source code files to link, where is the linker to locate the separate pieces of code? We see how this is handled in the following examples.

12.2.1 Link example 1 – single segment

In this example, the linker locates two pieces of code in sequential memory locations. We will write two source code files and place the code in a single relocatable segment. Both source code files are then assembled independently to produce two `*.rel` files. In producing the `*.rel` files, the assembler tool will assemble each of the `*.asm` files as though it begins at memory location 0000. The linker tool will then concatenate[1] the two `*.rel` files according to the order specified in the linker command file, `*.lcf`. That is, the linker tool will read the `*.lcf` file to obtain the name of a relocatable file, and locate that file immediately after the preceding one.

Both the source files in this example, `LinkExample1_FileA.asm` and `LinkExample1_FileB.asm`, contain the `.seg MYCODE (rel)` directive. This indicates that the code in both files is to be contained within a relocatable segment named MYCODE.

Here is the assembly of `LinkExample1_FileA.asm`:

```
                        1    ; LinkExample1_FileA.asm
                        2    .seg MYCODE (rel)
         0000 3E 02     3    ld a, 2
         0002 06 04     4    ld b, 4
         0004 0E 06     5    ld c, 6
```

Here is the assembly of `LinkExample1_FileB.asm`:

```
                        1    ;LinkExample1_FileB.asm
                        2    seg MYCODE (rel)
         0000 48        3    ld c, b
         0002 47        4    ld b, a
         0004 79        5    d a, c
```

Here is the linker command file, `LinkExample1_FileA.lcf`; this instructs the linker to concatenate the two sources in the order shown:

---

[1] Join end to end.

```
C:\G80UserProgs\LinkExample1_FileA.rel
C:\G80UserProgs\LinkExample1_FileB.rel
```

Type the two files LinkExample1_FileA.asm and LinkExample1_FileB.asm and assemble both of them independently. With LinkExample1_FileA displayed in GDS (LinkExample1_FileB.lcf is not used), edit LinkExample1_FileA.lcf to make it as shown above, then run the linker tool. Now run the simulator and click on the Disassembly tab[2]. This shows the code that has been produced by the linker: observe that it is as though the following single source file had been written:

```
0000 3E 02      ld a, 2
0002 06 04      ld b, 4
0004 0E 06      ld c, 6
0006 48         ld c, b
0007 47         ld b, a
0008 79         ld a, c
```

The code in LinkExample1_A.rel is 6 bytes long and has been located to memory locations 0000 to 0005 inclusive. The code in LinkExample1_B.rel is 3 bytes long and has been located to the next memory locations 0006 to 0008 inclusive.

12.2.2 Link example 2 – multiple segments

Usually a source file will refer to data stored in RAM. Let us assume that the computer stores the program code in ROM chips beginning at location 0000 and has RAM beginning at 8000. We will write the program instructions in a relocatable segment named CODE and place data in another relocatable segment named RAM. We shall then use the linker to locate segment CODE at memory address 0000 and segment RAM at memory location 8000.

Here is the assembly listing of LinkExample2_FileA.asm:

```
                    1    ;LinkExample2_FileA.asm
                    2              .seg CODE (rel)
0000 3A`01`00       3              ld a, (sue)
0003 2F             4              cpl
0004 3A`00`00       5              ld a, (fred)
                    6    ;
                    7              .seg RAM (rel)
0000                8    fred:     .ds 1
0001                9    sue:      .ds 1
```

---

[2] The G80 disassembler performs the opposite function to the assembler; that is, it converts the 0s and 1s stored in the G80 memory into instruction mnemonics. It does not produce symbolic addresses, instead it shows the absolute address.

Here is the assembly listing of `LinkExample2_FileB.asm`:

```
                    1    ;LinkExample2_FileB.asm
                    2            .seg CODE (rel)
0000 4F             3            ld c, a
0001 32`00`00       4            ld (yoko), a
                    5    ;
                    6            .seg RAM (rel)
0000                7    yoko:   .ds 1
```

Here is the linker command file, `LinkExample2_FileA.lcf`.

```
-b CODE = 0x0000
-b RAM = 0x8000
C:\G80UserProgs\LinkExample2_FileA.rel
C:\G80UserProgs\LinkExample2_FileB.rel
```

The first two lines specify the base addresses of the two segments. (The first line is not strictly necessary since if the base address of a segment is not specified, the linker uses the value 0000.) The programmer must maintain the linker command file manually; GDS helps by automatically writing the basis of the file when a source code file is first assembled.

Use the disassembly function in the simulator to check that the resulting linked code is as though the following, single, source file had been written:

```
0000 3A 01 80          ld a, (sue)
0003 2F                 cpl
0004 3A 00 80          ld a, (fred)
0007 4F                 ld c, a
0008 32 02 80          ld (yoko), a
                 ;
                        .org 0x8000
8000            fred:   .ds 1
8001            sue:    .ds 1
8002            yoko:   .ds 1
```

Observe that the code in segments having the same name has been concatenated. That is, the 4 bytes in the CODE segment of `LinkExample2_FileB` have been located immediately after the 7 bytes in the CODE segment of `LinkExample2_FileA`. In addition, the 1 byte in the RAM segment of `LinkExample2_FileB` has been located immediately after the 2 bytes in the RAM segment of `LinkExample2_FileA`.

12.2.3 Link example 3 – global variables

Often two or more source files will refer to the same data that is stored in RAM. In this example, memory location `fred` is referenced in two source files. In order to make `fred` known to both files, we declare it as a **global** variable, using the assembler directive, `.globl`.

Here is the assembly listing of `LinkExample3_FileA.asm`:

```
                        1    ; LinkExample3_FileA.asm
                        2            .seg CODE (rel)
     0000 3E 2A         3            ld a, 42
     0002 32`00`00      4            ld (fred), a
                        5    ;
                        6            .globl fred
                        7            .seg DATA (rel)
     0000               8    fred: .ds 1
```

Here is the assembly listing of `LinkExample3_FileB.asm`:

```
                        1    ;LinkExample3_FileB.asm
                        2            .globl fred
                        3            .seg CODE (rel)
     0000 AF            4            xor a
     0001 3A`00`00      5            ld a, (fred)
                        ;Note: Location fred is defined in
                                    FileA.asm
```

The linker command file, `LinkExample3_FileA.lcf`, is:

```
-b CODE = 0x0000
-b DATA = 0x8000
C:\G80UserProgs\LinkExample3_FileA.rel
C:\G80UserProgs\LinkExample3_FileB.rel
```

The resulting linked code is as though a single source file had been written:

```
                             .org 0x0000
     0000 3E 2A               ld a, 42
     0002 32 00 80            ld (fred), a
     0005 AF                  xor a
     0006 3A 00 80            ld a, (fred)
                         ;
                             .org 0x8000
     8000           fred:     .ds 1
```

12.3 Intel format file   The G80 linker tool combines the various relocatable files into a file named `*.ihx`. The format of this file conforms to a standard for 8-bit microprocessors defined by Intel Corp. In practice, this file is read by a device[3], which writes the 0s and 1s into a read-only memory chip. This chip is then plugged into the computer circuit board so placing the program code into the computer memory[4]. When you invoke the G80 simulator tool, the `*.ihx` file is automatically loaded into the G80 memory.

---

[3] Such devices are called PROM programmers.
[4] Some microcontroller chips combine a microprocessor and ROM (and RAM and ports) on a single chip. In this case, the PROM programming device writes the *.ihx file to the ROM in the microcontroller.

12.4 High-level languages

Writing programs in assembly language is an expensive process. The programmer must be familiar with the physical architecture of the microprocessor and with its instruction set. The programmer must then exercise her ingenuity to write code that uses efficient use of the microprocessor characteristics, and include many comments in order to make the intentions of the code clear. All this amounts to a considerable, and costly, effort. To reduce this effort, John Backus and his colleagues at IBM produced a programming language called FORTRAN (Formula Translator) in 1954 to 1957. This **high-level language** allows programs to be written without the need to understand the details of the microprocessor. The language is translated into assembly code using a **compiler** program. Many other high-level languages and their compilers followed, notably COBOL (Commercial and Business Orientated Language), BASIC (Beginners All-purpose Symbolic Instruction Code), Pascal, Ada, and C. For many years, C has been popular and manufacturers of modern day microprocessors often arrange for a C compiler to be available to produce code for their hardware products. Usually, these compilers run on a desktop PC. Because they run on one computer yet produce code for another microprocessor, they are called **cross-compilers**.

The aim of the programmer is to produce the binary code that will be executed by the microprocessor to produce the required outcome. When a high-level language is used, the programmer has to rely on the compiler to make best use of the architecture of the microprocessor. Thus, the compiler and the microprocessor should be regarded as a combination that implements the intentions of the programmer as described by the high-level language. Since the compiler produces relocatable files that are subsequently linked, a programmer may still choose to write some parts of her program in assembly language (or another high-level language) and link them with those produced by the compiler program. This is called **mixed-language programming**.

12.5 Problems

1   Change the order of the files specified in `LinkExample1_FileA.lcf` and run the linker. Using the disassembler tool in the simulator, observe that the order of the two pieces of code has been changed.

2   Change the base address of segment RAM in `LinkExample2_FileA.lcf` to `0x1000` and run the linker. Using the disassembler tool in the simulator, observe that the data is now located at 0x1000.

3   Modify the code for program `X5Sub.asm`, so that the main routine is in a file named `X5Main.asm` and the X5 subroutine is in a file named `X5.asm`. Build the complete program and test that it produces the correct result.

4   Modify the code for programs `String1.asm` and `CntChar.asm`, so that the main routine is in a file named `TestCntChar.asm` and the `CntChar` subroutine is in a file named `CntCharSub.asm`. Build the complete program and test that it produces the correct result.

13 The control unit

We have seen that the activity of the computer is determined by the instructions that are stored in memory as patterns of 0s and 1s. In this chapter, we consider two approaches to the design of the control unit within the G80 microprocessor. The first approach results in a **hard-wired controller**, while the second results in a **micro-programmed controller**. We begin by asking what the control unit must do.

13.1 Requirements of the control unit

In order to process a particular instruction the G80 must first fetch the instruction from memory and then execute that instruction. In the **fetch phase** the operation code at the memory location pointed to by the Program Counter is read and transferred into the Instruction Register, IR. This pattern of bits within the IR determines what the G80 does next, that is, it determines what the G80 activity is during the **execute phase**. During this phase, the control unit must generate the signals that control the logic circuits within the G80 in such a way as to perform the required instruction. We call these **micro-signals**. Thus, in order to execute the instruction ld a,(0x4926) the control unit must produce the micro-signals that load the Memory Address Register, MAR, with 0x4926 to address the required memory location, then assert MREQ and RD. After allowing time for the memory to place its data on the Data Bus, the control unit must assert the micro-signal that loads register A with the data currently on the Data Bus. This is followed by the fetch of the next instruction.

The computer contains registers which hold data to be processed, such as registers A and B, and other registers that contain information necessary to control the operation of the computer, such as the Program Counter, PC, and the Instruction Register, IR. The external memory may also be regarded as a collection of registers, some hold data and others hold instructions. All these registers are interconnected so that the contents of one can be transferred to another. Sometimes the data is passed through the Arithmetic and Logic Unit, ALU, in order to modify the data in some way. Essentially, an instruction is executed by transferring the contents of a register, or the output of the ALU, into another register.

13.2 Register transfers

We saw in an earlier chapter how data can be transferred between registers. Referring back to Figure 5.5 (page 74), to transfer the data in register R0 to R2, the required sequence of steps is:

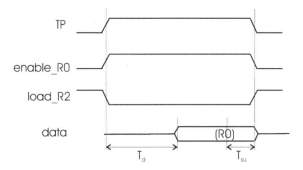

Figure 13.1 *Timing of register transfer*

    Step 1   enable_R0 = 1   load_R2 = 0
             ;*The data from R0 passes through the three-state buffers and*
    settles on the bus.
    Step 2   enable_R0 = 0   load_R2 = 1
             ;*Rising edge of load_R2 loads data into R2.*

Suppose we want this data transfer to take place when a signal, TP, is asserted. In Figure 13.1, enable_R0 = TP and load_R2 = /TP. When TP is first asserted, enable_R0 is also asserted and load_R2 is de-asserted. The data in R0 appears on the bus after a time, T_d, which is the sum of the times for the data to pass through the three-state buffers and for it to settle on the bus. When TP is de-asserted, load_R2 is asserted. The rising edge of load_R2 loads the data from the bus into R2. At the same time, enable_R0 is de-asserted so removing the data from the bus. Thus, the transfer of data is completed. In practice, TP must be asserted for a period that is greater than $T_d + T_{su}$,where T_{su} is the set-up time of the flip-flops in R2. The set-up time of a flip-flop is the period that the data must be present at the input of the flip-flop before the data is loaded into the flip-flop.

    This data transfer may be written concisely as

        TP: R2 ← (R0)[1]

which is read as 'During the period when TP is asserted, transfer the contents of register R0 to register R2.' We refer to such statements as **micro-operations**. These statements are written so that the expression to the right of the arrow evaluates to a data value and the expression to the left evaluates to a register or memory location. Thus 'R2' refers to register R2 while '(R0)' refers to the contents of register R2. Similarly, M[*adrs*] refers to the memory location having address *adrs* while (M[*adrs*]) refers to the contents of that memory location. These statements form part of a **register transfer language** that is useful in describing sequences of micro-operations. The control unit must cause different sequences of micro-operations that fetch and execute the different instructions. These micro-operations are performed at particular cycles of the system clock. Specific clock cycles may be identified

---

[1] Some people prefer to write TP: (R0) → R2.

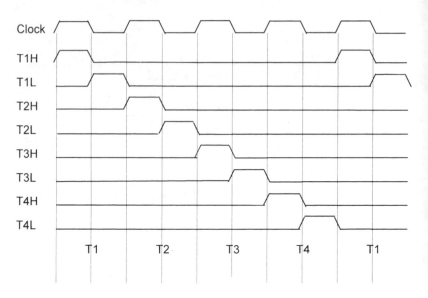

Figure 13.2 *Timing waveforms*

by a timing waveform generator circuit, Figure 13.2, which produces a sequence of timing pulses or **T-state** signals.

13.3 Instruction fetch

The first byte of an instruction is the operation code, which indicates what the instruction is to do. Thus, the first step is to read the operation code into the Instruction Register, IR, of the G80. This step is called the **instruction fetch**. The instruction fetch sequence transfers the contents of the memory location that is pointed to by the PC into the IR, that is, IR ← (M[PC]). This may be broken down into the micro-operation sequence:

Operation code Fetch micro-instruction, IR ← (M[PC])

```
T1H:   MAR ¨ (PC)      ;During T1H, put contents of PC
                        onto ABus.
T1L:   MREQ 5 1        ;During T1L, set MREQ.
       RD 5 1          ;During T1L, set RD.
T2H:   PC ¨ (PC) 1 1   ;During T2H, increment PC.
T2L:                   ;During T2L, do nothing
T3H:   IR ¨ (DBus)     ;During T3H, op code into IR.
       MREQ 5 0        ;During T3H, reset MREQ.
       RD 5 0          ;During T3H, reset RD.
T3L:                   ;Instruction decoder logic
                        settles.
```

This is an example of a **memory-read cycle**; it generates the external signals shown in the timing diagram, Figure 13.3. The signals MREQ and RD are shown as being asserted when low since this is common practice.

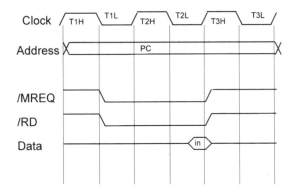

Figure 13.3 *Fetch cycle*

13.4 Examples of instruction execution

Following the op code fetch, the G80 executes the instruction indicated by the pattern of bits in IR. Since the op code fetch occurs during T-states T1 to T3, the execution of an instruction always begins at T-state T4. We consider some typical examples here.

13.4.1 ld d, c

This is a single byte instruction with op code 0x51. It performs the operation D ← (C). It may be executed during T-state T4 as follows:

      T1 to T3:   Op code Fetch
      J51 . T4H: D ← (C)
      J51 . T4L: Timing Generator reset.

The second line is read as: 'When the content of IR is 51 AND T-state T4H is asserted, transfer the contents of register C to register D.' The total time for the fetch and execution of this instruction is four clock cycles. The final micro-operation resets the Timing Generator so that the next T state will be T1H which begins the next op code Fetch cycle.

13.4.2 Add a, b

This is a single byte instruction with op code 0x80. It performs the operation A ← (B) + (A). It may be performed as follows:

      T1 to T3:   ;Op code Fetch cycle
      J80 . T4H: T ← (B)
                    ALU_mode = ADD   ;Set the mode control of the
                                          ALU to ADD
      J80 . T4L: A ← (ALU output)
             Timing Generator reset.

The fetch and execution of this instruction requires four clock cycles.

13.4.3 ld a, n

This is a 2-byte instruction: the number n is stored in the memory location following the op code 0x3E. After the op code fetch sequence, the PC is pointing to this location so the execution of this instruction is simply a memory-read cycle.

```
T1 to T3: ;Op code Fetch cycle
- - - Here is a memory read cycle A ← (M[PC]) - - -
J3E.T4H:  MAR ← (PC)          ;Contents of PC onto
Address Bus.
J3E.T4L:  MREQ = 1            ;Assert MREQ
          RD = 1              ;Assert RD
J3E.T5H:  PC ← (PC) + 1       ;Increment PC
                              ;Memory puts the contents
J3E.T5L:                      ;of addressed location onto
                              the Data Bus
J3E.T6H:  A ← (DBus)          ;Load A from Data Bus
          MREQ = 0            ;De-assert MREQ
          RD = 0              ;De-assert RD
J3E.T6L:  Timing Generator reset
```

The fetch and execution of this instruction requires six clock cycles.

13.4.4 Add a, (hl)

This is a single byte instruction with op code 0x86. It performs the operation $A \leftarrow (M[HL]) + (A)$ and thus requires a read of external memory. It may be performed as follows:

```
T1 to T3:    ;Op code Fetch cycle
- - - Here is a memory read cycle T ← (M[HL]) - - -
J86 . T4H:   MAR ← (HL)
J86 . T4L:   MREQ = 1
             RD = 1
J86 . T5H:   PC ← (PC) + 1
             ALU_mode = ADD     ;Set the mode control
                                of the ALU to ADD.
J86 . T5L:
J86 . T6H:   T ← (DBus)         ;Memory has by now
                                placed contents of
                                ;addressed location onto
                                Data Bus
             MREQ ← 0
             RD ← 0
- - - Here store the output of the ALU in A - - -
J86 . T6L:   A ← (ALU output)
             Timing Generator reset
```

The total time for the fetch and execution of this instruction is six clock cycles. Note that during periods T4, T5, and T6, the external signals will appear similar to Figure 13.3 since during these periods the G80 is performing a memory-read cycle.

13.4.5 ld (nn), a

This instruction performs the operation M[nn] ← (A) . The op code 0x32 is followed in the memory by the two bytes of *nn*. After transferring the op code into IR, the control unit transfers these bytes into the G80. To provide storage within the G80 for these two bytes, we add two 8-bit registers, called U and V, and also provide that these can be read as a single 16-bit register, UV.

```
T1 to T3:        Op code Fetch
- - - Here is a memory-read cycle V ¨ M[PC] - - -
J32 . T4H:       MAR ¨ (PC)
J32 . T4L:       MREQ 5 1
                 RD 5 1
J32 . T5H:       PC ¨ (PC) 1 1
J32 . T5L:
J32 . T6H:       V ¨ (DBus)      ;Data from memory now
                                  on Data Bus
                 MREQ 5 0
                 RD 5 0
- - - Here is a memory-read cycle U ¨ M[PC] - - -
J32 . T6L:       MAR ¨ (PC)
J32 . T7H:       MREQ 5 1
                 RD 5 1
J32 . T7L:       PC ¨ (PC) 1 1
J32 . T8H:
J32 . T8L:       U ¨ (DBus)      ;Data from memory now
                                  on Data Bus
                 MREQ 5 0
                 RD 5 0
- - - Here is a memory-write cycle M[UV] ¨ (A) - - -
J32 . T9H:       MAR ¨ (UV)      ;Required address onto
                                  Address Bus
J32 . T9L:       MREQ 5 1
                 DBus ¨ (A)      ;Data onto Data Bus
J32 . T10H:
J32 . T10L:      WR 5 1          ;Signal memory to write
                                  the data
J32 . T11H:
J32 . T11L:      WR 5 0
                 MREQ 5 0
                 Timing Generator reset
```

The execution of this instruction comprises two memory read cycles which read the argument *nn* from the memory, followed by a memory write cycle. The memory write cycle produces the external signals shown in Figure 13.4.

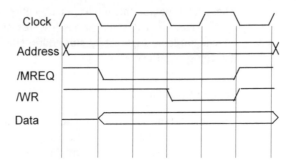

Figure 13.4 *Memory write cycle*

13.4.6 jp nn

This instruction performs the operation PC ← nn. The instruction is 3 bytes long; the first byte is the op code, while the second and third bytes contain the argument *nn*. The op code 0xC3 is read during the op code fetch cycle. Its execution requires that at the end of the execution phase, the 2 bytes following the op code are to be in the PC. We store these bytes temporarily in register UV, then copy UV to PC.

```
T1 to T3:      Op code Fetch
- - - Here is a memory read cycle V ¨ M[PC] - - -
JC3 . T4H:     MAR ¨ (PC)
JC3 . T4L:     MREQ 5 1
               RD 5 1
JC3 . T5H:     PC ¨ (PC) 1 1
JC3 . T5L:
JC3 . T6H:     V ¨ (DBus) ;Memory has placed its data
                           onto Data Bus
               MREQ 5 0
               RD 5 0
- - - Here is a memory read cycle U ¨ M[PC] - - -
JC3 . T6L:     MAR ¨ (PC)
JC3 . T7H:     MREQ 5 1
               RD 5 1
JC3 . T7L:     PC ¨ (PC) 1 1
JC3 . T8H:
JC3 . T8L:     U ¨ (DBus) ;Memory has placed its data
                           onto Data Bus
               MREQ 5 0
               RD 5 0
- - - Here is copy UV to PC - - -
JC3 . T9H:     PCL ¨ (V) - - - PCL is low byte of PC
JC3 . T9L:     PCH ¨ (U) - - - PCH is high byte of PC
               Timing Generator reset
```

The execution of this instruction comprises two memory read cycles, at the end of which UV contains the argument *nn*. During T-state T9, the contents of UV are copied to the PC, giving a total of nine clock cycles to fetch and execute this instruction.

13.4.7 jp z, nn

This instruction is similar to the `jp nn` instruction except that it performs the operation PC ← nn only if the Zero flag is set, otherwise it does nothing. The instruction is 3 bytes long; the first byte is the op code 0xCA, while the second and third bytes contain the argument *nn*. The argument *nn* is used only if the Zero flag is set. Thus, some micro-operations are conditional upon the state of the Z flag.

```
T1 to T3:           Op code Fetch
- - - Here is a memory read cycle V ¨ M[PC] - - -
Z . JCA . T4H:    MAR ¨ (PC)
Z . JCA . T4L:    MREQ 5 1
                  RD 5 1
Z . JCA . T5H:    PC ¨ (PC) 1 1
Z . JCA . T5L:
Z . JCA . T6H:    V ¨ (DBus)
                  MREQ 5 0
                  RD 5 0
- - - Here is a memory read cycle U ¨ M[PC] - - -
Z . JCA . T6L:    MAR ¨ (PC)
Z . JCA . T7H:    MREQ 5 1
                  RD 5 1
Z . JCA . T7L:    PC ¨ (PC) 1 1
Z . JCA . T8H:
Z . JCA . T8L:    U ¨ (DBus)
                  MREQ 5 0
                  RD 5 0
- - - Here is copy UV to PC - - -
Z . JCA . T9H:    PCL ¨ (V)     - - - PCL is low byte
                                      of PC
Z . JCA . T9L:    PCH ¨ (U)     - - - PCH is high byte
                                      of PC
                  Timing Generator reset
- - - If Z is not set, we simply increment the PC
      over the unused bytes - - -
/Z . JCA . T4H:   PC ¨ (PC) 1 1
/Z . JCA . T4L:   PC ¨ (PC) 1 1
/Z . JCA . T5H:   Timing Generator reset
```

The line `Z . JCA . T4H: MAR ¨ (PC)` is read as 'If the Z flag is set AND IR contains 0xCA AND T4H is asserted, copy the content of the PC to the MAR.'

Similarly, `/Z . JCA . T4H: PC ¨ (PC) 1 1` is read as 'If the Z flag is not set AND IR contains 0xCA AND T4H is asserted, increment the PC.'

The fetch and execution of this instruction takes nine clock cycles if the Zero flag is set, otherwise it takes five clock cycles.

13.5 Hardwired controller

From the previous section it is seen that each micro-operation is to occur when a logical term such as F . Jxx . Tyy becomes true, where F is the state of a flag, Jxx indicates that the Instruction Register holds xx, and Tyy indicates that the timing pulse generator is asserting T-state Tyy. This leads to the overall structure of the control unit shown in Figure 13.5.

The inputs to the block labelled Combinational Logic are from the decoder, the timing state generator, and the Status flags. Thus, each of the outputs from Combinational Logic depends on these inputs, as required by the micro-operation sequences derived in the previous section. This **hard-wired control unit** contains a considerable amount of combinational logic.

To determine the logic within the Combinational Logic block of Figure 13.5, a list of all micro-operations is made. Then, a particular micro-operation is chosen. The sequences of micro-operations for all instructions is searched to find the chosen micro-operation and to note the F . Jxx . Tyy condition, which determines when it is to be effected. For example, searching through the examples of micro-operation sequences given in section 13.4, it is seen that the micro-operation U ← (DBus) is required during J32.T8L, JC3.T8L, and Z.JCA.T8L. Thus we can write:

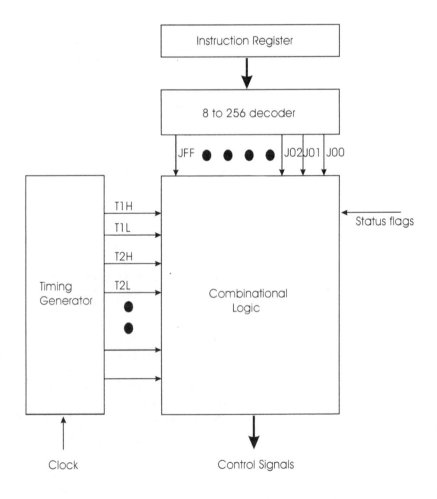

Figure 13.5 *Outline of hardwired controller*

$$U \leftarrow (DBus) = J32.T8L + JC3.T8L + Z.JCA.T8L$$

From this expression, the combinational logic circuit for the signal to load U from Dbus can be obtained.

Similarly, it is seen that the micro-operation $PC \leftarrow (PC) + 1$ is required during T2H, J3E.T5H, J86.T5H, J32.T5H, J32.T7L, JC3.T5H, JC3.T7L, Z.JCA.T5H, Z.JCA.T7L, /Z.JCA.T4H, and /Z.JCA.T4L. Thus we obtain:

$$PC \leftarrow (PC) + 1 =$$
$$T2H + J3E.T5H + J86.T5H + J32.T5H + J32.T7L$$
$$+ JC3.T5H + JC3.T7L + Z.JCA.T5H + Z.JCA.T7L$$
$$+ /Z.JCA.T4H + /Z.JCA.T4L$$

so giving the logic circuit for the signal to increment the PC.

Note that the Boolean expressions given above are derived from the example sequences in section 13.4 only. When the sequences for all the other instructions in the instruction set of G80 are taken into account, the expressions, and hence the logic circuit, becomes large.

13.6 More about the hardwired controller

The logic equations derived in the previous section can become long. The logic may be simplified by assigning the op codes to the instructions in such a way that each bit of the operation code carries information about the type of instruction. This may be done by forming similar instructions into groups. For example, one such group may be formed from instructions of the form ld r,s where r and s represent A, B, C, D, E, H, or L. In the G80, the op codes for these instructions have the binary format 01RRRSSS where:

Register	RRR, SSS
B	000
C	001
D	010
E	011
H	100
L	101
A	111

Thus, ld d,c has op code 01 010 001 or 0x51. When bit 7 of IR = = 0 AND bit 6 of IR = = 1, a transfer between two registers in the register file is indicated. Furthermore, bits 5, 4, 3 indicate the destination register and bits 2, 1, 0 indicate the source register. These bits may be connected directly to encoders that select the registers within the register file.

Similarly, many of the 8-bit arithmetical and logical instructions have op codes of the form 10 PPP RRR where RRR is as given above and PPP is:

Operation	PPP
add	000
adc	001
sub	010
sbc	011
and	100
xor	101
or	110
cp	111

Thus the op code for xor c is 10 101 001 or 0xA9.

The grouping of instructions allows the equations for the control signals to be written in terms involving just a few bits of IR instead of the fully decoded Jxx signals, so simplifying the logic considerably. However, the logic circuit of a hard-wired control unit is usually large and it can be expected to form a substantial proportion of the microprocessor circuitry.

13.7 Microprogrammed control

The microprogrammed control unit[2] is another form of control unit that is widely used in computing machines. We know that the control unit is required to output a different sequence of control signals in order to execute different instructions. The microprogrammed controller stores all these sequences in a ROM. To understand this idea, we begin by looking at how sequences may be generated using a ROM, called the control ROM, or CROM.

13.7.1 Sequence generator

The basic concept is illustrated in Figure 13.6. The CROM contains eight locations, each of which stores 4 bits, that is, it is an 8x4 ROM. The address input to the CROM is taken from a 3-bit counter that is incremented by a clock signal. Thus, each of the locations in the CROM is read out in sequence so generating a sequence of four output signals that are shown as waveforms. The sequence repeats since the counter overflows back to zero.

A development of this idea, Figure 13.7, is to replace the counter with a register, the CROM Address Register, and to store the next address within the CROM. The next address, as stored within the CROM, is loaded into the CROM Address Register on every clock pulse. The CROM now contains two fields, the Next Address field and the Control Signal field. Why do this?

---

[2] The microprogrammed control unit was described by M. V. Wilkes in the early 1950s.

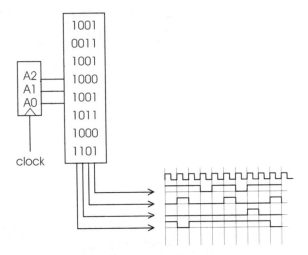

Figure 13.6 *ROM-based sequence generator*

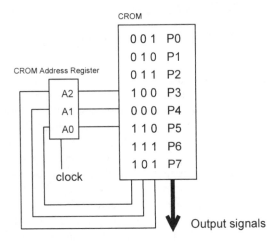

Figure 13.7 *CROM sequencer with Next Address field*

The answer is that the CROM can now generate any number of different sequences.

A close examination of the contents of the CROM shown in Figure 13.7 reveals that two different output signal sequences are stored in the CROM. One sequence begins at CROM location 0x00 while the other begins at CROM location 0x05. Thus, if the CROM Address Register, CAR, is initially 0x00, the output sequence will be:

P0, P1, P2, P3, P4, P0, P1, P2, ...

Alternatively, if the CAR is initially 0x05, the output sequence will be:

P5, P6, P7, P5, P6, P7, ...

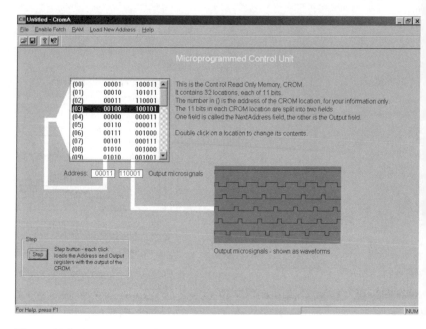

Figure 13.8 *Appearance of CromA.exe*

Run program `CROMA.exe`. The program appearance is shown in Figure 13.8. Click the Step button about a dozen times. Observe that the contents of the Control Signal field at CROM locations 0x00 to 0x04 are output cyclically. Now click on Load New Address in the menu and enter 00101 to load the CROM Address Register with 0x05. Click Step several times and observe that locations 0x05 to 0x07 are output cyclically. Now load the CROM Address Register with 01000 and click Step several times to observe that a sequence does not have to be stored in successive CROM locations.

To use the CROM sequence generator as a control unit in a computer, we need a sequence for every instruction in the instruction set of the computer. In practice this means that a large number of sequences will have to be stored in the CROM[3]. How is the appropriate sequence to be selected?

13.7.2 Selecting a sequence

The CROM sequence required to execute an instruction such as `ld a,(hl)` is determined by the operation code stored in the Instruction Register, IR, of the computer. An obvious possibility is to use the contents of the IR as the CROM address at which the control signal sequence for that instruction begins. That is, we load the CAR from the IR. We immediately recognize a problem: two operation codes may differ numerically by one. Thus 0x57 and 0x58 may both be legitimate operation codes in the computer so the sequence

---

[3] As noted in the discussion of the hardwired controller, the regularity within the operation codes of a computer helps to reduce the number of sequences required.

to execute the instruction with operation code 0x57 must occupy only one location in the CROM. There is a simple solution: CROM location 0x57 will contain a Next Address that refers to an unused location in the CROM where a sequence of any length may be placed. We will adopt this solution. The question now is how is the instruction fetch phase of the computer operation to be implemented?

For example, we will design our CROM contents so that the instruction fetch sequence occupies CROM locations 0x1E and 0x1F. This sequence of Control Signals is assumed to copy the next operation code from the RAM into the Instruction Register and into the CROM Address Register. At the end of each execution sequence, the Next Address field will be 0x1E so that the sequence to fetch the operation code of the next instruction will begin. This scheme is outlined in Figure 13.9. For simplicity, it is assumed that there are only four operation codes, 0x00 to 0x03.

Run program CROMA.exe and click on Enable Fetch in the menu. This loads the CROM with the data in Figure 13.9 and loads the CROM Address Register with 0x1E. Slowly click the Step button to see the Fetch sequence copy an operation code from RAM and then enter the appropriate Execute sequence. If you wish, you can change the program code in the RAM by clicking on RAM in the menu. (Remember that only 00 to 03 are valid op codes.)

CROM address	Next address	Control signals
00	04	First control signals to execute op code 0x00.
01	07	First control signals to execute op code 0x01.
02	1E	Only control signals to execute op code 0x02.
03	0B	First control signals to execute op code 0x03.
04	05	Second control signals to execute op code 0x00.
05	06	Third control signals to execute op code 0x00.
06	1E	Last control signals to execute op code 0x00.
07	08	Second control signals to execute op code 0x01.
08	09	Third control signals to execute op code 0x01.
09	0A	Fourth control signals to execute op code 0x01.
0A	1E	Last control signals to execute op code 0x01.
0B	0C	Second control signals to execute op code 0x03.
0C	1E	Last control signals to execute op code 0x03.
...	...	.
1E	1F	Control signal sequence to copy next operation code into IR and into the CAR. (Instruction Fetch)
1F	XX	

Figure 13.9 *CROM contents for microprogrammed controller*

13.7.3 Conditional branching

To accommodate conditional instructions, such as jp c, fred, two sequences must be generated by the control unit. Which one is actually followed must be made to depend on the state of the G80 status flags. One way of providing this facility is to add a Branch Address field and a Flags field to the CROM as shown in Figure 13.10. The Flags field is 3 bits, one for each of the C, S, and Z flags. The multiplexer[4] inputs come from the Next Address and Branch Address fields of the CROM. For instructions that do not depend on the state of a flag, the Flag field of the CROM contains three zeros so that Sel is always 0 and the multiplexer selects its input that comes from the Next Address field of the CROM. In these cases, the controller works as previously described.

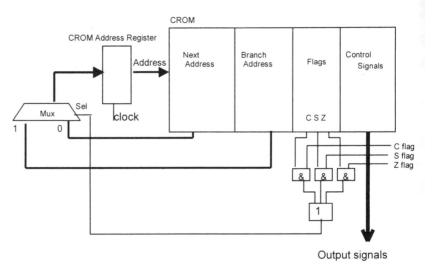

Figure 13.10 *Microprogrammed controller with Branching facility*

For an instruction that depends, say, on the Carry flag, the C bit of the Flag's field is made to be 1. Now, if the Carry flag is set, Sel is 1 and the multiplexer selects the Branch Address field, which is loaded into the CROM Address Register. However, if the Carry flag is not set, Sel is 0 and the multiplexer selects the Next Address field, which is loaded into the CROM Address Register. Thus, the Carry flag can determine which one of the two alternative sequences is generated by the controller. One of these sequences will generate the Control Signals for the case when the Carry flag is not set, while the other sequence generates the Control Signals for the case when the Carry flag is set.

The CROM in the control unit described here has one bit for each Control Signal and may be over a hundred bits wide. Many variations of the basic ideas discussed here are used in practice with the goal of providing a high

---

[4] The multiplexer behaves as a two-way switch, connecting one or other of its multi-bit inputs to its output. The position of the switch is determined by the control signal, Sel.

execution speed within an acceptable area of silicon. Note that the micro-programmed control unit effectively contains a program to generate the control signals. Indeed, each location is said to contain a **micro-instruction** and the CROM contains a **micro-program**. The technique is used in the design of some, but not all, modern microprocessors.

13.8 Problems

1   Derive a possible micro-operation sequence for the instruction jp z,nn. How does your sequence relate to the given sequence for jp z,nn?

2   Derive a possible micro-operation sequence for the instruction jp c,nn. How does your sequence relate to the given sequence for jp z,nn?

3   Derive a possible micro-operation sequence for the instruction jp nc,nn. How does your sequence relate to the given sequence for jp c,nn?

4   Derive a possible micro-operation sequence for the instruction push bc.

5   Derive a possible micro-operation sequence for the instruction pop bc.

The following problems require program CromA.exe.

6   Using the default data in the CROM, click Step about a dozen times. Sketch the micro-signal waveforms generated for the first 11 steps.

7   Determine the contents of the CROM that produce the sequence of output signals shown in Figure P13.1. Assume the sequence begins at CROM location 00 and that the sequence repeats forever. Use CromA.exe to check your answer.

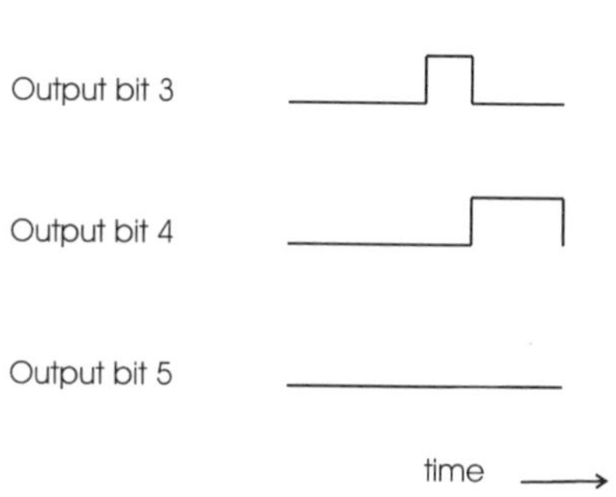

Figure P13.1

PART 3

Larger Computers

14 Larger computers

In this part of the book, we consider how we can extend the basic techniques used in the G80 to make a microprocessor capable of meeting the demands of a modern general-purpose personal computer as found on desks throughout the world. In this chapter, we take a brief look at the history of the development of general-purpose computers, look more closely at the organization of memory within a computer, introduce the locality of reference properties of a program, and identify the major components of an operating system.

14.1 General-purpose computers

The computers we have considered up to now are intended to run just one program. The program code is written into a ROM device and thus appears in the computer memory space, ready to run when the computer is powered up. A computer based on a microprocessor such as the G80 is quite adequate for very many embedded systems; indeed, similar computers were used for the control of early space exploration vehicles.

We can, of course, use a microprocessor to make a general-purpose computer, such as the ubiquitous Personal Computer or PC. Such computers effectively use the program stored in ROM to load a program called the **operating system**[1] from a hard disk. Computers based on microprocessors similar to the G80 were amongst the first to bring computers into popular use in the office, on the factory floor, and in the home. They used the Zilog Z80 or the Intel 8080/8085 with an operating system called CP/M and ran applications such as word processors and spreadsheets. The CP/M operating system required the user to type commands from the keyboard. Some of these commands were quite complex. Much of the present-day popularity of computers amongst home and office users is due to the ease of use provided by a **graphical user interface**, or GUI.

A GUI simplifies the manner by which the user interacts with the computer. It allows the user to give commands to the computer using a mouse click while pointing to a graphical object on the computer display. This supplements the earlier method of entering, from the keyboard, text-based commands to the computer. Along with this development was the ability of the computer to store several programs at the same time (even though there is not enough RAM in the computer to store all the program code) and allow the user to switch from one to the other using the GUI. These developments put great demands on the computer system and were possible only because of the development of larger and faster microprocessors.

In passing, we note that although these developments are very impressive, we should not lose sight of the fact that some computing applications are

---

[1] These operating systems are usually known as a Disk Operating System or DOS.

extremely demanding. For example, the identification and tracking of the thousands of man-made objects that orbit our planet require a huge amount of computation. The implementation of these very demanding applications often lies in building a computer whose hardware comprises hundreds of microprocessors, and has software that causes them to work together in an efficient manner. Many of the techniques used in current PCs were developed in historically significant, but expensive, computers and these techniques are now available to the computer user at a vastly reduced financial cost. We can reasonably expect still more improvements to PCs.

14.2 Memory bottleneck

The microprocessor, built on a single piece of silicon, is the fastest part of a computer system. Its operation is slowed whenever it makes a request for data that is stored outside it. Since most of these data requests by the microprocessor are to the RAM or **main memory**, the connection between the microprocessor and main memory has been likened to a bottleneck, through which data to and from the microprocessor is squeezed. The ideal main memory would be fast enough to allow the microprocessor to access it without introducing a delay. The ideal main memory would also be very large so that it could store many programs and their associated data. However, a large main memory constructed from very fast RAM devices is financially expensive. Before considering techniques for speeding up access to the main memory, we remind ourselves of the various types of memory that are available.

14.3 Storage within a computer

A general-purpose computer, such as popular personal computers, contains various storage devices, such as main memory, magnetic disks, and optical disks. Optical disks and floppy magnetic disks are used principally to store programs and data on a device that is external to the computer. These storage media are convenient for the retail distribution of programs and for the archiving of data in a way that is secure against a failure of the computer. Magnetic hard disks are used to store programs and data in a form that is ready to be accessed by the computer without the user having to insert an optical or floppy disk. The main memory store in a computer is made from

Storage medium	Size	Access speed	Cost per byte
Secondary storage (magnetic and optical disks)	Large to very large	Slow	Very low
Main memory (RAM)	Large	Fast	Moderate
Microprocessor registers	Small	Extremely fast	Extremely high

Figure 14.1 *Memory hierarchy*

a number of RAM devices[2], and is used to store code and data for programs that the computer is currently using. Finally, the microprocessor itself contains registers that store the data that is currently being processed.

We can regard these storage devices as being in a hierarchy, ordered according to how close they are to the microprocessor, Figure 14.1. In general, a high access speed implies small size and high cost per byte.

14.4 Data bus width and memory address space

We wish to speed up the microprocessor's access to a program's code and data, which are stored in main memory. We want to do this without simply using very fast, expensive, RAM devices to build the main memory. An obvious solution is to increase the width of the data bus from 8 bits to, say, 32 bits. This will allow 4 bytes to be accessed simultaneously[3]. We also want to provide a large memory space, so we shall let the address bus be 32 bits wide. This will provide a memory space of $2^{32} = 4$ gigabyte, or 4 GB, which is adequate for the foreseeable future. Note that this does not imply that our computer will actually contain 4 GB of memory; we simply make provision for a memory of that size. A 32-bit memory address requires that the Program Counter must also be 32 bits wide. Because programs often compute a memory address, we will make the width of all of the microprocessor registers 32 bits. Because of this last property, we call this machine a **32-bit machine**. Most new designs of large microprocessors in recent years have been 32-bit machines.

14.5 Addressing modes

14.5.1 New addressing modes

Although the microprocessor has 32-bit registers, not all the data we want to process requires 32 bits; we will still want to be able to access 8-bit and 16-bit data. Therefore, we will provide instructions that refer to 8-bit and 16-bit data, in addition to 32-bit data. For example, we might refer to the 32-bit accumulator register as register EAX and the lower 16 bits as AX. The 2 bytes that comprise AX may be called AH and AL, as shown in Figure 14.2. We provide instructions[4] such as:

```
mov eax, 0x12345678    ;load 32-bit register
mov ax, 0x1234         ;load 18-bit register
mov ah, 0x12           ;load 8-bit register
```

We will also improve on the G80 indexed addressing mode, exemplified by ld a, (ix + 42). This is inflexible since the displacement (here 42) has to be known at the time the program is written. We will provide a **based indexed**

---

[2] A large main memory is usually constructed from dynamic RAM devices, DRAM. These are cheaper than Static RAM, SRAM, devices, since they use one transistor per bit whereas SRAM devices use four or six transistors per bit. The major disadvantage of DRAM devices is that they have a longer access time than SRAM devices.

[3] The currently popular Intel Pentium has a 64-bit data bus, while some microprocessors designed for playing games have a 128-bit data bus.

	31	24	23	16	15	8	7	0
EAX								
AX								
AH								
AL								

Figure 14.2 *Partitions of the 32-bit accumulator register*

addressing mode that allows the displacement to be the contents of a micro-processor register so that the displacement can be computed when the program is running. For example, mov eax, [ebx + esi] will load register EAX with the contents of the memory location whose address is given by the sum of the contents of registers EBX and ESI.

For yet more flexibility, we will provide a **based indexed with displacement** addressing mode that combines the features of the indexed mode and the based indexed mode. For example, mov eax, [ebx + esi + 42] will load register EAX with the contents of the memory location whose address is given by the sum of the contents of registers EBX and ESI and the constant 42. This will give the programmer great flexibility when specifying the address of a memory location. Whatever the addressing mode, the address of an operand that is referred to in an instruction is called the **effective address**.

14.5.2 Importance of compiler

The great flexibility in specifying the effective address makes it difficult for an assembly code programmer to use the addressing modes efficiently. In practice, we expect most programs for a large computer to be written in a high-level language, such as C. A compiler program then translates the high-level language to assembly code making the best use of the various addressing modes. In general, the compiler program will take advantage of the architecture of the computer for which it produces executable code. In turn, the design of a modern computer will be influenced by the needs of a compiler. Thus, there is close interaction between the computer architecture and the needs of its compiler. Indeed, it may be claimed that a large computer should be evaluated only by considering how well the hardware of the computer performs the program code produced by its associated compiler.

14.6 Organization of 32-bit memory

The organization of the 32-bit wide memory is shown in Figure 14.3. Each row in the memory comprises 4 bytes. Since an entire row is selected at a

---

[4] To distinguish these new instructions from those of the G80, we use mov (move) instead of ld (load).

FFFFFFFF	FFFFFFFE	FFFFFFFD	FFFFFFFC
...	...	...	...
00000013	00000012	00000011	00000010
0000000F	0000000E	0000000D	0000000C
0000000B	0000000A	00000009	00000008
00000007	00000006	00000005	00000004
00000003	00000002	00000001	00000000
Byte3	**Byte2**	**Byte1**	**Byte0**
To Data Bus via buffers			

Figure 14.3 *32-bit memory organization. Each rectangle represents a single-byte location, whose address is shown within the rectangle*

time, the lower 2 bits of the address are not needed[5]. The Address Bus therefore need carry only A31-A2; A1 and A0 are both effectively zero so that the Address Bus carries the address of a 4-byte **word**[6]. For example, when the Address Bus carries 0x0000 0008, all the 4 bytes at 0x0000 0008, 0x0000 0009, 0x0000 000A, and 0x0000 000B are selected. To allow the microprocessor to access just one of the 4 bytes, we will provide four signals called ByteEnables, BE0-BE3, which are derived from A1 and A0 within the microprocessor. These signals can be used to enable the four buffers that connect the memory to the Data Bus. Thus, if the microprocessor is actually requesting the single byte at 00000009, the Address Bus will carry word address 0x0000 0008[7] and ByteEnable, BE1, will be asserted, so connecting just the required memory location to the Data Bus.

14.6.1 Memory interleaving

It is a property of programs that most of their instructions are fetched from consecutive memory locations. This suggests that access to the memory can be speeded up by selecting two, or more, consecutive memory words at the same time. We can decrease the *average* access time of the memory by organizing it such that words with odd word-addresses (A2 = = 1) are placed in a separate module, or bank, to those with even word-addresses (A2 = = 0), Figure 14.4[8]. The required memory address appears at the address inputs of both banks, and logic within the banks simultaneously selects two consecutive

---

[5] All binary numbers that are multiples of 4 end in 00.

[6] We use 'word' here to mean 4 bytes. However, this definition is not used universally; in some writing 'word' may refer to a different number of bytes.

[7] That is, 0x0000 0009 with the lower 2 bits forced to zero gives 0x0000 0008.

[8] This is called two-times interleaving. Some computers employ four- or eight-times memory interleaving, that, is they have four or eight banks.

Bank 1 – Odd word addresses			
FFFFFFFF	FFFFFFFE	FFFFFFFD	FFFFFFFC
...	...	...	...
0000001F	0000001E	0000001D	0000001C
00000017	00000016	00000015	00000014
0000000F	0000000E	0000000D	0000000C
00000007	00000006	00000005	00000004

Bank 0 – Even word addresses			
FFFFFFFB	FFFFFFFA	FFFFFFF9	FFFFFFF8
...	...	...	...
0000001B	0000001A	00000019	00000018
00000013	00000012	00000011	00000010
0000000B	0000000A	00000009	00000008
00000003	00000002	00000001	00000000

Figure 14.4 *Two-times memory interleaving. Each rectangle represents a single-byte storage location, whose address is shown within the rectangle*

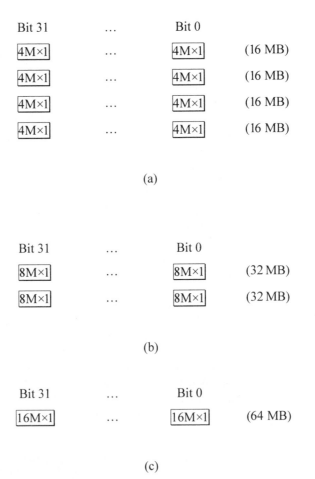

(a)

(b)

(c)

Figure 14.5 *64 MB memory: (a) made from 128 off 4M × 1 DRAM chips; (b) made from 64 off 8M × 1 DRAM chips; (c) made from 32 off 16M × 1 DRAM chips*

words. Assuming a memory read operation, both banks store their output in a data buffer. We now have two consecutive words from memory stored in the buffers. The microprocessor will read the currently addressed word and, as is likely, the microprocessor next accesses the following word, that word will be immediately available from the buffer. At the same time, the other memory bank can begin to access the following word in memory.

If we are designing a computer for a special purpose, say fingerprint recognition, we have the freedom to design the best memory system for that application. However, if we are designing a computer for home and office use, we have to provide for the different sizes of memory users require. For this type of computer, memory interleaving becomes less attractive as the size of DRAM chips becomes larger. Consider a memory size of 64 MB. In a computer that has a 32-bit data bus, the memory must be organized as 16M words. If the memory is made from $4M \times 1$ DRAM chips (4M locations, each of 1 bit), the organization is shown in Figure 14.5(a). This can be easily organized as either four banks of 16 MB or two banks of 32 MB. Using $8M \times 1$ chips, the organization is shown in Figure 14.5(b). This can only be organized as two banks of 32 MB. Finally, using $16M \times 1$ chips, the organization is shown in Figure 14.5(c). This cannot be organized into more than one bank. If we wish to allow a user to add more memory after the initial purchase of the computer, the variety of available DRAM chip sizes makes the logic that selects the appropriate bank complicated. For more than two banks, the operation of the logic begins to reduce the benefit gained by using multiple banks.

14.6.2 Burst cycle memory access

The internal organization of DRAM devices allows them to be designed so that consecutive locations may be accessed in a **burst**. This mode of operation provides that once the first location has been accessed, which takes two or more clock cycles, successive locations can be accessed on every clock cycle. We will assume our microprocessor can read and write main memory in bursts.

14.7 Instruction queue

A **queue** is a memory organized like a queue or waiting line at a supermarket. The first data stored in a queue is the first data that is removed from it; thus, a queue is a **first-in, first-out** store. It will be beneficial if we place the next few instructions from the main memory into a small, say 16-byte, queue made from fast flip-flops. Then, the microprocessor will be able to obtain the next instruction from the queue with minimal delay. This is a form of **instruction pre-fetching**. Of course, this scheme will work best when all the instructions in the queue will be executed in a sequence. If an instruction is a program branch, the remaining instructions in the queue will be invalid and the queue must be refilled with instructions beginning at the branch target address[9].

---

[9] The target address of a branch instruction is the address that will be loaded into the Program Counter if the branch is taken, that is, if the condition for the branch is true.

The immediate problem is: how are we to keep the queue filled? The G80 control unit causes an instruction fetch followed by the execution of that instruction. We now require that, while the microprocessor is executing an instruction, it is *at the same time* able to fetch another instruction from main memory and place it in the queue. Clearly, this implies that the functions of fetching an instruction and executing an instruction must be put into two separate units.

14.8 Locality of reference

Because instructions and data in a program are stored in sequential memory locations, when a program is being executed, it will usually refer to memory locations that have addresses that follow previous references. This is called the **spatial locality** property of a program. In addition, since programs usually contain loops, references to memory locations that have occurred in the recent past are likely to occur again in the near future. This is called the **temporal locality** property of a program. Thus, however large the program, over a short period the microprocessor spends most of its activity referring to a few, small clusters of instructions and data. These spatial and temporal properties of a program are referred to as the **locality of reference** properties of a program.

Both the temporal and locality properties of a program indicate that, over a short period, only a few clusters of instructions or data within a program need to be made available to the microprocessor. This suggests that these active clusters of main memory locations can be copied into a separate, high-speed memory so that the microprocessor can gain access to these clusters more rapidly. This separate memory is called a **cache**. We consider the design and use of cache memory in Chapter 15.

The same principle applies to what is stored in main memory and what is stored on the disk. Because of the locality of reference properties of a program, only those parts of the program that are currently being accessed by the microprocessor need actually be in main memory. When the microprocessor refers to a part of a program that is not in main memory, we can arrange that another part, currently in main memory, but no longer required, is replaced by the required new part. Thus, if a program is too big to fit into the available main memory, it will still be able to be run. Similarly, the currently needed parts of a number of different programs may be present in main memory, so allowing any of them to be run. The required techniques are called **memory management** and are considered in Chapter 16.

14.9 Operating systems

A general-purpose computer system will have, at least, a keyboard and visual display that allow the user to enter commands and view the results. After the computer is powered up, it must automatically run a program that waits for the user to enter a command, either via the graphical user interface or via the keyboard. Whatever the input method, the program that accepts and carries out the commands from the user is a part of the operating system, OS. The OS is complex and many of its functions cannot be carried out entirely in software without introducing unacceptable delays. Thus, large microprocessors, such as those used in personal computers, include special hardware that speed up the operation of the OS. A modern operating system is therefore a program that interacts closely with special hardware within the microprocessor.

We have seen, in program `Switch1.asm`, how a keyboard can be used to select a piece of code to be run. This program is an example of a very simple **command processor**, the part of the OS that interprets and executes the user's commands. Typically, when the user types the name of an application program, the command processor will locate the disk file that contains the application program, and load it into the main memory of the computer. The OS will then run the application and, when the application ends, the OS will return to wait for another user command. (Some operating systems allow several applications to be run at the same time.) Thus, the OS program is responsible for running the user's application programs. The term **task** or **process** is used to refer to an application program that the OS runs. That is, from the point of view of the OS, the user's application programs are tasks.

The OS will need to read and write to various peripheral devices such as the keyboard, the mouse, and the disk. Thus, the code to perform these actions forms a part of the OS, the **input/output control system**. Since these actions are often needed by the user's application program, they exist in the OS as subroutines that can be called by the application. Thus, the writer of the application does not need to be concerned about the details of devices such as the disk store; instead, the programmer simply makes a call to the appropriate subroutine in the OS. The collection of all the facilities of the OS that are available to a programmer is often called the **application program interface**, API.

14.9.1 Booting the operating system*

The OS is a large program that resides on a disk store and so is not in the main memory of the computer when it is powered up. How is it to be started? This problem has been likened to that of trying to lift yourself up by pulling on the laces or straps of your boots; hence, it is called the **bootstrap** problem. The solution is to have a relatively small **bootstrap program** stored in ROM so that when the computer is powered up, the bootstrap program runs and loads the OS from the disk store. However, there is a problem in doing this; the problem arises from the fact that the machines on which we want the OS to run may use hardware from a variety of manufacturers.

There would be no problem if the hardware of every computer that runs a particular OS were completely standardized, that is, all computers running the OS have exactly the same hardware. However, if the disk drive, or any other peripheral device, were to be replaced by one from another manufacturer, it would require a different sequence of logic control signals to make it work. How can we make the OS accommodate different hardware?

To allow an OS to work with devices from different manufacturers, the common solution is to separate the device-dependent parts of the OS by putting those parts of the code into various **device driver** files on the hard disk. These can be transferred from the hard disk into the main memory either when the OS starts running or when the OS requires access to that particular device.

We are still left with the problem of how to provide that the bootstrap program can run on computers with peripheral devices from different manufacturers. In particular, the bootstrap requires access to the keyboard, the visual display, and the hard disk. The common solution is to put the core of the driver code for these devices into the BIOS (**Basic Input Output System**), which is stored in one or more ROM devices. A basic keyboard driver is stored in the same BIOS ROM that stores the bootstrap code itself. This ROM is usually located on the motherboard of the computer hardware. The BIOS routines for the visual display and hard disk are stored in a ROM on the circuit cards of these devices. When the bootstrap program runs it detects the presence of the ROM for the visual display (it is located at a defined location in the memory space) and runs the code in the visual display BIOS. This initializes the display device so that it can be used to display information about what is happening during the boot process. (The first information displayed is often about the visual display itself.) Similarly, the bootstrap program will discover the presence of the BIOS ROM for the hard disk and execute the routines within it so that the hard disk can be accessed by later parts of the bootstrap program. From this point in the bootstrap program it can use the visual display and keyboard to communicate with the user and access the hard disk. The bootstrap program can now load the OS from the disk.

It is common for the boot program to perform some self-testing, such as checking that all the main memory chips are working. In order to do this test, data about the expected size of the main memory has to be available. This information is stored in a CMOS[10] RAM device that is automatically powered by a battery when the computer is switched off. This memory may also be used to store other information such as which disk drive holds the operating system files.

---

[10] CMOS or complementary metal oxide silicon is the name of an integrated circuit technology that uses very low power.

15 Cache memory

This chapter addresses the problem of how we can increase the speed of access to the main memory without simply making the main memory from RAM chips having a shorter access time. A main memory made from fast RAM chips would be financially expensive, take up a lot of board space, and consume a large amount of energy. We shall see that a very substantial increase in access speed can be achieved by the use of a relatively small, but fast, additional memory, called a cache.

15.1 Basic operation of cache

The locality of reference properties of a program, discussed in Chapter 14, suggests that, over short periods, only the currently active clusters of instruction code and data need to be made available to the microprocessor. We will therefore introduce another memory, a **cache memory**, into the computer. This will be made from fast, static RAM, and be large enough to hold the currently active clusters of instruction code and data that the microprocessor needs. The microprocessor will access the cache rather than main memory and so will have faster access to the code and data that it requests. To further improve the access time to the cache, we will either place the cache on the same chip as the microprocessor, or provide a separate, short-length, high-speed, bus between the microprocessor and the cache. This will avoid the delays inherent in driving signals on long bus wires.

The memory hierarchy in the computer is now as shown in Figure 15.1.

Assume that the cache has been partly filled by copying parts of main memory into it. When the microprocessor makes a request to read a particular word (instruction code, or data) in main memory, the address of the word appears both at main memory and at the cache. If the requested word is present in the cache, the cache hardware will assert a signal, *hit*. If *hit* is asserted, the required word will be read from the cache, otherwise, the word will be read from main memory. Because of the temporal locality of reference property, we expect that this word will be referenced again in the near future, so we will also store the word in the cache.

Consider the execution of the following loop written in G80 code and assuming we have a cache.

```
       ...form sum of 200 numbers at (hl)
       ld b, 200
       xor a
again: add a, (hl)
       inc hl
       djnz again
```

Microprocessor registers

Cache memory

Main memory

Secondary memory

Figure 15.1 *Memory hierarchy*

The last three instructions constitute the body of the loop, which is executed 200 times. Assuming the cache is initially empty, every instruction generates a cache miss[1], causing the instruction to be cached. At the end of the first pass through the loop, all the code for the loop body will be in the cache so that the next 199 passes will be executed at much higher speed.

We can improve this further by making use of the spatial locality of reference property of a program. Instead of caching only the code for the instruction, we will cache a block or **line**[2] of main memory locations that includes the requested instruction. We do this because the line is likely to contain the code for the next few instructions that the microprocessor will require in the immediate future. Thus, in the example above, it is likely that the whole of the loop body will be cached when the first instruction is read from main memory, so giving a further speed improvement.

Before looking at the engineering problems to be solved, we will calculate the potential speed improvement that can be expected. We calculate the average access time of memory as follows.

Let: t_S = average access time of memory system
 t_C = access time of cache
 t_M = access time of main memory

Define the *hit ratio*, h:

$$h = \frac{\text{number of times required word is in the cache}}{\text{total number of memory references}}$$

Then, a cache hit gives access in t_C while a cache miss gives access in $t_C + t_M$ since both the cache and main memory are accessed.

Thus $t_S = h.t_C + (1 - h).(t_C + t_M) = t_C + (1 - h).t_M$.
For example, say $t_C = 10$ns and $t_M = 50$ ns.
For a hit ratio, h = 0.80: $t_S = 10 + 0.2 \times 50 = 20$ ns

---

[1] A cache miss is indicated by the *hit* signal not being asserted.
[2] We will assume that the length of the line is 16 bytes.

That is, the average access time of memory system is reduced from 50 ns with no cache to 20 ns with the cache. If the hit ratio is 0.90, the average access time is 15 ns while a hit ratio of 0.98 gives an average access time of 11 ns. Clearly, the engineering challenge is to make the hit ratio as close to 1 as possible, since then the average access time approaches that of the cache memory.

Two major design problems arise: how is the data to be organized in the cache, and how is the computer to determine which parts of main memory to store in the cache? In addition, if the microprocessor writes to the cache, so modifying its contents, when should the main memory be updated?

15.2 Cache organization – direct mapping

We assume that the cache contains 8 KB of data. Now, since following a cache miss we will copy a line of 16 bytes from main memory into the cache, we let each cache storage location hold 16 bytes. Therefore, the cache contains $8K/16 = 512$ lines, each line containing 16 bytes, Figure 15.2.

Our computer has a 32-bit address bus and can access a 4-byte word over its 32-bit data bus. Only the upper 30 bits of an address appear on the address bus since main memory is organized into 4-byte words. How are we to use the upper 30 bits of the address from the microprocessor to select one of the 512 lines in the cache?

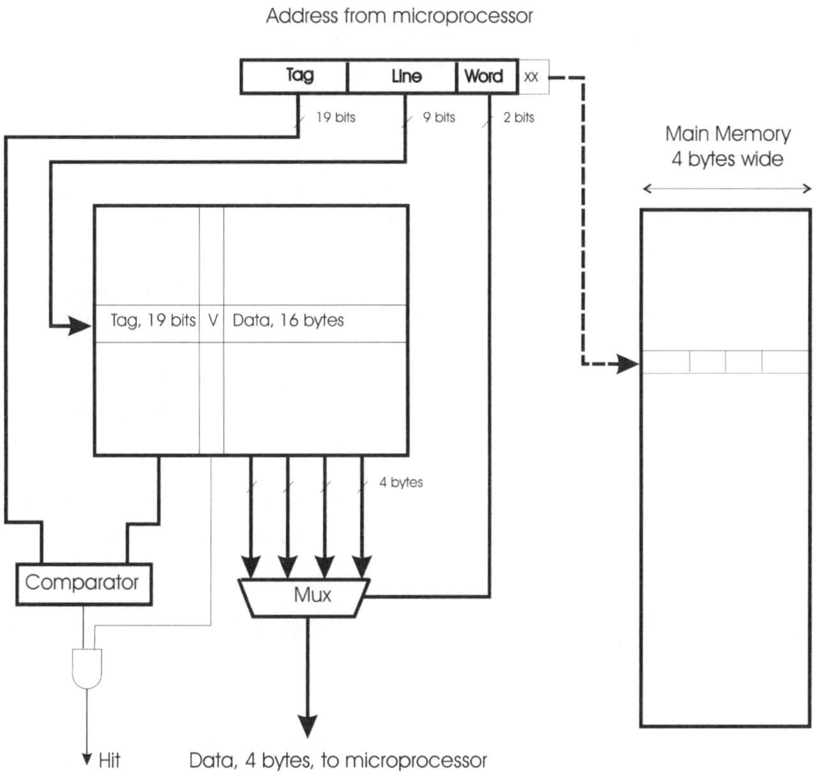

Figure 15.2 *Organization of directly mapped cache*

A31...............A13	A12...........A4	A3.A2
Tag	Line	Word
19 bits	9 bits	2 bits

Tag	Valid	Data
9 bits	1 bit	Four, 4-byte words = 16 bytes.

Figure 15.3 (a) *Partitions of address;* (b) *cache line entry*

A possible solution is to use **direct mapping** of the address from the microprocessor to a cache address. The 9 bits, A12 to A4, of the address from the microprocessor are used as the cache address, even though many different addresses from the microprocessor will map to the same cache line[3]. In order to overcome this ambiguity, we store the upper 19 bits of the address from the microprocessor in the cache in addition to the line of data. These bits are called the **tag**. Thus, the address from the microprocessor is regarded as comprising a 19-bit tag, a 9-bit line number, and a 2-bit **word selector**, A1 and A0 not being used, Figure 15.3(a).

When the microprocessor generates an address, the line number part of the address is used as the cache address. The content of the addressed line in the cache is read out and a hardware comparator compares the tag in the address from the microprocessor with the tag stored in the cache. If they are the same, the data in the cache is that requested by the microprocessor, and the *hit* signal is asserted. At the same time, the 2-bit word selector is input to a 4-way selector that selects the required 4-byte word from the 16 bytes stored in the cache line. Thus, the requested word is made available to the microprocessor. If *hit* is not asserted (a cache miss), the word is read from main memory, and the 16-byte aligned[4] memory line that contains the word is read in a single burst from main memory and stored in a cache line.

Following power-up or reset, the cache holds invalid data and then gradually fills with valid data. Thus, before the cache is full, some of its content will be invalid and must not be used. The obvious solution is to add a **valid bit** to each cache line. On power-up, the cache is **flushed** by setting all the valid bits to zero; when the line in the cache is filled with data, the valid bit for the line is set to one. This bit is ANDed with the output of the comparator thereby causing the *hit* signal to be de-asserted if the cache line is invalid. Each cache location then contains the entry shown in Figure 15.3(b).

---

[3] For example, all microprocessor addresses xxxx xxxx xxxx xxxx xxx1 1111 1111 00•• will map to cache line 1 1111 1111.
[4] A 16-byte aligned memory block begins at location xxxxxxx0 and ends at xxxxxxxF.

15.2.1 Memory write operations

When the microprocessor performs a memory write operation, and the word is not in the cache, the new data is simply written into main memory. However, when the word is in the cache, both the word in main memory and the cache must be written in order to keep them the same. The question is: when is the main memory to be written? The simplest answer is to write to both the cache and main memory at the same time. This is called a **write-through** policy. The main memory then always contains the same data as the cache. This is important if there are any other devices in the computer that also access main memory[5]. We can overcome the slowing down due to the main memory write operation by providing that subsequent cache reads proceed concurrently with the write to main memory. Since more than 70% of memory references are read operations, it is likely that the cache can continue to be read while the write to main memory proceeds.

An alternative policy, called **write-back** or **copy-back**, is to write the new data to the cache only. At the same time, a flag in the cache line is set to indicate that the line has been modified. Immediately before the cache location is replaced with new words from main memory, if the flag is set, the line will be copied back into main memory. Of course, if the flag is not set, this copying is unnecessary.

15.2.2 How many words should be stored in a cache line?

In the previous discussion, we assumed that each cache line stores four 4-byte words. But what is the 'best' number of words to store in a cache line? In the following discussion, we assume a fixed cache data size. The cache data size is the product of the number of locations and the number of words stored in each line. Thus, more words per line imply fewer locations in the cache and, conversely, fewer words per line imply more locations in the cache. We approach this problem by considering very small and very large line sizes.

If each cache line holds only one word, there will be a large number of locations in the cache and it will exploit temporal locality to the full because the cache holds the maximum number of recently used words. However, there is little or no exploitation of spatial locality since consecutive words in main memory are not stored in the line.

On the other hand, if each cache line holds very many words, there will be a small number of locations in the cache and it exploits spatial locality more fully, because each line will hold instructions that are likely to be used in the near future. However, exploitation of temporal locality is reduced because there are fewer lines in the cache. There is also a decreasing likelihood that the copied words will actually be used. This arises because, if the line contains instruction code, it may include a branch instruction and the remaining code in the line becomes irrelevant before all of it is used.

The 'best' line size is somewhere between one word and 'very many'

---

[5] For example, some input and output is performed by direct memory access, DMA.

words. Experimental investigations indicate that the cache hit ratio increases as the line size increases from one to a 'few' words, but then decreases for larger line sizes. Our chosen line size of 16 bytes is reasonable.

15.2.3 Critique

The direct mapping of the address from the microprocessor to a cache address is simple, which implies that it can be implemented at low cost in high-speed hardware. It has been used in many commercial computers. However, consider two frequently occurring addresses from the microprocessor both of which map to the same cache location. For example, 0000 0000 0000 0000 0001 0000 0000 00•• and 0000 0000 1111 0000 0001 0000 0000 00•• both map to cache line 256. The cache line will be replaced every time one of these addresses occurs resulting in a dramatic drop in the hit ratio. We *could* reduce the probability of these repeated collisions by making the cache larger; however, we will seek out other ways of organizing a cache.

15.3 Cache organization – set-associative mapping

In the directly mapped cache organization, two frequently occurring addresses, both of which map to the same cache line, cause the hit rate to fall. A common, and simple, solution is to place a number of directly mapped caches side by side. Figure 15.4 shows this organization for two directly

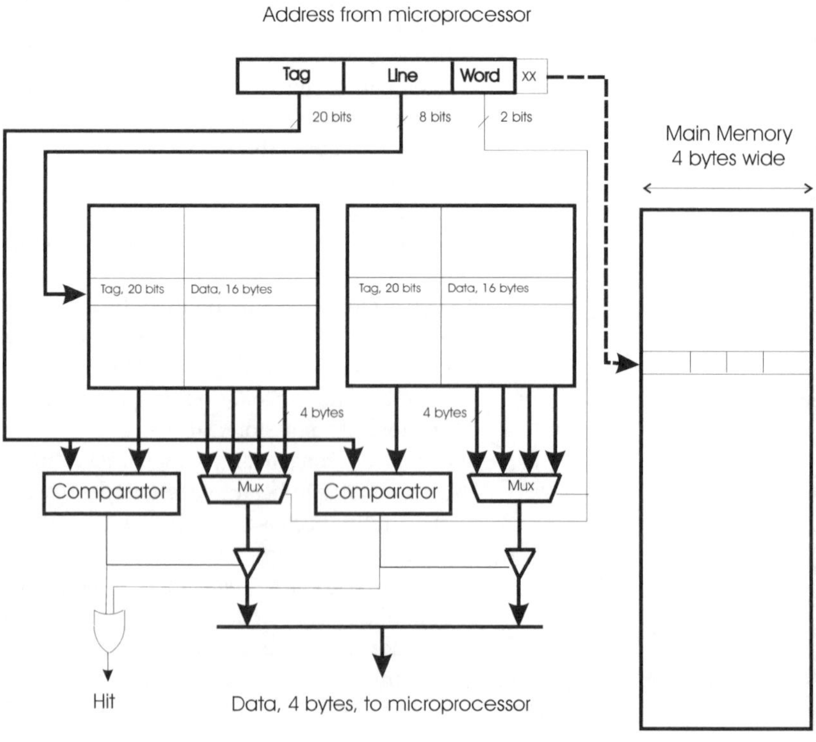

Figure 15.4 *Organization of two-way set-associative cache*

A31...............A11	A10...........A4	A3.A2
Tag	Set	Word
21 bits	7 bits	2 bits

Figure 15.5 *Partitions of address*

mapped caches side by side. (The Valid bits have been omitted for clarity.) As before, we assume that a line of data comprises 16 bytes, but now two lines of data are stored in each cache location. The two lines in each cache location are collectively called a **set**. Now, when two addresses from the microcomputer map to the same cache set, both lines of data can be stored in the set. Of course, there will still be a drop in hit ratio if more than two frequently occurring addresses from the microcomputer map to the same cache set; the solution is to increase the number of lines in each set to, say, four, giving a four-way set.

Assume a four-way set, that is, each location in the cache stores four lines of data, and each line contains 16 bytes. Then, for a total cache data size of 8 KB, there will be 128 locations, since 128 locations × 4 lines/location × 16 bytes/line = 8 KB. The address of one of 128 locations in the cache will be obtained from the 7 bits, A10 to A4, in the address from the microprocessor. Thus, the address from the microprocessor is regarded as comprising a 21-bit tag, a 7-bit line number, and a 2-bit word selector, A1 and A0 not being used, Figure 15.5.

The operation of this cache organization is the same as for the directly mapped cache except that there are now four *hit* signals. Not more than one of these will be asserted and so can be used to determine which of the four lines in the set contains the required data.

15.3.1 Line replacement

When a requested word is not in the cache, a new line of data is copied from main memory into the cache. Assuming a four-way set, bits A10 to A4 of the address from the microprocessor indicate the cache location where the new line is to be stored, but which of the four lines in the set stored at that location is to be replaced? This decision must be made entirely by hardware because software will be much too slow. Clearly, if the Valid bit in a line indicates that the line is not in use, that line is the one to be replaced. However, when the Valid bits indicate that all four of the lines are in use, a policy for the replacement of a line is needed.

The simplest policy is the **random replacement policy**; a line within the selected set is chosen at random. Since we need a random number between 0 and 3, the policy can be implemented by having a single 2-bit counter that is incremented whenever a particular operation occurs. The current count is used to select the line within the set. This is simple to implement and surprisingly effective. However, we seek a more rational policy.

A rational approach suggests that the least recently used (accessed) line is the least likely to be needed in the near future. This policy is the **least** recently used policy, LRU, and, in one form or another, is in wide use. A strict method for this policy is to have a counter for each line, four counters in our four-way set cache. When a line is referenced, its counter is set to zero while the other three counters are incremented. Each line count thus indicates the age of the line since it was last referenced; the line with the highest count is the oldest and is the one to be replaced. This is expensive to implement in hardware, so we look for an approximation to the LRU policy that is simpler to implement.

Consider a two-way set-associative cache. We can store a single bit, B, in the set to indicate which line was last used. Call the two lines in the set L0 and L1. Then, when L0 is accessed, bit B is set to 1, else it is set to 0. The bit thus indicates which line was most/least recently accessed. This scheme can be expanded to cope with four-way sets by dividing the four lines into three pairs[6]. Let there be three LRU bits, B0, B1, and B2. These are all set to 0 when the cache is flushed, and are updated on every cache hit or replacement. Call the four lines in the set, L0, L1, L2, and L3. Divide these four lines into two pairs of lines, pair L01 comprising lines L0 and L1, and pair L23 comprising lines L2 and L3. Let bit B0 indicate whether pair L01 or L23 was last accessed. That is, if either L0 or L1 is accessed, B0 is set to 1, while if either L2 or L3 is accessed, B0 is set to 0. Let bit B1 indicate which line in pair L01 is accessed. That is, if L0 is accessed, B1 is set to 1, else B1 is set to 0. Similarly, bit B2 indicates which line in pair L23 is accessed. That is, if L2 is accessed, B2 is set to 1, else B2 is set to 0.

When all lines in a set are in use (all Valid bits are 1), the replacement mechanism works as follows. If $B0 == 0$, a line in pair L01 is to be replaced, else the line is in L23. If the line is in pair L01 and $B1 == 0$, L0 is to be replaced, else L1 is to be replaced. If the line is in pair L23 and $B2 == 0$, L2 is to be replaced, else L3 is to be replaced.

15.4 Cache organization – fully associative mapping

This method of cache organization uses a very simple idea: we simply store the address from the microprocessor in the cache along with its associated data. Assume, as before, that the microprocessor produces a 32-bit address and that each cache location stores a 16-byte line of data. Then, the address from the microprocessor is regarded as comprising a 28-bit tag, and a 2-bit word selector, A1 and A0 not being used, Figure 15.6(a). The content of each cache location is shown in Figure 15.6(b).

When the microprocessor requests a memory address, we see if the required data is in the cache by comparing all the tags stored in the cache with the upper 28 bits of the address from the microprocessor. If there is a match, we have a cache hit and the data in the cache may be accessed. However, the comparison of all the tags stored in the cache with the requested main memory address would be unacceptably slow unless done by hardware. This requires a special form of memory called an **associative memory** or **content addressable memory,** CAM, Figure 15.7. Each cache location has a comparator circuit attached to it. The upper 28 bits of the address from the microprocessor are presented to the CAM and all the comparators in CAM

---

6 This is the replacement policy used in the Intel 80486 internal cache.

A31...............A4	A3.A2
Tag	Word
28 bits	2 bits

Valid	Tag	Data
1 bit	28 bits	16 bytes

Figure 15.6 (a) *Partitions of address;* (b) *cache entry*

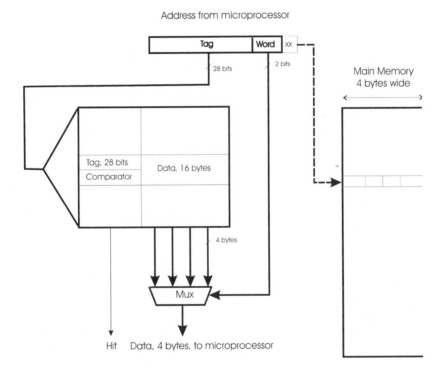

Figure 15.7 *Content-addressable memory*

simultaneously compare these 28 bits with the tags stored in the CAM. Where there is a match, the *hit* signal is asserted and the data in the cache location is output from the CAM.

This form of cache is very flexible since any address from the micro-processor can be stored anywhere in the cache. Thus, there is a wide choice of which line in the cache to replace when there is a cache miss. However, it is not always practicable to take advantage of this freedom because complex replacement policies are expensive to implement. Clearly, associative memory is very expensive in terms of transistors per location, because of the comparator circuit for each location. For this reason, this form of cache organization is currently used only for the small caches that are used in other parts of the microprocessor.

15.5 Problems

1   Assume that the financial cost of a cache byte is 100 times that of a main memory byte, that the main memory contains 128 MB, and the cache contains 8 KB. Calculate the average financial cost of each byte in units of the cost of a main memory byte.

2   Determine the average read time of a memory system using a cache, given that the average access time of main memory is 10 ns, the cache access time is 2 ns, and the hit ratio is 0.9.

3   A computer employs a 32-bit address space, a 32-bit data bus, and a cache that holds 4 KB of data.

Determine the number of bits in the tag, line, and byte fields of the address from the microprocessor, assuming the following organizations:

(a) Direct mapping with a line size of 8 bytes.
(b) Direct mapping with a line size of 16 bytes.

4   A computer employs a 32-bit address and a cache of 4 KB.

Determine the number of bits in the tag, set, and byte fields of the address from the microprocessor, assuming the following organizations:

(a) Two-way set-associative mapping with a line size of 4 bytes.
(b) Four-way set-associative mapping with a line size of 4 bytes.

5   Show that for a 32-bit main memory address and a directly mapped cache holding 64 KB of data:

(a) if there are 4 bytes in each line and a single Valid bit, the total cache size is 1.53×64 KB;
(b) if there are 16 bytes in each line and a single Valid bit, the total cache size is 1.13×64 KB.

6   (a) The LRU policy described in section 15.3.1 uses 3 LRU bits, B2, B1, and B0, to indicate the least recently used line in a four-way set. Show that the signal to replace L0, ReplaceL0, is given by /B1./B0. Similarly, show that ReplaceL1 = B1./B0, ReplaceL2 = /B2.B0, and ReplaceL3 = B2.B0.
(b) All the LRU bits were set to 0, and then lines L0, L3, L1, and L2 were filled. The next six accesses result in cache misses. Determine the behaviour of the replacement policy.

7   In the directly mapped cache, suggest how the AND of the signal from the comparator and from the Valid bit may be avoided by incorporating it into the comparator.

16 Memory management

In Chapter 15 we saw how the cache provides fast access to those portions of main memory that are likely to be needed in the near future. In this chapter, we regard the main memory as a form of cache for the hard disk store. That is, we shall use the main memory as a store for those portions of the disk store that are likely to be needed in the near future. This will allow us to execute a program even though not all the program code and data can fit into the main memory of the computer. In turn, this will allow us to store parts of a number of programs within the main memory and be able to run any of them.

16.1 Virtual and physical addresses – imaginary and real memory

The original idea[1] was to allow a program to use the disk store as though it was an extension of main memory. Thus, if the program requested access to part of the program that was not currently stored in main memory, the system automatically transferred that part of the program from the disk into the main memory. The program was then able to continue to run. By this means, a program that is too large to fit into the main memory could be executed by the computer.

The modern interpretation of this idea is that we allow a programmer to write her program as if all the memory-address space of the computer is actually filled with memory devices. For a computer with a 32-bit address bus, this means that the programmer may write a program assuming that 4 GB of memory physically exists. Since it is most unlikely that the computer will

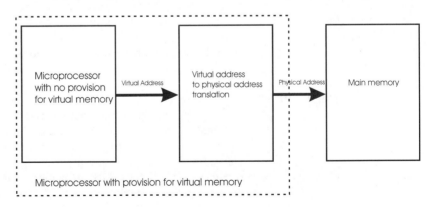

Figure 16.1 *Concept of virtual memory system*

---

[1] A 'one-level storage system' was first implemented in the early 1960s by T. Kilburn and his colleagues who designed the Atlas computer at Manchester University, UK.

actually contain 4 GB of memory chips, the program may refer to a memory location that does not physically exist in the computer. We regard addresses from the microprocessor as imaginary or **virtual addresses**. Now, an address generated by the program would normally appear on the address pins of the microprocessor, but a **virtual memory system**, Figure 16.1, modifies the virtual address before it is actually placed on the address bus. The modified address is that of a memory location that physically exists in the computer; it is called a **physical address**.

16.2 Pages and page frames

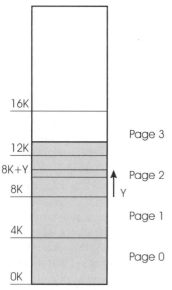

Figure 16.2 *A program divided into pages*

A program may generate a request to access anywhere within the 4 GB memory-address space of the computer. An immediate question is to ask what the virtual memory system is to do when the program refers to a memory location that does not physically exist. Before finding a solution to this problem, we must consider what is to happen when the computer user invokes[2] the program. We shall assume that the OS contains a **loader program** that transfers code from the disk to main memory. Further, the loader will transfer as much of the program code from the disk to main memory as will fill the available space in the main memory. We now ask how and where this code is to be located in main memory. A commonly used solution is to regard program code as being divided into fixed-size blocks or **pages**.

We shall choose a page size of 4 KB[3]. Further, we will regard the code for a task as consisting of a number of pages, Figure 16.2. For example, we regard location 8K + Y in the code as being located at **offset** Y within page 2. Since the page size is 4 KB (4K = 2^{12}), the number Y is a 12-bit number, yyyy yyyy yyyy. Writing 8K + Y in binary, we have (assuming a 32-bit address) 8K + Y = 0000 0000 0000 0000 0010 yyyy yyyy yyyy. The upper 20 bits indicate the page number, here 2, while the lower 12 bits indicate the offset within the page.

We also regard the main memory address space as being divided into **page frames.** Thus, a 4 GB memory address space that is divided into 4K page frames has $2^{32}/2^{12} = 2^{20}$ page frames. Each page frame begins at a physical memory address that is a multiple of 4K[4]. One of the requirements of the virtual memory system is that it can transfer a page of task code and data from the disk to a page frame in memory.

16.3 Page Tables

A page of code may be transferred from the disk to any page frame in main memory. Hence, the virtual memory system must keep a record of the physical address in main memory where each page transferred from the disk is stored. We shall use a look-up table, the **Page Table**, which has one row, or entry, for every page in the program. Since a programmer may write her program as if all the 4 GB of memory address space is available for her program, the page table will have 2^{20} entries. In Figure 16.3(a), pages 504

---

[2] The term 'invokes' in this context means 'starts to run'.
[3] We will consider the appropriate size of a page later.
[4] We say the page frames are **4K-aligned**. That is, each one begins at an address that is a multiple of 4K. These addresses end in 12 zeros.

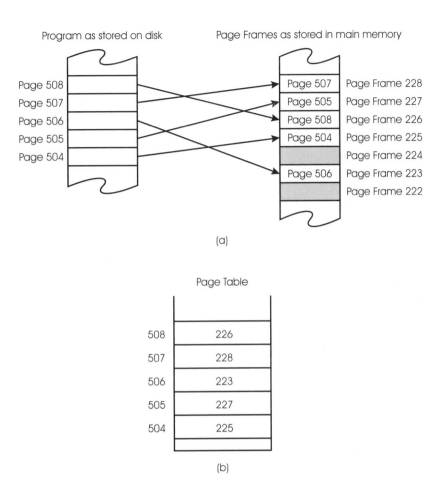

Figure 16.3 *Showing how pages of program code are stored in physical memory*

to 508 of a program, which is stored on disk, are shown. In this example, the code in page 504 on the hard disk has been stored in page frame 225 in main memory, the code in page 505 is stored in page frame 227, and so on. A small part of the page table containing the **physical page number** where pages 504 to 508 are stored is shown in Figure 16.3(b). This shows that page 504 of the program is stored in main memory page frame 225, page 505 of the program is stored in page frame 227, and so on.

A program may make a request to access any memory location within the 4 GB address space. When it does so, the physical address is looked up in the Page Table as shown in Figure 16.4. Note that the lower 12 bits, the offset, is the same in both the virtual address and the physical address because page frames always start at a physical address ending with 12 zeros. The physical address is used to access the required location in main memory. For example, if the Page Table is as shown in Figure 16.3(b), and the virtual page number (bits 31–12 in the address from the microprocessor) is 504, the

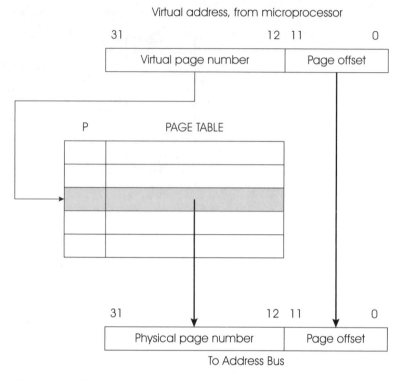

Figure 16.4 *Page Table showing how a virtual address is mapped to a physical address*

physical page number will be 225. Since not all pages of the program may be actually stored in main memory, the P (Present) flag indicates whether that page is currently in main memory or on the disk.

Each program, or task, that the computer has stored in its main memory has its own Page Table. These may be stored in the main memory with the address of the start of the Page Table held in a special register within the microprocessor, called the **Page Table Register**. This register is loaded when the OS switches to a new task. Each time the virtual memory system transfers a page from disk into main memory, the physical page number is stored in the Page Table at the appropriate row, and the P flag is set.

16.4 Handling a page fault

If the Present flag, P, in the Page Table indicates that the requested page is not in main memory, a **page fault** has occurred, and the requested page must be loaded from disk into main memory. This is **demand paging** – a page is loaded only when it is needed, that is, on demand. In order to do this, we arrange for a page fault to generate an exception[5]. The exception service

---

[5] An exception is an interrupt that is generated by the microprocessor itself. The term 'interrupt' is usually used to refer to interrupts from outside the microprocessor, typically from input and output devices. Other exceptions may be generated, for example by the floating-point unit when commanded to perform a division by zero.

routine, in the virtual memory system, will find the requested page on the disk, transfer it into a page of main memory, update the Page Table entry, and, finally, continue to run the task.

The address of the requested page on the disk may be stored in the Page Table. Thus, when the task is first started or created[6], we make the virtual memory system fill the Page Table with the disk address (track and sector) of each page in the task. If there are not enough bits in the Page Table to hold a disk address, we can set up another table in parallel with the Page Table. Also, in order to speed up the disk access, we can copy pages of the task into a more readily accessible **swap file** on the disk.

Deciding where to place the new page in main memory is straightforward if there is an unused page frame in main memory. However, we must expect that all the main memory will be in use so that the virtual memory system must decide which page in the main memory to replace. Ideally, we would like an algorithm that will identify the page that will not be needed for the longest time in the future. This is the most suitable page to replace. Since we cannot predict the future, practical **page replacement policies** approximate this ideal. Consequently, a practical policy will occasionally produce bad decisions; however, the objective is to arrive at a policy that makes reasonably good decisions most of the time and is as simple as possible. Fortunately, we have more freedom in choosing these policies than we had in choosing cache line replacement policies because a page replacement policy can be performed in software. This is because the time taken by software to determine which page to replace is very small compared to the relatively extremely long time taken to access the disk when responding to a page fault. The speed benefit obtained by implementing the policy in hardware would be very little and not worth giving up the flexibility obtained by using a software implementation.

Before considering the most popular policies for selecting a page for replacement, we ask what the memory management system is to do if any data in the page being replaced has been modified by the task. A modified page must be copied back to the disk in order to save the new data. However, we want the virtual memory system to do this only if the page has been modified, otherwise we waste time with an unnecessary disk write. Therefore, we will introduce a D (Dirty) flag that is set whenever the contents of the page are modified. This flag is stored in the Page Table alongside the P flag. If it is not set, the virtual memory system will not waste time writing the page back to the disk.

16.4.1 Least-recently used

An obvious page replacement policy is to replace the page that has not been used for the longest time, the **least-recently used**, LRU, policy. The rationale for this is that pages that have been referenced in the near past are likely to be referred to in the near future so it is desirable to keep them in main

---

[6] When the OS responds to a request for a new task, it creates the data structures needed by the task.

memory. Conversely, the page that has not been accessed for the longest time is the most suitable candidate for replacement. A strict implementation of this policy requires that each time a page is referenced the current time be recorded. Currently, most microprocessors do not have special hardware to do this, and software is too slow. A similar algorithm, based on the least frequently used page is often used.

16.4.2 Least-frequently used

The rationale for the **least-frequently used**, LFU, page replacement policy is that the page that has been least frequently accessed within the recent past is the most likely candidate for replacement. Obviously, this requires that the virtual memory system is able to determine how often a page has been accessed within the recent past. This is implemented by providing an A (Accessed) flag in the Page Table in addition to the P flag. Every time a page is accessed, the A flag is set and, periodically (say, every 1000 ns), the virtual memory system scans all the Page Table entries, looking at the A flag. If the A flag is set, the virtual memory system increments the frequency count for the page and resets the A flag. When a page in main memory has to be replaced, the page with the lowest frequency count is selected for replacement.

One disadvantage of this policy is that a page that has just been brought into memory is vulnerable to replacement since its frequency count is low, yet it may be needed many times in the near future. A refinement of this algorithm is to give a newly loaded page a frequency count at the middle point of the range of the possible frequency count values. As before, the frequency count is incremented if the A flag is set, but it is decremented if the A flag is not set. Thus, pages that have not been accessed within the sample period become more likely to be replaced.

16.4.3 Not used recently

The **not used recently**, NRU, page replacement policy uses both the A (Accessed) flag and the D (Dirty) flag. Modified pages are regarded as less attractive for replacement because they must be written to the disk when they are replaced. When a task is first loaded into main memory, none of its pages has been accessed or modified, that is, $<AD> = = <00>$. As the task is executed, these flags are modified so that, at any time, each page falls into one of the four categories, $<AD> = = <00>$, $<01>$, $<10>$, or $<11>$. The policy assumes that the lower the value of AD, the more attractive the page is for being replaced. Thus, a page that has not been accessed and is not Dirty, $<AD> = = <00>$, is a very likely candidate for replacement while a page that has been accessed and is dirty is a least likely candidate for replacement.

When finding a page for replacement, the virtual memory system scans the pages to find a page with $<AD> = = <00>$. The scan begins with the page immediately following the last page swapped and, when it reaches the last page, it continues with the first page; that is, the scan is circular. If a page with <AD> = = <00> is not found, the scan is repeated, this time searching for a page with the next higher category, <AD> = = <01>. The circular scans are repeated until a page is found for replacement. At regular intervals, the A flag on all the pages is reset; thus, category <AD> = = <01>, not accessed but dirty, can exist.

16.5 Page size

When designing a virtual memory system, we must be aware of the characteristics of the hard disk store. The read/write head within a disk store takes an extremely long time[7] to move until it is at the required distance from the centre of the disk, the radius. Once the head is at the required radius, the disk must make, on average, a half-revolution before the required sector containing the data comes under the head. This delay is called the **disk latency**. However, once the required sector is under the head, the data is read much more rapidly. Thus, reading two or more adjacent sectors from the disk will result in a lower average read time per byte than if only one sector is read because the disk latency is shared over the number of sectors accessed. Hence, to make efficient use of the disk, we shall use it to read a number of sectors at a time.

We have assumed that a page contains 4 Kbytes. We now ask how we are to choose the 'best' page size. A strong influence is the extremely high time cost of loading a page from disk when a page fault occurs. A large page size shares, or amortizes, the disk latency more effectively than a small page size. A large page size also reduces the length of the Page Table, since there are fewer pages. However, some of the code in the page is likely to be unused because of program jumps. This is both a waste of memory space and the time it took to fill it from disk. There are too many variables to allow us to calculate the 'best' page size; instead, we shall have to resort to the use of a program that simulates the design of the virtual memory system and test it when it is running various types of user applications. The result of these simulations suggests that 4 KB is a reasonable choice for the 32-bit address computer we have been considering. However, the Intel Pentium II microprocessor introduced the facility for both 4 KB and 4 MB pages. The very large 4 MB page is suited to user application programs that make extensive use of large data structures such as visual images and by the OS program itself.

The expectations of the users of computers will continue to increase the demands on the computer designer. It is reasonable to expect that the 32-bit address space will become too small, and this will be accompanied by faster hard disks or other secondary storage technologies. These expected developments would have a substantial effect on the 'best' page size for a virtual memory system.

16.6 Two-level paging*

As noted earlier, there is a row, or entry, in the Page Table for each page frame of the physical address space. For a microprocessor that has a 32-bit

---

[7] Time here is measured in units of the period of the clock signal that drives the microprocessor and so sets the basic unit of time in the computer system.

address and uses a 4 KB (2^{12}) page, the number of entries in the Page Table is $2^{32}/2^{12} = 2^{20}$. If each Page Table entry comprises 4 bytes, the size of the Page Table is $4 \times 2^{20} = 4$ MB. Since each task has its own Page Table, the memory space required for the Page Tables for all the tasks loaded into the computer is embarrassingly large. Indeed, the tables may use up most of the physically available memory!

To reduce the amount of main memory required by the Page Tables, we will split each Page Table into pages so that parts of a Page Table itself can be stored on disk. We can do this conveniently by using a **two-level paging** scheme. Consider that the 20-bit virtual page number part of the virtual address is split into two 10-bit fields, called Directory and Table, Figure 16.5. A register within the microprocessor, the **Page Directory Physical Base Address Register**, holds the physical address of the start of the **Page Directory**, which is a look-up table with only 2^{10} (1024) entries. The 10-bit Directory field of the virtual address is added[8] to the contents of the Page Directory Physical Base Address Register to obtain the physical address of an entry in the Page Directory, which is stored in main memory. Each of the 1024 Page Directory Entries contains the address of the start of a Page Table. In turn, each Page Table holds 1024 Page Table Entries, each of which holds the address of a page frame in main memory. All these addresses are 20 bits followed by 12 zeros, since they all point to 4K-aligned locations in main memory. As before, the lower 12 bits of the virtual address are used to indicate the offset within the main memory page.

Each table has 1024 entries each of which uses 4 bytes. Thus, each table is 4 KB, so that each table can be stored in a single page frame. We store the Page Directory in main memory. If it points to a Page Table that is not currently in main memory, a page fault will be generated and the virtual memory system software will load the required Page Table, itself one page long, from the disk.

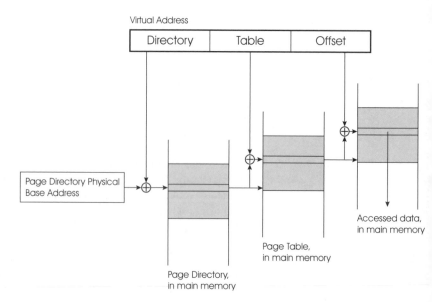

Figure 16.5 *Two-level paging scheme*

---

[8] Since all addresses are aligned to a page, the addition is actually achieved by concatenation.

16.7 Translation look-aside buffer

The conversion of a virtual address to a physical address involves many actions; the two-level paging scheme requires three accesses to memory in order to access the requested memory location. These, of course, will slow the computer. To overcome this difficulty, we will again make use of the locality of reference property of a program. Thus, when a translation has been made, it is likely to be needed again in the near future. This suggests that recently used translations should be stored in a special cache; this cache is called the **translation look-aside buffer**, TLB.

The TLB is a cache that stores recent mappings of virtual addresses to physical addresses. Now, instead of looking up the physical page number in the Page Tables on every memory reference, the microprocessor first looks up the virtual page number in the TLB. If there is a hit, the physical page number is read from the TLB. This will be concatenated with the page offset to form the 32-bit physical address, which is placed on the address bus. If there is a miss, we arrange for the full address translation process to be executed and the upper 20 bits of the physical address will be stored in the TLB for future accesses. In the Intel 80486, a TLB storing just 32 page references[9] results in a hit rate of about 0.98 so that the two-level page look-up is invoked in only about 2% of all memory references.

16.8 Memory protection

The virtual memory scheme has an additional, useful property, namely **memory protection**. Since a given main memory page frame only appears in the Page Table for a single task, one task cannot access the memory used by another task. This is beneficial since we do not want a programming error in one task to generate an access to the memory used by another task. However, there remains the possibility that instructions in one user task could modify the Page Tables in such a way as to give that task access to pages belonging to another task. Thus, we must prevent a user task from executing any microprocessor instructions that modify the Page Tables; these modifications should be made only by the OS. This implies that we have, at least, two modes of operation of the microprocessor: a **user mode**, and an OS or **supervisor mode**[10].

When the microprocessor is in user mode, it will not be able to execute instructions that change the data structures that are used by the OS to control the execution of user tasks. If a user task attempts to execute an instruction that is only available in supervisor mode, we arrange for an exception to be generated, so that the OS will be informed of the attempted violation. The OS will normally display a message to the user, informing her of the violation and what, if anything, can be done about it.

We can introduce additional protection by adding flags to the Page Table entries. Thus, one flag will indicate whether or not the page is allowed to be written, while another flag will indicate whether the page is for access by a user task or by the OS only. Collectively, these flags define the **access rights** of a page. Every time a task accesses a page these bits will be checked and

[9] This TLB cache uses four-way set-associative organization.
[10] These modes are sometimes distinguished by a number indicating their **privilege level.**

any attempt by a task to violate these conditions will generate an exception. The exception routine will normally produce an appropriate message to the computer user.

Nevertheless, sometimes it is desirable that more than one user task can have access to the same pages of code and data. For example, the user may wish to draw a diagram using one application and use the data that encodes the diagram in a word processing application so that, when changes are made to the diagram, they automatically appear in the word processing application. We can arrange for this by allowing the virtual memory system to include the pages of the diagram code to be in both page tables.

16.9 Problems

1   What are the main objectives of a memory management system?

2   When a programmer writes a program for a computer having a 32-bit address space, what limitations on memory are imposed?

3   Many commercial computer designs have eventually failed because they did not provide a sufficient number of bits for the physical memory address.

   (a) Why is this an important parameter?
   (b) Why is it difficult to increase the number of address bits in an existing computer architecture?

4   What benefit would accrue from increasing the number of address bits from 32? Why might address spaces greater than 32 bits be required?

5   Assume a strict least-recently used page replacement policy is implemented by hardware that writes the time of the last access of a page into the Page Table entry. In principle, how might the memory management system make use of this information? How might the determination of the oldest page be speeded?

6   The LFU page replacement policy has an additional weakness not mentioned in the text. It results from the fact that during the time that the task is initialized, the pages containing the initialization code are used frequently. Consider the time following the task initialization and suggest why the LFU policy has a weakness.

Appendix A: G80 instruction set

The constants used in the formation of the operation codes are shown below. These are chosen arbitrarily, for example only. They must be replaced by the actual value of the arguments in a particular instruction. For example, the code for ld a,0x42 is 3E 42 instead of the 3E 20 shown in this list.

```
n      = 0x20        ;One byte quantity
nn     = 0x1234      ;Two byte quantity
dd     = 0x55        ;Displacement for index registers
fred   = 0x01C3      ;Relative address
```

8E	adc a,(hl)	A3	and a,e	FD CB 55 66	bit 4,(iy+dd)
DD 8E 55	adc a,(ix+dd)	A4	and a,h	CB 67	bit 4,a
FD 8E 55	adc a,(iy+dd)	A5	and a,l	CB 60	bit 4,b
8F	adc a,a	E6 20	and a,n	CB 61	bit 4,c
88	adc a,b			CB 62	bit 4,d
89	adc a,c	CB 46	bit 0,(hl)	CB 63	bit 4,e
8A	adc a,d	DD CB 55 46	bit 0,(ix+dd)	CB 64	bit 4,h
8B	adc a,e	FD CB 55 46	bit 0,(iy+dd)	CB 65	bit 4,l
8C	adc a,h	CB 47	bit 0,a	CB 6E	bit 5,(hl)
8D	adc a,l	CB 40	bit 0,b	DD CB 55 6E	bit 5,(ix+dd)
CE 20	adc a,n	CB 41	bit 0,c	FD CB 55 6E	bit 5,(iy+dd)
ED 4A	adc hl,bc	CB 42	bit 0,d	CB 6F	bit 5,a
ED 5A	adc hl,de	CB 43	bit 0,e	CB 68	bit 5,b
ED 6A	adc hl,hl	CB 44	bit 0,h	CB 69	bit 5,c
ED 7A	adc hl,sp	CB 45	bit 0,l	CB 6A	bit 5,d
		CB 4E	bit 1,(hl)	CB 6B	bit 5,e
86	add a,(hl)	DD CB 55 4E	bit 1,(ix+dd)	CB 6C	bit 5,h
DD 86 55	add a,(ix+dd)	FD CB 55 4E	bit 1,(iy+dd)	CB 6D	bit 5,l
FD 86 55	add a,(iy+dd)	CB 4F	bit 1,a	CB 76	bit 6,(hl)
87	add a,a	CB 48	bit 1,b	DD CB 55 76	bit 6,(ix+dd)
80	add a,b	CB 49	bit 1,c	FD CB 55 76	bit 6,(iy+dd)
81	add a,c	CB 4A	bit 1,d	CB 77	bit 6,a
82	add a,d	CB 4B	bit 1,e	CB 70	bit 6,b
83	add a,e	CB 4C	bit 1,h	CB 71	bit 6,c
84	add a,h	CB 4D	bit 1,l	CB 72	bit 6,d
85	add a,l	CB 56	bit 2,(hl)	CB 73	bit 6,e
C6 20	add a,n	DD CB 55 56	bit 2,(ix+dd)	CB 74	bit 6,h
09	add hl,bc	FD CB 55 56	bit 2,(iy+dd)	CB 75	bit 6,l
19	add hl,de	CB 57	bit 2,a	CB 7E	bit 7,(hl)
29	add hl,hl	CB 50	bit 2,b	DD CB 55 7E	bit 7,(ix+dd)
39	add hl,sp	CB 51	bit 2,c	FD CB 55 7E	bit 7,(iy+dd)
DD 09	add ix,bc	CB 52	bit 2,d	CB 7F	bit 7,a
DD 19	add ix,de	CB 53	bit 2,e	CB 78	bit 7,b
DD 29	add ix,ix	CB 54	bit 2,h	CB 79	bit 7,c
DD 39	add ix,sp	CB 55	bit 2,l	CB 7A	bit 7,d
FD 09	add iy,bc	CB 5E	bit 3,(hl)	CB 7B	bit 7,e
FD 19	add iy,de	DD CB 55 5E	bit 3,(ix+dd)	CB 7C	bit 7,h
FD 29	add iy,iy	FD CB 55 5E	bit 3,(iy+dd)	CB 7D	bit 7,l
FD 39	add iy,sp	CB 5F	bit 3,a		
		CB 58	bit 3,b	DC 34 12	call c,nn
A6	and a,(hl)	CB 59	bit 3,c	FC 34 12	call m,nn
DD A6 55	and a,(ix+dd)	CB 5A	bit 3,d	D4 34 12	call nc,nn
FD A6 55	and a,(iy+dd)	CB 5B	bit 3,e	C4 34 12	call nz,nn
A7	and a,a	CB 5C	bit 3,h	F4 34 12	call p,nn
A0	and a,b	CB 5D	bit 3,l	EC 34 12	call pe,nn
A1	and a,c	CB 66	bit 4,(hl)	E4 34 12	call po,nn
A2	and a,d	DD CB 55 66	bit 4,(ix+dd)	CC 34 12	call z,nn

CD 34 12	call nn	ED 60	in h,(c)		4E	ld c,(hl)	
		ED 68	in l,(c)		DD 4E 55	ld c,(ix+dd)	
3F	ccf				FD 4E 55	ld c,(iy+dd)	
		34	inc (hl)		4F	ld c,a	
BE	cp (hl)	DD 34 55	inc (ix+dd)		48	ld c,b	
DD BE 55	cp (ix+dd)	FD 34 55	inc (iy+dd)		49	ld c,c	
FD BE 55	cp (iy+dd)	3C	inc a		4A	ld c,d	
BF	cp a	04	inc b		4B	ld c,e	
B8	cp b	03	inc bc		4C	ld c,h	
B9	cp c	0C	inc c		4D	ld c,l	
BA	cp d	14	inc d		0E 20	ld c,n	
BB	cp e	13	inc de		56	ld d,(hl)	
BC	cp h	1C	inc e		DD 56 55	ld d,(ix+dd)	
BD	cp l	24	inc h		FD 56 55	ld d,(iy+dd)	
FE 20	cp n	23	inc hl		57	ld d,a	
		DD 23	inc ix		50	ld d,b	
ED A9	cpd	FD 23	inc iy		51	ld d,c	
ED B9	cpdr	2C	inc l		52	ld d,d	
ED A1	cpi	33	inc sp		53	ld d,e	
ED B1	cpir				54	ld d,h	
		ED AA	ind		55	ld d,l	
2F	cpl	ED BA	indr		16 20	ld d,n	
		ED A2	ini		5E	ld e,(hl)	
27	daa	ED B2	inir		DD 5E 55	ld e,(ix+dd)	
					FD 5E 55	ld e,(iy+dd)	
35	dec (hl)	C3 34 12	jp nn		5F	ld e,a	
DD 35 55	dec (ix+dd)	E9	jp (hl)		58	ld e,b	
FD 35 55	dec (iy+dd)	DD E9	jp (ix)		59	ld e,c	
3D	dec a	FD E9	jp (iy)		5A	ld e,d	
05	dec b				5B	ld e,e	
0B	dec bc	DA 34 12	jp c,nn		5C	ld e,h	
0D	dec c	FA 34 12	jp m,nn		5D	ld e,l	
15	dec d	D2 34 12	jp nc,nn		1E 20	ld e,n	
1B	dec de	C2 34 12	jp nz,nn		66	ld h,(hl)	
1D	dec e	F2 34 12	jp p,nn		DD 66 55	ld h,(ix+dd)	
25	dec h	EA 34 12	jp pe,nn		FD 66 55	ld h,(iy+dd)	
2B	dec hl	E2 34 12	jp po,nn		67	ld h,a	
DD 2B	dec ix	CA 34 12	jp z,nn		60	ld h,b	
FD 2B	dec iy				61	ld h,c	
2D	dec l	18 08	jr fred		62	ld h,d	
3B	dec sp	38 06	jr c,fred		63	ld h,e	
		30 04	jr nc,fred		64	ld h,h	
F3	di	20 02	jr nz,fred		65	ld h,l	
		28 00	jr z,fred		26 20	ld h,n	
10 10	djnz .+0x12				6E	ld l,(hl)	
					DD 6E 55	ld l,(ix+dd)	
FB	ei	7E	ld a,(hl)		FD 6E 55	ld l,(iy+dd)	
		DD 7E 55	ld a,(ix+dd)		6F	ld l,a	
E3	ex (sp),hl	FD 7E 55	ld a,(iy+dd)		68	ld l,b	
DD E3	ex (sp),ix	7F	ld a,a		69	ld l,c	
FD E3	ex (sp),iy	78	ld a,b		6A	ld l,d	
		79	ld a,c		6B	ld l,e	
08	ex af,af'	7A	ld a,d		6C	ld l,h	
EB	ex de,hl	7B	ld a,e		6D	ld l,l	
D9	exx	7C	ld a,h		2E 20	ld l,n	
		7D	ld a,l				
76	halt	3E 20	ld a,n		ED 47	ld i,a	
		46	ld b,(hl)		ED 57	ld a,i	
ED 46	im 0	DD 46 55	ld b,(ix+dd)				
ED 56	im 1	FD 46 55	ld b,(iy+dd)		02	ld (bc),a	
ED 5E	im 2	47	ld b,a		12	ld (de),a	
		40	ld b,b		0A	ld a,(bc)	
DB 20	in a,(n)	41	ld b,c		1A	ld a,(de)	
ED 78	in a,(c)	42	ld b,d				
ED 40	in b,(c)	43	ld b,e		77	ld (hl),a	
ED 48	in c,(c)	44	ld b,h		70	ld (hl),b	
ED 50	in d,(c)	45	ld b,l		71	ld (hl),c	
ED 58	in e,(c)	06 20	ld b,n		72	ld (hl),d	

73	ld (hl),e
74	ld (hl),h
75	ld (hl),l
36 20	ld (hl),n
DD 77 55	ld (ix+dd),a
DD 70 55	ld (ix+dd),b
DD 71 55	ld (ix+dd),c
DD 72 55	ld (ix+dd),d
DD 73 55	ld (ix+dd),e
DD 74 55	ld (ix+dd),h
DD 75 55	ld (ix+dd),l
DD 36 55 20	ld (ix+dd),n
FD 77 55	ld (iy+dd),a
FD 70 55	ld (iy+dd),b
FD 71 55	ld (iy+dd),c
FD 72 55	ld (iy+dd),d
FD 73 55	ld (iy+dd),e
FD 74 55	ld (iy+dd),h
FD 75 55	ld (iy+dd),l
FD 36 55 20	ld (iy+dd),n
32 34 12	ld (nn),a
ED 43 34 12	ld (nn),bc
ED 53 34 12	ld (nn),de
22 34 12	ld (nn),hl
ED 73 34 12	ld (nn),sp
DD 22 34 12	ld (nn),ix
FD 22 34 12	ld (nn),iy
3A 34 12	ld a,(nn)
ED 4B 34 12	ld bc,(nn)
ED 5B 34 12	ld de,(nn)
2A 34 12	ld hl,(nn)
ED 7B 34 12	ld sp,(nn)
DD 2A 34 12	ld ix,(nn)
FD 2A 34 12	ld iy,(nn)
01 34 12	ld bc,nn
11 34 12	ld de,nn
21 34 12	ld hl,nn
31 34 12	ld sp,nn
DD 21 34 12	ld ix,nn
FD 21 34 12	ld iy,nn
F9	ld sp,hl
DD F9	ld sp,ix
FD F9	ld sp,iy
ED A8	ldd
ED B8	lddr
ED A0	ldi
ED B0	ldir
ED 44	neg
00	nop
B6	or a,(hl)
DD B6 55	or a,(ix+dd)
FD B6 55	or a,(iy+dd)
B7	or a,a
B0	or a,b
B1	or a,c
B2	or a,d
B3	or a,e
B4	or a,h
B5	or a,l

F6 20	or a,n
ED BB	otdr
ED B3	otir
ED 79	out (c),a
ED 41	out (c),b
ED 49	out (c),c
ED 51	out (c),d
ED 59	out (c),e
ED 61	out (c),h
ED 69	out (c),l
D3 20	out (n),a
ED AB	outd
ED A3	outi
F1	pop af
C1	pop bc
D1	pop de
E1	pop hl
DD E1	pop ix
FD E1	pop iy
F5	push af
C5	push bc
D5	push de
E5	push hl
DD E5	push ix
FD E5	push iy
CB 86	res 0,(hl)
DD CB 55 86	res 0,(ix+dd)
FD CB 55 86	res 0,(iy+dd)
CB 87	res 0,a
CB 80	res 0,b
CB 81	res 0,c
CB 82	res 0,d
CB 83	res 0,e
CB 84	res 0,h
CB 85	res 0,l
CB 8E	res 1,(hl)
DD CB 55 8E	res 1,(ix+dd)
FD CB 55 8E	res 1,(iy+dd)
CB 8F	res 1,a
CB 88	res 1,b
CB 89	res 1,c
CB 8A	res 1,d
CB 8B	res 1,e
CB 8C	res 1,h
CB 8D	res 1,l
CB 96	res 2,(hl)
DD CB 55 96	res 2,(ix+dd)
FD CB 55 96	res 2,(iy+dd)
CB 97	res 2,a
CB 90	res 2,b
CB 91	res 2,c
CB 92	res 2,d
CB 93	res 2,e
CB 94	res 2,h
CB 95	res 2,l
CB 9E	res 3,(hl)
DD CB 55 9E	res 3,(ix+dd)
FD CB 55 9E	res 3,(iy+dd)
CB 9F	res 3,a
CB 98	res 3,b
CB 99	res 3,c
CB 9A	res 3,d

CB 9B	res 3,e
CB 9C	res 3,h
CB 9D	res 3,l
CB A6	res 4,(hl)
DD CB 55 A6	res 4,(ix+dd)
FD CB 55 A6	res 4,(iy+dd)
CB A7	res 4,a
CB A0	res 4,b
CB A1	res 4,c
CB A2	res 4,d
CB A3	res 4,e
CB A4	res 4,h
CB A5	res 4,l
CB AE	res 5,(hl)
DD CB 55 AE	res 5,(ix+dd)
FD CB 55 AE	res 5,(iy+dd)
CB AF	res 5,a
CB A8	res 5,b
CB A9	res 5,c
CB AA	res 5,d
CB AB	res 5,e
CB AC	res 5,h
CB AD	res 5,l
CB B6	res 6,(hl)
DD CB 55 B6	res 6,(ix+dd)
FD CB 55 B6	res 6,(iy+dd)
CB B7	res 6,a
CB B0	res 6,b
CB B1	res 6,c
CB B2	res 6,d
CB B3	res 6,e
CB B4	res 6,h
CB B5	res 6,l
CB BE	res 7,(hl)
DD CB 55 BE	res 7,(ix+dd)
FD CB 55 BE	res 7,(iy+dd)
CB BF	res 7,a
CB B8	res 7,b
CB B9	res 7,c
CB BA	res 7,d
CB BB	res 7,e
CB BC	res 7,h
CB BD	res 7,l
C9	ret
D8	ret c
F8	ret m
D0	ret nc
C0	ret nz
F0	ret p
E8	ret pe
E0	ret po
C8	ret z
ED 4D	reti
ED 45	retn
CB 16	rl a,(hl)
DD CB 55 16	rl a,(ix+dd)
FD CB 55 16	rl a,(iy+dd)
CB 17	rl a,a
CB 10	rl a,b
CB 11	rl a,c
CB 12	rl a,d
CB 13	rl a,e
CB 14	rl a,h
CB 15	rl a,l
17	rla

```
CB 06       rlc a,(hl)          CB C7       set 0,a       DD CB 55 FE set 7,(ix+dd)
DD CB 55 06 rlc a,(ix+dd)       CB C0       set 0,b       FD CB 55 FE set 7,(iy+dd)
FD CB 55 06 rlc a,(iy+dd)       CB C1       set 0,c       CB FF       set 7,a
CB 07       rlc a,a             CB C2       set 0,d       CB F8       set 7,b
CB 00       rlc a,b             CB C3       set 0,e       CB F9       set 7,c
CB 01       rlc a,c             CB C4       set 0,h       CB FA       set 7,d
CB 02       rlc a,d             CB C5       set 0,l       CB FB       set 7,e
CB 03       rlc a,e             CB CE       set 1,(hl)    CB FC       set 7,h
CB 04       rlc a,h             DD CB 55 CE set 1,(ix+dd) CB FD       set 7,l
CB 05       rlc a,l             FD CB 55 CE set 1,(iy+dd)
07          rlca                CB CF       set 1,a       CB 26       sla (hl)
                                CB C8       set 1,b       DD CB 55 26 sla (ix+dd)
CB 1E       rr a,(hl)           CB C9       set 1,c       FD CB 55 26 sla (iy+dd)
DD CB 55 1E rr a,(ix+dd)        CB CA       set 1,d       CB 27       sla a
FD CB 55 1E rr a,(iy+dd)        CB CB       set 1,e       CB 20       sla b
CB 1F       rr a,a              CB CC       set 1,h       CB 21       sla c
CB 18       rr a,b              CB CD       set 1,l       CB 22       sla d
CB 19       rr a,c              CB D6       set 2,(hl)    CB 23       sla e
CB 1A       rr a,d              DD CB 55 D6 set 2,(ix+dd) CB 24       sla h
CB 1B       rr a,e              FD CB 55 D6 set 2,(iy+dd) CB 25       sla l
CB 1C       rr a,h              CB D7       set 2,a
CB 1D       rr a,l              CB D0       set 2,b       CB 2E       sra (hl)
1F          rra                 CB D1       set 2,c       DD CB 55 2E sra (ix+dd)
                                CB D2       set 2,d       FD CB 55 2E sra (iy+dd)
CB 0E       rrc a,(hl)          CB D3       set 2,e       CB 2F       sra a
DD CB 55 0E rrc a,(ix+dd)       CB D4       set 2,h       CB 28       sra b
FD CB 55 0E rrc a,(iy+dd)       CB D5       set 2,l       CB 29       sra c
CB 0F       rrc a,a             CB DE       set 3,(hl)    CB 2A       sra d
CB 08       rrc a,b             DD CB 55 DE set 3,(ix+dd) CB 2B       sra e
CB 09       rrc a,c             FD CB 55 DE set 3,(iy+dd) CB 2C       sra h
CB 0A       rrc a,d             CB DF       set 3,a       CB 2D       sra l
CB 0B       rrc a,e             CB D8       set 3,b
CB 0C       rrc a,h             CB D9       set 3,c       CB 3E       srl (hl)
CB 0D       rrc a,l             CB DA       set 3,d       DD CB 55 3E srl (ix+dd)
0F          rrca                CB DB       set 3,e       FD CB 55 3E srl (iy+dd)
                                CB DC       set 3,h       CB 3F       srl a
                                CB DD       set 3,l       CB 38       srl b
C7          rst 0x00            CB E6       set 4,(hl)    CB 39       srl c
CF          rst 0x08            DD CB 55 E6 set 4,(ix+dd) CB 3A       srl d
D7          rst 0x10            FD CB 55 E6 set 4,(iy+dd) CB 3B       srl e
DF          rst 0x18            CB E7       set 4,a       CB 3C       srl h
E7          rst 0x20            CB E0       set 4,b       CB 3D       srl l
EF          rst 0x28            CB E1       set 4,c
F7          rst 0x30            CB E2       set 4,d
FF          rst 0x38            CB E3       set 4,e       96          sub (hl)
                                CB E4       set 4,h       DD 96 55    sub (ix+dd)
9E          sbc a,(hl)          CB E5       set 4,l       FD 96 55    sub (iy+dd)
DD 9E 55    sbc a,(ix+dd)       CB EE       set 5,(hl)    97          sub a
FD 9E 55    sbc a,(iy+dd)       DD CB 55 EE set 5,(ix+dd) 90          sub b
9F          sbc a,a             FD CB 55 EE set 5,(iy+dd) 91          sub c
98          sbc a,b             CB EF       set 5,a       92          sub d
99          sbc a,c             CB E8       set 5,b       93          sub e
9A          sbc a,d             CB E9       set 5,c       94          sub h
9B          sbc a,e             CB EA       set 5,d       95          sub l
9C          sbc a,h             CB EB       set 5,e       D6 20       sub n
9D          sbc a,l             CB EC       set 5,h
DE 20       sbc a,n             CB ED       set 5,l       AE          xor (hl)
                                CB F6       set 6,(hl)    DD AE 55    xor (ix+dd)
ED 42       sbc hl,bc           DD CB 55 F6 set 6,(ix+dd) FD AE 55    xor (iy+dd)
ED 52       sbc hl,de           FD CB 55 F6 set 6,(iy+dd) AF          xor a
ED 62       sbc hl,hl           CB F7       set 6,a       A8          xor b
ED 72       sbc hl,sp           CB F0       set 6,b       A9          xor c
                                CB F1       set 6,c       AA          xor d
37          scf                 CB F2       set 6,d       AB          xor e
                                CB F3       set 6,e       AC          xor h
CB C6       set 0,(hl)          CB F4       set 6,h       AD          xor l
DD CB 55 C6 set 0,(ix+dd)       CB F5       set 6,l       EE 20       xor n
FD CB 55 C6 set 0,(iy+dd)       CB FE       set 7,(hl)
```

G80 instruction set – organized by instruction type

There are about 150 different instructions that the G80 can execute. These are based on the instruction set of the Zilog Z80 microprocessor. To help remember these instructions they are shown below in groups of similar instructions. A programmer must remember these groups, but not necessarily all the instructions within a group. Thus, if the programmer wishes to perform a particular type of operation, she can search for a suitable instruction in the relevant group.

The letter R is used to stand for any of the 8-bit registers A, B, C, D, E, H, L.

The phrase 'Memory location (bc)' is to be read as 'the memory location whose address is held in register pair BC'.

8-bit load

ld destination, source

Source

Destination	Any 8-bit register, R	Memory location (hl)	Memory location (bc)	Memory location (de)	Memory location (ix+disp)	Memory location (iy+disp)	8-bit quantity, N
Register a	ld a, R	ld a, (hl)	ld a, (bc)	ld a, (de)	ld a, (ix+Q)	ld a, (iy+Q)	ld a, N
Any 8-bit register, R	ld R, R	ld R, (hl)	x	x	ld R, (ix+Q)	ld R, (iy+Q)	ld R, N
Memory location given by hl, (hl)	ld (hl), R	x	x	x	x	x	ld (hl), N
Memory location given by ix, (ix+Q)	ld (ix+Q), R	x	x	x	x	x	ld (ix+Q), N
Memory location given by iy, (iy+Q)	ld (iy+Q), R	x	x	x	x	x	ld (iy+Q), N

ld (bc), a	ld a, (bc)	ld (de), a	ld a, (de)	ld (NN), a	ld a, i	ld i, a

16-bit load

ld destination source

Destination

Destination	Source						
	bc	de	hl	ix	iy	16-bit number, NN	(NN)
bc	x	x	x	x	x	ld bc, NN	ld bc, (NN)
de	x	x	x	x	x	ld de, NN	ld de, (NN)
hl		x	x	x	x	ld hl, NN	ld hl, (NN)
ix		x	x	x	x	ld ix, NN	ld ix, (NN)
iy		x	x	x	x	ld iy, NN	ld iy, (NN)
Memory location NN	ld (NN), bc	ld (NN), de	ld (NN), hl	ld (NN), ix	ld (NN), iy	x	x

push af	push bc	push de	push hl	push ix	push iy
pop af	pop bc	pop de	pop hl	pop ix	pop iy
ld sp, hl	ld sp, ix	ld sp, iy	ld sp, NN	ld sp, (NN)	ld (NN), sp

8-bit arithmetic and logic

Operation	Source				
	Any 8-bit register, R	Memory location (hl)	Memory location (ix+Q)	Memory location (iy+Q)	8-bit quantity, N
Add to A	add a, R	add a, (hl)	add a, (ix+Q)	add a, (iy+Q)	add a, N
Add with carry to A	adc a, R	adc a, (hl)	adc a, (ix+Q)	adc a, (iy+Q)	adc a, N
Subtract from A	sub R	sub (hl)	sub (ix+Q)	sub (iy+Q)	sub N
Subtract with carry from A	sbc R	sbc (hl)	sbc (ix+Q)	sbc (iy+Q)	sbc N
Logical AND with A	and R	and (hl)	and (ix+Q)	and (iy+Q)	and N
Logical XOR with A	xor R	xor (hl)	xor (ix+Q)	xor (iy+Q)	xor N
Logical OR with A	or R	or (hl)	or (ix+Q)	or (iy+Q)	or N
Compare with register A	cp R	cp (hl)	cp (ix+Q)	cp (iy+Q)	cp N
Increment	inc R	inc (hl)	inc (ix+Q)	inc (iy+Q)	x
Decrement	dec R	dec (hl)	dec (ix+Q)	dec (iy+Q)	x

Complement register A	cpl
Multiply register A by −1	neg

16-bit arithmetic

Operation	Source					
	bc	de	hl	sp	ix	iy
Add to hl	add hl, bc	add hl, de	add hl, hl	add hl, sp	x	x
Add to ix	add ix, bc	add ix, de	x	add ix, sp	add ix, ix	x
Add to iy	add iy, bc	add iy, de	x	add iy, sp	x	add iy, iy
Add with carry to hl	adc hl, bc	adc hl, de	adc hl, hl	adc hl, sp	x	x
Subtract with carry to hl	sbc hl, bc	sbc hl, de	sbc hl, hl	sbc hl, sp	x	x
Increment	inc bc	inc de	inc hl	inc sp	inc ix	inc iy
Decrement	dec bc	dec de	dec hl	dec sp	dec ix	dec iy

Shifts and rotates

The different type of shifts and rotates are described in Chapter 5

Source

Operation	Any 8-bit register, R	Memory location (hl)	Memory location (ix+disp)	Memory location (iy+disp)
Rotate left circular	rlc R	rlc (hl)	rlc (ix+Q)	rlc (iy+Q)
Rotate right circular	rrc R	rrc (hl)	rrc (ix+Q)	rrc (iy+Q)
Rotate left	rl R	rl (hl)	rl (ix+Q)	rl (iy+Q)
Rotate right	rr R	rr (hl)	rr (ix+Q)	rr (iy+Q)
Shift left arithmetical	sla R	sla (hl)	sla (ix+Q)	sla (iy+Q)
Shift right arithmetical	sra R	sra (hl)	sra (ix+Q)	sra (iy+Q)
Shift right logical	srl R	srl (hl)	srl (ix+Q)	srl (iy+Q)

rlca = rlc a	rrca = rrc a	rla = rl a	rra = rr a

Jumps

Also called branches

	Condition								
	Always	Jump if Carry flag is set	Jump if Carry flag is not set	Jump if Zero flag is set	Jump if Zero flag is not set	Jump if Sign flag is set	Jump if Sign flag is not set	Jump if Parity is even	Jump if Parity is odd
Jump	jp NN	jp c, NN	jp nc, NN	jp z, NN	jp nz, NN	jp m, NN	jp p, NN	jp pe, NN	jp po, NN
Jump[1]	jr Q	jr c, Q	jr nc, Q	jr z, Q	jr nz, Q	x	x	x	x

Jump to location given in register pair	jp (hl)	jp (ix)	jp (iy)
Decrement B, jump[1] if B not 0	djnz Q	x	x

Note 1: Q is a relative address. The location to be jumped must be within <-128, 127> of the current value in the PC.

Call and return

Condition

	Always	If Carry flag is set	If Carry flag is not set	If Zero flag is set	If Zero flag is not set	If Sign flag is set	If Sign flag is not set	If Parity is even	If Parity is odd
Call	call NN	call c, NN	call nc, NN	call z, NN	call nz, NN	call m, NN	call p, NN	call pe, NN	call po, NN
Return	ret	ret c	ret nc	ret z	ret nz	ret m	ret px	ret pe	ret po

Return from maskable interrupt	reti
Return from non-maskable interrupt	retn
Restart	rst K = call K, where K is 0x00, 0x08, 0x10, 0x18, 0x20, 0x28, 0x30, 0x38

Single-bit manipulations

Operation	Any 8-bit register, R	Source Memory location (hl)	Memory location (ix+disp)	Memory location (iy+disp)
Set bit B, b = 0...7	set B, R	set B, (hl)	set B, (ix+Q)	set B, (iy+Q)
Reset bit B, b = 0...7	reset B, R	reset B, (hl)	reset B, (ix+Q)	reset B, (iy+Q)
Bit test, if the bit is 0, set Z, else reset Z	bit B, R	bit B, (hl)	bit B, (ix+Q)	bit B, (iy+Q)

Input and output

Input to register A from port	in a, (port)
Input to any 8-bit register from the port whose address is in register C	in R, (c)
Output from register A to port	out (port), a
Output any 8-bit register to the port whose address is in register C	out (c), R

Exchanges

Exchange af and af'	ex af, af'
Exchange bc, de, hl with bc', de', hl'	exx
Exchange de, hl	ex de, hl
Exchange top of stack, (sp), and hl	ex (sp), hl
Exchange top of stack, (sp), and ix	ex (sp), ix
Exchange top of stack, (sp), and iy	ex (sp), iy

Block operations

Copy a block of data from (hl) to (de)	Load (de) from (hl), increment hl and de, decrement bc	ldi
Register bc counts the number of bytes	Same as ldi, repeat until bc = 0	ldir
	Load (de) from (hl), decrement hl and de, decrement bc	ldd
	Same as ldd, repeat until bc = 0	lddr
Search a block of data pointed to by hl for a match with register A	Compare (hl) with register A, increment hl, decrement bc	cpi
	Same as cpi, repeat until bc = 0 or match found	cpir
Register bc counts the number of bytes	Compare (hl) with (de), decrement hl, decrement bc	cpd
	Same as cpd, repeat until bc = 0 or match found	cpdr
Input a block from port	Input from the port (c), increment hl, decrement bc	ini
Register bc counts the number of bytes	Same as ini, repeat until bc = 0	inir
	Input from the port (c), decrement hl, decrement bc	ind
	Same as ind, repeat until bc = 0	indr
Output a block of data	Output to the port (c), increment hl, decrement bc	outi
Register bc counts the number of bytes	Same as outi, repeat until bc = 0	otir
	Output to the port (c), decrement hl, decrement bc	outd
	Same as ioutd, repeat until bc = 0	outdr

Miscellaneous operations

Set the Carry flag	scf
Complement the Carry flag	ccf
No operation	nop
Halt	halt
Disable interrupts	di
Enable interrupts	ei
Set interrupt mode 0	im 0
Set interrupt mode 1	im 1
Set interrupt mode 2	im 2

Appendix B: ASCII character codes

		Least significant hex digit															
		0	1	2	3	4	5	6	7	8	9	A	B	C	D	E	F
Most significant digit	0	NUL	SOH	STX	ETX	EOT	ENQ	ACK	BEL	BS	HT	LF	VT	FF	CR	SO	SI
	1	DLE	DC1	DC2	DC3	DC4	NAK	SYN	ETB	CAN	EM	SUB	ESC	FS	GS	RS	US
	2	spc	!	“	#	$	%	&	‘	(	)	*	+	,	_	.	/
	3	0	1	2	3	4	5	6	7	8	9	:	;	<	=	>	?
	4	@	A	B	C	D	E	F	G	H	I	J	K	L	M	N	O
	5	P	Q	R	S	T	U	V	W	X	Y	Z	[	\	]	^	_
	6	`	a	b	c	d	e	f	g	h	i	j	k	l	m	n	o
	7	p	q	r	s	t	u	v	w	x	y	z	{	}	|	~	del

ASCII stands for the American Standard Code for Information Interchange. It has become adopted as an international standard by the International Standards Organization, ISO. Virtually all devices that handle characters, such as printers and keyboards, use this code.

It is convenient to remember the ASCII codes for the characters ‘0’ to ‘9’; these are 0x30 to 0x39. Thus, it is easy to convert a 4-bit number in the range 0 to 9 to ASCII by simply logically ORing the number with 0x30.

Appendix C: Specifications of the input and output devices

Summary

Input device	Port Address		Function
	Mnemonic	Value	
Toggle switches	SWS	0x90	Data – state of switches
Keypad	KEYPAD	0x80	Data – key number
	KEYPAD_C	0x81	Control – interrupt control
ASCII keyboard	PCKBD	0xC0	Data – ASCII code of key
Digital potentiometer	POT	0x40	Data – position of slider

Output device			
Light-emitting diodes	LEDS	0x20	Data – state of LEDs
Seven-segment displays	SSEGL	0xA0	Data – left hand display
	SSEGR	0xA1	Data – right hand display
Liquid crystal display	LCD	0xD0	Data – ASCII code of character
Chart recorder	CHART	0x30	Data – position of plotted point
	CHRED	0x31	Data – value of red marker
	CHGRN	0x32	Data – value of green marker
	CHBLU	0x33	Data – value of blue marker
Stepper motor	MOTOR	0xB0	Data – step and sensor state
Beeper	BEEP	0x60	Data – irrelevant

Complex devices			
Counter	CTR	0xE0	Data – down-counter and time constant
		0xE1	Control – interrupt control
Timer	TIM	0x70	Data – down-counter & Time constant
	TIM_C	0x71	Control – interrupt control
Calendar	CALNDR	0x10	Data – day of week
	CALNDR + 1	0x11	Data – year
	CALNDR + 2	0x12	Data – month
	CALNDR + 3	0x13	Data – day of month
	CALNDR + 4	0x14	Data – hour
	CALNDR + 5	0x15	Data – minute
	CALNDR + 6	0x16	Data – second
Pottery kiln	KTEMP	0xF0	See specification for use of these ports.
	KCTRL	0xF1	

Unattached ports			
		0x00	See specification for use of these ports.
		0x01	
		0x02	
		0x03	

Device: Toggle Switches
Data port address: SWS = 0x90

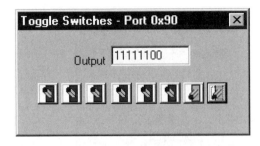

Function:
This device is a bank of eight toggle switches. When the data port SWS is read, this device returns a byte of data each bit of which indicates the state of a switch. The current value of the data port is shown in the 'Output' box. A switch toggles when clicked.

Example:

```
in a, (SWS)    :Copy switches into register A.
```

Device: Keypad
Data port address: KEYPAD = 0x80
Control port address: KEYPAD_C = 0x81

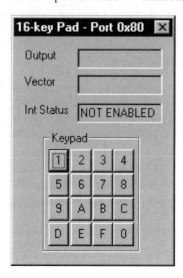

Function:

When the data port KEYPAD is read, this device returns a byte of data that contains the value of the keypad key that has been 'pressed'. To press a key, click on it.

The current value of the data port is shown in the 'Output' box. The lower 4 bits of the port are the value of the pressed key, 0x0 to 0xF. Bit 7 is the DataReady signal. It is set when a key is pressed and automatically reset when the data port is read. Bits 6, 5, and 4 are unused.

This device may be programmed to generate an interrupt request when a key is pressed by writing 0x83 to the control port, KEYPAD_C. This facility is disabled by writing 0x03 to the control port.

When used with the G80 programmed to have a vectored interrupt response, the interrupt vector is stored in this device by writing the vector, which must be an even number, to the control port.

The current state of the interrupt request may be obtained by reading the control port. Bit 7 is the interrupt flag; when an interrupt request has been made, the control port contains 0x80, otherwise it contains 0x00. Reading the control port automatically resets the interrupt flag.

These properties are summarized in the following table.

	Read	**Write**
KEYPAD	DataReady flag (bit 7) and key value (bits 3, 2, 1, 0)	No effect.
KEYPAD_C	Bit 7 is the interrupt request flag – 0x00 no interrupt requested, 0x80 interrupt requested. Read resets port to 0x00.	0x83 Enable interrupt. 0x03 Disable interrupt. Even number = vector.

Example programs:

```
Pad_LCD.asm      Handshaking
Int1.asm         Interrupt
```

Device: ASCII keyboard
Data port address: PCKBD = 0xC0
This device is the keyboard on the host computer.

Function:
When this data port is read a dialog box appears inviting the user to press a key on the keyboard of the host computer. The data returned is the ASCII code for the key.

Example:

```
in a, (PCKBD)     :Copy host keyboard into register A.
```

Device: Digital Potentiometer

Data port address: POT = 0x40

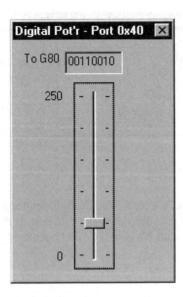

Function:
This device outputs the position of its slider. The position has a value between 0 and 250. The output position is updated when the slider is released.
The slider is moved by dragging it using the mouse cursor with the left button held down. The Page Up and Page Down host computer keys move the slider in steps of 50 while the arrow keys move the slider one step.

Example:

```
    in  a,  (POT)        :Copy potentiometer into register A.
```

Device: Light-emitting Diodes

Data port address: `LEDS = 0x20`

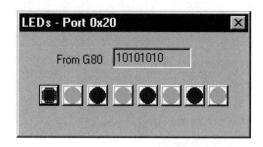

Function:
This device is a bank of eight light-emitting diodes. Each LED is connected to the corresponding bit in the data port. If the data bit is 1, the LED becomes red; if the data bit is 0, the LED becomes green.

Example:

    `out (LEDS), a`   :Send contents of register A to LEDS.

Device: Seven-segment Display

Data ports addresses: SSEGL = 0xA0
                         SSEGR = 0xA1

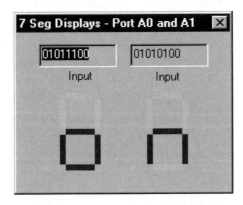

Function:
This device comprises two seven-segment displays. A segment is illuminated by writing data that contains a 1 in the bit position corresponding to the segment.

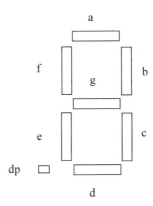

Bit	7	6	5	4	3	2	1	0
Segment	dp	g	f	e	d	c	b	a

Example:

```
out (SSEGL), a    :Send contents of register A to left-hand display.
```

Device: Liquid Crystal Display

Data port address: `LCD = 0xD0`

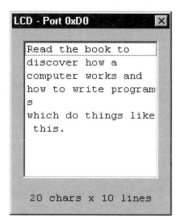

LCD - Port 0xD0

Read the book to
discover how a
computer works and
how to write program
s
which do things like
 this.

20 chars x 10 lines

Function:
The LCD displays the character whose ASCII code is written to the data port. The display has ten lines, each of 20 characters. A line longer than 20 characters automatically wraps to the next line. The display automatically scrolls when more than ten lines are written to it.

A character is written at the current cursor position. The cursor position is automatically moved to the next character position when a character has been displayed.

Some codes, and sequences of codes, control the display as described in the following table.

Action	Code (hex)	Code (dec)
Clear the LCD	0xFF	255
Start a new line	0x0A	10
Cursor on	0x1B, 0x00, 0x00	27, 0, 0
Cursor off	0x1B, 0x00, 0x01	27, 0, 1
Move cursor to column, row	0x1B, column, row	27, column, row
	column = <1 . . . 20>, and row = <1 . . . 10>. The top left-hand position is column 1, row 1	

Note: Commercial LCDs usually require a handshake in order to write data to them. This is because they take quite a long time to display a character and so signal when they are ready to receive a new character. For simplicity, the LCD specified here is assumed to be always ready to receive data from the G80.

Example:

```
out (LCD), a       :Send contents of register A to LCD.
```

Device: Chart Recorder

Data port addresses: CHART = 0x30
                             CHRED = 0x31
                             CHGRN = 0x32
                             CHBLU = 0x33

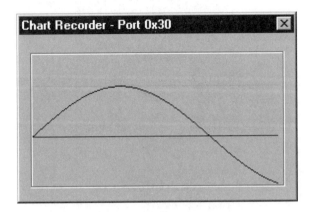

Function:
This device is a strip chart recorder that plots the input of an 8-bit unsigned integer (0 to 255) on a strip of paper. Every time data is written to port CHART of the device, the data is plotted as an analogue and the drawing position moves on a small step.

Up to three markers may also be plotted. To use a marker, write to one or more of ports CHRED, CHGRN, CHBLU of the recorder before it is used to plot data. The markers plot as red (CHRED), green (CHGRN), and blue (CHBLU) horizontal lines. The default value of all markers is zero. When a marker has a value of zero, it is not plotted.

Example:

    `out (CHART), a`   :Send contents of register A to chart recorder.

Device: Stepper Motor

Data port address: `MOTOR = 0xB0`

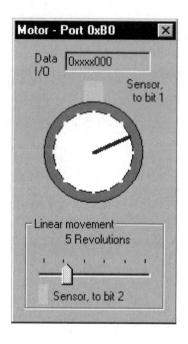

Function:
The motor steps through an angle of 22.5° when bit 0 changes from 0 to 1.
The direction of the step is controlled by bit 7; when 0 the motor steps clockwise, when 1 the motor steps counter-clockwise. When stepped, the motor must be allowed a short time to move before another step can be initiated.

The data port may be read and written.
When the motor reaches the 12 o'clock position, the sensor connected to bit 1 of the data port is activated.
The motor drives a mechanism such that five complete rotations, 80 steps, of the motor move the traverse from end to end. The traverse wraps from the end to the start. When the traverse is at the start, the sensor connected to bit 2 is activated.

Example program:

```
Pad_Step.asm
```

Device: Beeper
Data port address: `BEEP = 0x60`

This device is actually the beeper on the host computer.

Function:
A write of any data to this port produces a beep or a click sound.

Example:

```
out (BEEP), a      :Beep once.
```

Device: Conveyor Belt Counter
Data port address: CTR = 0xE0
Control port address: CTR_C = 0xE1

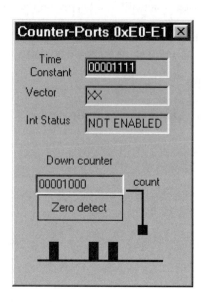

Function:
This device is a model of a factory conveyor belt in which articles are carried by the conveyor belt and pass under a sensor. The output of the sensor is connected to a counter. Each time an article passes under the sensor, the counter is decremented. When the counter reaches zero, it is automatically reloaded with the value shown in the Time Constant box. If the interrupt in the counter circuit has been enabled, an interrupt request is generated to the G80.

To initialize the device, write an 8-bit unsigned integer to port CTR. This number appears in the Time Constant box. (The term 'time constant' is used because commercial devices are often 'timer–counters'; that is, they will count pulse inputs from an external device or count system clock pulses.) When the conveyor belt begins to run, the time constant is copied into the Down counter and the pulses from the object detector decrements this counter. When the Down counter reaches zero, the Zero detect logic reloads the time constant into the Down counter and the process repeats. The contents of the Down counter may be read at any time by reading port CTR.

This device may be programmed to generate an interrupt request when the Down counter reaches zero by writing 0x83 to the control port CTR_C. This facility is disabled by writing 0x03 to the control port.

When used with the G80 programmed to have a vectored interrupt response, the interrupt vector is stored in this device by writing the vector, which must be an even number, to the control port CTR_C.

The current state of the interrupt request flag is obtained by reading the control port. Bit 7 is the interrupt flag; when an interrupt request has been made, the control port contains 0x80, otherwise it contains 0x00. Reading the control port automatically resets the interrupt flag.

These properties are summarized in the following table.

	Read	Write
CTR	Current value of the Down counter.	Data stored as Time Constant.
CTR_C	Bit 7 is the interrupt request flag – 0x00 no interrupt requested, 0x80 interrupt requested. Read resets port to 0x00.	0x83 Enable interrupt. 0x03 Disable interrupt. Even number = vector.

Example program:

```
Belt1.asm
```

Device: Timer
Data port address: TIM = 0x70
Control port address: TIM_C = 0x71

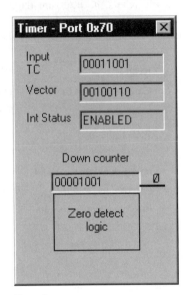

Function:
The timer is essentially a hardware counter that is decremented by the system clock. (While this is true for real timers, the simulator decrements the counter in a way that allows you to single step through your programs that use the timer. Because of this the timer is *not* decremented at equal intervals of time.)

To initialize the device, write an 8-bit unsigned integer to port TIM. This number, the **time constant**, appears in the Input TC box. When the timer begins to run, the time constant is copied into the Down counter and the system clock (∅) decrements this counter. When the Down counter reaches zero, the Zero detect logic reloads the time constant into the Down counter and the process repeats. The contents of the Down counter may be read at any time by reading port TIM.

This device may be programmed to generate an interrupt request when the Down counter reaches zero by writing 0x83 to the control port TIM_C. This facility is disabled by writing 0x03 to the control port.

When used with the G80 programmed to have a vectored interrupt response, the interrupt vector is stored in this device by writing the vector, which must be an even number, to the control port.

The current state of the interrupt request flag may be obtained by reading the control port. Bit 7 is the interrupt flag; when an interrupt request has been made, the control port contains 0x80, otherwise it contains 0x00. Reading the control port automatically resets the interrupt flag.

These properties are summarized in the following table.

	Read	Write
TIM	Current value of the Down counter.	Data stored as Time Constant.
TIM_C	Bit 7 is the interrupt request flag – 0x00 no interrupt requested, 0x80 interrupt requested. Read resets port to 0x00.	0x83 Enable interrupt. 0x03 Disable interrupt. Even number = vector.

Example program:

```
Timer1.asm
```

Device: Calendar
Data port base address: `CLNDR = 0x10`
This device is actually the calendar in the host computer.

Function:
The calendar is a series of seven counters that keep track of the current date and time. The counters are incremented every second.
Each counter is connected to an 8-bit port. The ports are read only.

Port address	Value
CLNDR+0	Day of week, 1 . . . 7. Sunday = 1
CLNDR+1	Year – 2000: 00..99
CLNDR+2	Month, 1 . . . 12. January = 1
CLNDR+3	Day of month, 1 . . . 31
CLNDR+4	Hour, 00 . . . 23
CLNDR+5	Minute, 00 . . . 59
CLNDR+6	Second, 00 . . . 59

Example:

```
in  a,  (CLNDR + 3)  ;Get Day of Month
```

Device: Pottery Kiln

Data port address: KTEMP = 0xF0
Control port address: KCTRL = 0xF1

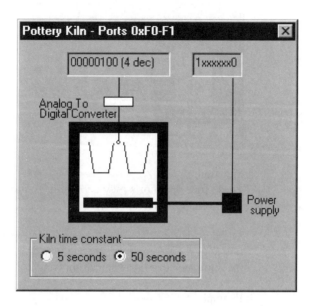

Function:

This device is a model of a pottery kiln. The kiln heater is switched on or off by bit 0 of port KCTRL. A temperature sensor is connected to an amplifier and an 8-bit analogue-to-digital converter (ADC). The output of the ADC is connected to port KTEMP. The ADC is configured to automatically convert the temperature to a digital value at regular intervals of time. On completing a conversion, the ADC sets bit 7 of port KCTRL, so indicating that a new temperature value is available. When the temperature is read from port 0xF0, bit 7 of port KCTRL is automatically reset.

The value of the least significant bit of the ADC output is 5°C. Thus, when the ADC output is 60, the kiln temperature is 300°C. The kiln temperature ranges from 20°C, the ambient temperature, to 1250°C, the maximum temperature.

The model of the kiln dynamic behaviour is that of a first order system. The heating time constant used in the model defaults to 'long' but may be set to 'short' to reduce the time required to test a program that controls the kiln. The cooling time constant is five times the heating time constant.

Example program:

```
Kiln1.asm
```

Device: Ports with no attached devices and with no interrupt logic
Data port addresses: 0x00, 0x01, 0x02, 0x03

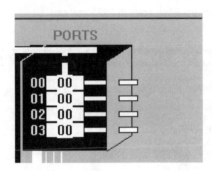

Function:

These four data ports may be read or written. The ports contain no logic for generating an interrupt request.

The port data is shown in the appropriate port data register. The contents of this data register may be changed by double-clicking in the ports region of the simulator display when in the single-step mode.

Example:

```
in a, (2)      :Copy port 2 into register A.
out (1), a     :Send contents of register A to port 1.
```

Device: Ports with no attached devices and with interrupt logic for mode 0
Data port addresses: 0x00, 0x01, 0x02
Control port address: 0x03

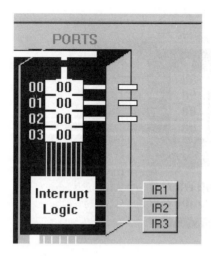

Function:
Ports 0x00, 0x01, and 0x02 may be read or written. However, port 0x03 is used as the control port for the interrupt logic.

When any of the interrupt request buttons, IR1, IR2, or IR3, is asserted by clicking on it, the port logic circuit asserts the interrupt request signal, INT, to the G80. At the same time, the port logic circuit loads port 0x03 with the code for one of the **restart** instructions. If IR1 is asserted, the logic in the port loads port 0x03 with the code for the rst 10 instruction. Thus, the interrupt service routine for IR1 must start at memory location 0x0010. Similarly, the interrupt service routine for IR2 must begin at location 0x0020, and that for IR3 at 0x0030.

The port data is shown in the appropriate port data register. The contents of this data register may be changed by double-clicking in the ports region of the simulator display when in the single-step mode.

Example program:
    Int0.asm

Device: Ports with no attached devices and with interrupt logic for mode 1
Data port addresses: 0x00, 0x01, 0x02
Control port address: 0x03

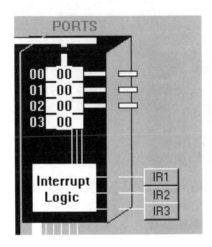

Function:
Ports 0x00, 0x01, and 0x02 may be read or written. However, port 0x03 is used as the control port for the interrupt logic.

When any of the interrupt request buttons, IR1, IR2, or IR3, is asserted by clicking on it, the port logic asserts interrupt request signal, INT, to the G80. At the same time, the port logic sets the lower bits of port 0x03 according to which of the IRx buttons was asserted. IR1 causes bit 0 to be set, IR2 causes bit 1 to be set, and IR3 causes bit 2 to be set. Thus, the interrupt service routine must read port 0x03 in order to determine which of the IRx inputs caused the interrupt request.

The port data is shown in the appropriate port data register. The contents of this data register may be changed by double-clicking in the ports region of the simulator display when in the single-step mode.

Example program:

```
Int1.asm
```

Device: Ports with no attached devices and with interrupt logic for mode 2

Data port addresses: 0x00, 0x02
Vector port addresses: 0x01, 0x02

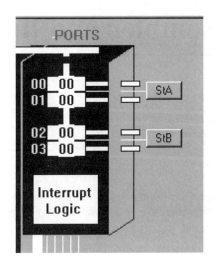

Function:

Ports 0x00 and 0x02 may be read or written. However, port 0x01 holds the interrupt vector for port 0x00, and port 0x03 holds the interrupt vector for port 0x01.

When either of the interrupt request buttons, StA or StB, is asserted by clicking on it, the port logic asserts the interrupt request signal, INT, to the G80.

The port data is shown in the appropriate port data register. The contents of this data register may be changed by double-clicking in the ports region of the simulator display when in the single-step mode.

Example program:

```
Int2.asm
```

Appendix D: The GDS assembler and linker

1 Format of the assembly source program

An assembler statement may have as many as four fields. The general format of a statement is:

```
[label:]    Operator    Operand    [;Comment]
```

The label and comment fields are optional. The operator field may be an assembler directive or an assembly mnemonic. Some operators do not require an operand, e.g. cpl.

1.1 Label field

If present, a label must be the first field in a source statement and must be terminated by a colon (:). Multiple labels may appear on successive lines. For example:

```
Fred:
Sue:
        ld a, 42
```

The legal characters for defining labels are:

Letters A to Z
Letters a to z
Digits 0 to 9

A label must have not more than 32 characters. A label must not start with a digit.

1.2 Operator field

The operator field specifies the action to be performed. It may consist of an instruction mnemonic or an assembler directive. When the operator is an instruction mnemonic, a machine instruction is generated and the assembler evaluates the addresses of the operands which follow. When the operator is a directive, the assembler performs certain control actions or processing operations during assembly of the source program.

Leading and trailing spaces or tabs in the operator field have no significance; such characters serve only to separate the operator field from the preceding and following fields.

An operator is terminated by a space, tab, or end of line.

1.3 Operand field

When the operator is an instruction mnemonic, the operand field contains program variables that are to be evaluated/manipulated by the operator.

Operands may be expressions or symbols, depending on the operator. Multiple expressions used in the operand fields must be separated by a comma. An operand should be preceded by an operator field; if it is not, the statement will give an error. All operands following instruction mnemonics are treated as expressions.

The operand field is terminated by a semicolon when the field is followed by a comment. For example, in the following statement:

```
Label:    ld a, fred   ;Comment field
```

The white space after `ld` terminates the operator field and defines the beginning of the operand field; a comma separates the operands `a` and `fred` and a semicolon terminates the operand field and defines the beginning of the comment field. When no comment field follows, the operand field is terminated by the end of the source line.

1.4 Comment field

The comment field begins with a semicolon and extends to the end of the line. This field is optional and may contain any 7-bit ASCII character except null. Comments do not affect assembly processing or program execution.

2 Symbols and expressions

The following characters are legal in source programs:

1 The letters A to Z. Both upper- and lower-case letters are acceptable. The assembler is case sensitive; i.e. ABCD and abcd are different symbols.
2 The digits 0 to 9.
3 The characters: period/full stop (.), dollar sign ($), and underscore (_).
4 The special characters listed below:

Colon (:)	Label terminator.
Equal sign (=)	Direct assignment operator.
Space or Tab	Item or field terminator.
Comma (,)	Operand field separator.
Semicolon (;)	Start of Comment field.
Left parenthesis (	Expression delimiter.
Right parenthesis)	Expression delimiter.

Plus sign (+ `fred`)	Positive value of `fred`.
Minus sign (– `fred`)	Produces the negative (two's complement) of `fred`.
Tilde (~`fred`)	Produces the one's complement of `fred`.
Single quote (`'d`)	Produces the ASCII code of the character `d`.
Plus sign (`fred + sue`)	Arithmetic addition operator.
Minus sign (`fred – sue`)	Arithmetic subtraction operator.
Asterisk (`fred*sue`)	Arithmetic multiplication operator (signed 16 bit).
Slash (`fred/sue`)	Arithmetic division operator (signed 16-bit quotient).
Ampersand (`fred & sue`)	Logical AND operator.
Bar (`fred | sue`)	Logical OR operator.
Percent sign (`fred % sue`)	Modulus operator (16-bit value).
Circumflex (`fred ^ sue`)	Exclusive OR operator.
`0b, 0B`	Binary radix operator.
`0x, 0h, 0X, 0H`	Hexadecimal radix operator.

2.1 Symbols

The following rules govern the creation of user-defined symbols:

1 Symbols can be composed of alphanumeric characters, dollar signs ($), periods (.), and underscores (_) only.
2 The first character of a symbol must not be a digit.
3 The symbol must have not more than 32 characters.
4 Spaces and tabs must not be embedded within a symbol.

2.2 Numbers

All numbers in the source program are interpreted in decimal radix unless otherwise specified. Individual numbers can be designated as binary, octal, or hexadecimal through the temporary radix prefixes.

Negative numbers must be preceded by a minus sign. The G80 assembler translates such numbers into two's complement form. Positive numbers may (but need not) be preceded by a plus sign.

2.3 Terms

A term is a component of an expression and may be one of the following:

1 A number.
2 A symbol. (An undefined symbol is assigned a value of zero and inserted in the Symbol Table as an undefined symbol.)
3 A single quote followed by a single ASCII character, or a double quote followed by two ASCII characters.

4 An expression enclosed in parentheses. Any expression so enclosed is evaluated and reduced to a single term before the remainder of the expression in which it appears is evaluated. Parentheses, for example, may be used to alter the left-to-right evaluation of expressions (as in fred*sue + yoko versus fred*(sue + yoko)), or to apply a unary operator to an entire expression (as in -(fred + sue)). Where a left parenthesis is at the start of an expression, preface it with 0+. For example, 0 + (fred + sue)*8.

5 A unary operator followed by a symbol or number.

2.4 Expressions

Expressions are combinations of terms joined together by binary operators. Expressions reduce to a 16-bit value.

Expressions are evaluated with an operand precedence as follows:

First	*	/	%	multiplication, division, and modulus.
Second	+	−		addition and subtraction.
Third	<<	>>		left shift and right shift.
Fourth	^			logical XOR.
Fifth	&			logical AND.
Last	|			logical OR, except that unary operators take precedence over binary operators.

3 Assembler directives

An assembler directive is placed in the operator field of the source line. Only one directive is allowed per source line. Each directive may have a blank operand field or one or more operands. Legal operands differ with each directive.

3.1 .byte and .db directives

The .byte or .db directive is used to generate successive bytes of binary data in the object module.

```
Format:   .byte exp           ;Stores the binary value
          .db exp             ;of the expression in the next byte.
          .byte exp1,exp2,     ;Stores the binary values of the list
             expn
          .db exp1,exp2,expn  ;of expressions in successive bytes.
```

where exp represent expressions that will be truncated to 8 bits of data.

Each expression will be calculated as a 16-bit word expression, the high-order byte will be truncated. Multiple expressions must be separated by commas.

3.2 .word and .dw directives

The `.word` or `.dw` directive is used to generate successive words of binary data in the object module.

Format:	`.word exp`	;Stores the binary value
	`.dw exp`	;of the expression in the next word
	`.word exp1,exp2,expn`	;Stores the binary values of the list
	`.dw  exp1,exp2,expn`	;of expressions in successive words

where `exp` represent expressions that will occupy 2 bytes of data. Each expression will be calculated as a 16-bit word expression.
   Multiple expressions must be separated by commas.

3.3 .blkb, .blkw, and .ds directives

The `.blkb` and `.ds` directives reserve byte blocks in the object module; the `.blkw` directive reserves word blocks.

Format:	`.blkb  N`	;reserve N bytes of space
	`.blkw  N`	;reserve N words of space
	`.ds  N`	;reserve N bytes of space

3.4 .ascii directive

The `.ascii` directive places 1 binary byte of data for each character in the string into the object module.

Format:	`.ascii /string/`

where `string` is a string of printable ASCII characters bracketed between the delimiting characters. These delimiters may be any paired printing characters, as long as the characters are not contained within the string itself. If the delimiting characters do not match, the `.ascii` directive will give an error.

3.5 .asciz directive

This is the same as the `.ascii` directive except that a 0x00 byte is appended to terminate the character string.

Format:	`.asciz /string/` where `string` is a string of printable asciz characters.

3.6 .seg directive

The `.seg` directive provides a means of defining and separating multiple programming and data sections.

Format: `.seg name [(options)]`

where `name` represents the symbolic name of the program section. This name may be the same as any user-defined symbol as the segment names are independent of all symbols and labels.

The name is the segment label used by the assembler and the linker to collect code from various separately assembled modules into one section. The name may be from 1 to 8 characters in length.

`options` specifies the type of program or data segment, either absolute (`abs`), or relocatable (`rel`).

Multiple invocations of the `.seg` directive with the same name must specify the same option or leave the option field blank, this defaults to the previously specified options for this program segment.

3.7 .org directive

Format: `.org exp`

where `exp` is an absolute expression that indicates where the code is to be located. The `.org` directive is valid only in an absolute program section and will give an error if used in a relocatable program area.

3.8 .globl directive

The `.globl` directive defines (and thus provides linkage to) symbols not defined within a module. Because object modules are linked by global symbols, these symbols are vital to a program. All internal symbols appearing within a given program must be defined at the end of pass 1 or they will be considered undefined.

Format: `.globl sym1,sym2,...,symn`

where `sym1`, `sym2`, `symn` represent legal symbolic names. When multiple symbols are specified they must be separated by commas.

A `.globl` directive may also have a label field and/or a comment field.

4 Linker command   This specifies a segment base address; the expression may contain constants and/or defined symbols from the linked files.

Format: `-b seg = expression`

E.g.   `-b CODE = 0x8000`

This sets the base address of the segment named CODE to 0x8000. Each definition must be on a separate line.

Index